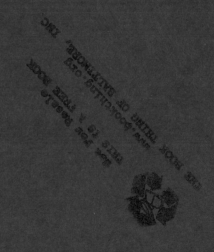

The Abolition of Britain

From Winston Churchill to Princess Diana

PETER HITCHENS

ENCOUNTER BOOKS

San Francisco

First U.S. edition published in 2000 by Encounter Books, an activity of Encounter for Culture and Education, Inc., a nonprofit tax exempt corporation.

First published in 1999 by Quartet Books Limited, London.

Encounter Books website address: www.enounterbooks.com

Jacket design by Nick Collier

Manufactured in the United States and printed on acid-free paper.

The paper used in this publication meets the minimum requirements of ANSI/NISO Z39.48-1992 (R 1997) (*Permanence of Paper*).

Library of Congress Cataloging-in-Publication Data

Hitchens, Peter, 1951–
    The abolition of Britain : from Winston Churchill to Princess Diana / Peter Hitchens.—1st ed.
      p.   cm.
    Includes bibliographical references
    ISBN 1-893554-18-X (acid-free paper)
      1. Great Britain—Civilization—20th century.   2. Great Britain—Social Condition—20th century.   I. Title.
    DA566.4 .H5 2000
    941.085—dc21   00-061032

10   9   8   7   6   5   4   3   2   1

For Rebecca, Daniel and Jonathan

Contents

	Preface to the Second Edition	vii
	Introduction: A Modern Man	1
ONE	The Warrior and the Victim	17
TWO	Born Yesterday	44
THREE	Class War	64
FOUR	The Pink Bits	84
FIVE	Hell Freezes Over	105
SIX	The Telescreen Triumphs	128
SEVEN	Forty Years On	144
EIGHT	A Real Bastard	162
NINE	The Queen's English	177
TEN	Difficulties with Girls	190
ELEVEN	Last Exit to Decency	207
TWELVE	Suburbs of the Mind	221
THIRTEEN	The Pill That Cured Morality	232
FOURTEEN	Health Warning	248
FIFTEEN	Is Britain Civilized?	263
SIXTEEN	Year Zero	273
	Conclusion: Chainsaw Massacre	289

Notes   319
Acknowledgements   327
Works Cited   329

Preface to the Second Edition

This book was originally published with an entire chapter missing. It was not a matter of censorship. I decided to remove the chapter after I was urged to do so by people whose judgement I respect. They feared that this one chapter would cause so much fuss that the rest of the book would then be ignored or forgotten, and that this would be a waste.

This chapter, about the strange new orthodoxy on homosexuality, has now been revised and restored, and it seems to me now—as it did then—mild, measured and reasonable. But all the other chapters too seem to me restrained and cautious, especially when I consider the grievous bodily harm done to this country during my lifetime, and the worse things likely to follow before too long.

From the moment when I sketched out its first rough outline, *The Abolition of Britain* has repeatedly proved its own point: that a whole system of thought and belief was fast becoming unthinkable and unsayable. An agent who had been urging me for months to get between hard covers flatly declined to handle this project, saying quite frankly that this was because he did not agree with it. When I then placed it in the hands of another agent, several publishers rejected the outline, some on openly political grounds.

The reviews, upon publication, which I had expected to be hostile and in many cases hoped would be hostile, were often personally abusive. I think this was due to the widespread belief that failure to conform with today's orthodoxy is a moral failing. For supporters of Newspeak, Newthought and the Big Tent, opposition and dissent cannot be simply legitimate or reasoned, but must result from a flaw in character. Thus, Polly Toynbee, who is always perfectly civil to me when we meet, felt able to call my book 'mad'; Will Hutton said on the radio that it was 'barmy'; a prominent BBC presenter told me—off the air—that he thought it was 'potty'. One interviewer seemed to think that by writing this polemic I had given him the right to launch into a sort of psychoanalysis of my character—for which I suppose he is as well-qualified as anyone else—in which everything from sibling rivalry to my mother's suicide and my partly Jewish ancestry was relevant. He concluded that I suffered from low self-esteem, which to those familiar with my colossal vanity was a rather good joke.

The idea that my book might be justified by historical truth and accurate observation, and that my views might be shared by many reasonable, kind and wise people, was apparently insupportable. Therefore it had to be explained by some failing within me. It has been said in various places that I am known to both my friends and my enemies as 'bonkers', to which I will only say that anyone who calls me by this unpleasant and profoundly intolerant name is mistaken if he thinks that he is my friend. And if he wishes to be my enemy, he will have to do an awful lot better than that.

My critics believe in a number of things which I find odd and extremist. They think it sensible to abolish our national currency and hand over our national wealth to a centralized supranational power over which we have no democratic control. They believe that government can spend our money better than we can. Many of them used to believe that the best way to deal with the Soviet threat was to disarm ourselves and smile. They think that the best response to terrorist blackmail is to lick the blackmailer's toecaps and give him what he wants. They release convicted criminals by the score long before their sentences are over, and appear to believe that the only people in this country who should have firearms are criminals and the IRA. They think it is right to bomb innocent civilians so that we can feel more comfortable about watching atrocity reports from the Balkans on the nine o'clock news. They defend the mass slaughter of unborn infants. They even think that the schools are getting better.

It is no shame to be called an extremist by people who think that such opinions are, or even ought to be, in the mainstream. But I will not return the compliment, because I don't believe in avoiding arguments by dismissing my opponents as illegitimate or marginal. As for dragging half-understood psychiatric terms into political discourse, I disdain it. That way lies the classification of dissidents as insane, the methods of the Soviet Serbsky Institute, where glinting doctors truss the dissident in a straitjacket or subject him to obscene 'treatment' because he refuses to love Big Brother. That way also lies the idea that those who disagree with you are personally at fault and ought perhaps to disappear, or be made to disappear—a creepy idea in the mouths of British progressives, a terrifying one in the mouths of the regimes that such people so often support or at least excuse.

I will treat my critics in the way most of them, with some honourable exceptions, will not treat me: I will accept that they are decent human beings and that they have a coherent, thoughtful vision of the world they would like to see and the British people's place in it. One of the happiest effects of this book was that it provided the excuse for several debates, with my brother Christopher, and with Jonathan Freedland, author of *Bring Home the Revolution*. These exchanges were civilized, reasonable and good-humoured without being soft-edged, and entirely in the decent old British tradition of honest and robust disagreement. Both Jonathan and Christopher are republicans, and my final chapter owes much to a fiercely fought clash with Jonathan on the importance of the Crown, a discussion in which I came to the conclusion that the friends of liberty in this country may find the monarchy an important ally. A typically British paradox.

What shocked me about my brother's position, and that of many supporters of the European Union, was how little account they seemed to have taken of the profoundly author-itarian and illiberal institutions which govern the EU, whose increasing power in these islands has done much to bring about the disappearance of Britishness. I am always puzzled by the unwillingness of my opponents to deal with this difficulty, but I am specially perplexed when at the same time they rail against the vestigial powers of throne and Privy Council. And I am shocked by the laziness of their arguments for obliterating the hereditary element in the House of Lords, who were abolished not because they were undemocratic but because they were independent. Despite my critics' claims that they stand for more liberty, I think that in reality they stand for less. The modern Left's scorn for freedom is rapidly becoming an issue in its own right. This is shown by the actions of the increas-ingly illiberal Blair government, which instinctively reaches for the authoritarian solution to every problem, from limiting jury trial to demanding DNA and drug testing of suspects.

I think the Left's project, despite some attractive spokes-men, is a profoundly unattractive vision, and I suspect that many of them lack the imagination to see just how dismal it is. Some of them, more honest with themselves or simply more intelligent, recognize that their new order will be less free and less democratic than anything we have known in this country for centuries. Presumably, they believe that powerful higher motives justify this loss. Such people always *do* think that. In that case it is odd that so few will come out openly and argue their case. It seems they prefer to ignore the opposition, and to characterize it as paranoid or lunatic when it cannot be pushed to the margins of society. Do they fear that their own position is weak or do they simply know that—clearly stated—

it will be unacceptable to millions of people? I do not know. What I *do* know is that the publication of this book has strengthened my belief that a great civilization, whose greatest possession is liberty, is on the edge of extinction and that we have very little time to save it.

I am a modern man. I am part of the rock and roll generation—the
Beatles, colour TV, that's the generation I come from.
—Tony Blair, in a speech at Stevenage, 22 April 1997

INTRODUCTION

A Modern Man

THE PRIME MINISTER DID NOT realize how significant these words were when he blurted them out in the middle of the most puzzling and mysterious general election campaign in modern British history. He may have known that they were important, but did he know why? For they offer the best explanation for his victory, and a convincing reason to believe that the Tories will never again hold power in Britain. During the next few years it will become clear that the 1997 election was a historic choice between two utterly different ideas of Britain, a choice which had little to do with economics, or even politics, and everything to do with the far more important issue of *what kind of people we are.*

Many of those born, raised and educated in surroundings normally associated with Tory thinking and values no longer actually share those values. Few people under the age of fifty now possess what could be described as a Conservative imagination. Their attitude towards sexuality, drugs, manners, dress, food, swear-words, music and religion has little or nothing in common with the traditional idea of Conservative behaviour. As the far-from-leftist commentator Richard Littlejohn cackled derisively shortly before the election, 'John Major is probably the last man left in Britain who wears a tie on Saturdays.'

In these words a dozen other messages are contained about a generation and a way of existence which seem doomed.

Since the election, the death of Princess Diana has widened the crevasse between the old culture and the new. Because it was the first royal death for more than a generation, it gave Britain an unexpected opportunity to take its own temperature, and to discover that it was suffering from a rather unpleasant fever. Those brought up in the older tradition were astonished, puzzled and even hurt to hear pop songs and applause at a funeral, and to see mourners who wept at one moment and took photographs of the cortège a few minutes later. Those brought up since the changes took hold were equally surprised, puzzled and annoyed by the restraint and self-discipline of the other half of the nation, seeing it as a failure to show correct emotion.

There was no doubt about which half dominated. Television, by taking the side of the new, emotional, victim-loving faction, made it seem as if the pro-Diana, anti-Windsor mood was universal and unchallenged, causing many people to wonder if they were personally flawed because they did not feel the sensations that TV was reporting and encouraging. This was a bizarre dictatorship of grief, quickly noticed by the Prime Minister's public relations men, who then used Diana's glamour and appeal to imply that Labour's radical programme of constitutional change was in some way a vindication of Diana's life. The brilliant, cynical phrase 'The People's Princess' frightened those who knew anything about the way in which dictatorships are born. Diana had become a grotesque combination of Marilyn Monroe, Eva Perón and John Lennon, martyred by the mythical 'establishment', the strange false enemy whose alleged existence was and is the excuse for Labour's slow-motion *coup d'état*.

Once, such a coup would have been impossible because, the British people would have been instinctively suspicious of it and rejected it. Yet in the thirty years before the 1997 election, a long and profound set of changes in the British way of life had brought to maturity a generation to whom the past was not just a foreign country, but a place of mystery which was easier to mock than understand. Born in the collapse of British confidence which followed the diplomatic, economic, military, religious and imperial decay of the 1950s, the new culture simply was not interested in many of the concerns which the Tories tried to drag into the campaign.

These seemingly superficial changes were far more important than they appeared. Into the vacuum left by the end of British self-confidence a new conformism has come rushing, probably more powerful than the one which went before. This is often dismissed, half-jokingly, with the casual phrase 'political correctness'. But this imported expression does not even begin to encompass the power and danger of the thing. The new empire of ideas reaches into the most intimate areas of life, and those who do not accept it are judged to be personally at fault, not simply politically or philosophically wrong. Unmitigated by any lingering attempt to loathe the sin rather than the sinner, unshakeable in its certainty that personal righteousness is reserved for those who share its views about South Africa, landmines and the homeless, it is the most intolerant system of thought to dominate the British Isles since the Reformation.

This overthrow of the past has not been planned—such things cannot be orchestrated though they can be skilfully guided—but has followed the coincidental disappearance of rival or alternative moral and cultural forces and structures. So many features of this country's life crumbled at once, that the new culture had to take the place of patriotism, faith, morality and literature. The issue of what a person knows or believes has been confused, as it never used to be, with the idea of what sort of citizen he or she is.

This revolution, though well under way, is not complete. Still to come are the destruction or at least the serious diminishing of the monarchy, the reduction of the power of the House of Commons, the transformation of the practice of law, the end of the pre-eminence of privileged institutions like the universities of Oxford and Cambridge, the disestablishment of the Church of England and the dissolution of the 1707 union of England with Scotland. Its effect on education, broadcasting, newspapers, customs and institutions has been so devastating that it is fair to compare it directly with Mao Zedong's concentrated effort to bury China's past, thirty years ago. The most important difference between the Chinese Cultural Revolution and the British one is that ours is still going on, long after China has halted and even reversed its attack on tradition and ancient institutions. (Deng Xiaoping made an immense effort to restore proper examinations and academic rigour to Chinese schools and universities.) The obvious differences are less significant. Of course we have not dragged aged professors through the streets in dunce's caps, burned our libraries or murdered those who resisted. But we have gravely devalued knowledge and academic qualifications, made many thoughts almost unthinkable, sundered many of the invisible bonds which once held our society together, and inflicted upon our country a permanent and irreversible change in morals, values, customs, taboos, language, humour, art and even eating habits.

At the centre of all this change is a deep shift in the way the British people view themselves, their past and their future. Fewer each day now consider themselves to be British. Instead they are choosing the narrower loyalties of the UK's smaller nations—to such an extent that even the English have begun to feel a vague nationalism and the forgotten St George's Cross has reappeared in the hands of English football supporters after two centuries when it flew only from church towers. The Church of England, the only other purely English institution, is barely known to most football supporters, who probably think that churches flying the red-and-white flag are joining in the general soccer fervour. This may seem to be a 'symptom' rather than something important in itself, but there are far too many such symptoms and they amount to a transformation with enormous significance. Until now, historians and commentators have dealt with its many aspects one by one, but there are so many important connections between them that they make more sense taken as a whole, *because they show how many pillars of the old order collapsed at once.*

This is not to suggest that there has been some sort of conspiracy with a central Red Guard command plotting the next step, but that a series of important coincidences have combined with the spirit of the age and the growth of a new type of middle class, mainly state-educated and state-employed, to bring about an entirely new culture. It is that culture which produced the Labour election victory on 1 May 1997 and which, having voted for the breakup of the United Kingdom, is now about to be persuaded to accept the incorporation of the remains into some sort of European federal state. How can such a thing happen, only fifty-five years after Britain emerged from the Second World War as a great power, its national spirit strong, its culture confident and its independence and integrity confirmed by victory?

A good starting point for this era is Sir Winston Churchill's funeral in 1965, and a good finishing point is the startlingly different funeral of Princess Diana in 1997. The death of Churchill, an unchallengeable father figure, was a final farewell to a reassuring past. By travelling back to that not-very-distant time it is possible to see the extent of the changes which have overtaken us. Even in the commonplace features of life, a comparison between the day before yesterday and today reveals differences which are more than a mere adaptation to the modern world. Examine school textbooks, especially on history and geography, from forty years ago, and set them beside their equivalents today. Do the same with advertisements, guidebooks and other unselfconscious documents which show how we really felt about ourselves and our way of life at the time. You will find that you are investigating the inner life of a wholly foreign country.

Many of these trends and tremors began long before 1965, and it is necessary to go further into the past to examine them. Some of the changes in our society began with campaigns or fashions in thought which started before the First World War. Most are more recent, finding their roots in events like the Lady Chatterley trial, the satire boom, and the mysterious birth of British rock music.

One of the great blows to stability has been the change in family life, from the first appearance of the teenager in the late 1930s, to Edmund Leach's disturbing Reith lectures of 1967, which blamed the traditional family for most of society's problems. There has been a transformation in the way in which people arrange and furnish their houses, the sort of food they eat and where and how they eat it. Cheap pre-cooked fast food, the freezer and the microwave, have practically ended the formal meal around the table, and allowed family members to remain in front of the television or at the computer keyboard without needing to interrupt their activities. The spread of central heating and double glazing has allowed even close-knit families to avoid each other's company in well-warmed houses, rather than huddling round a single hearth forced into unwanted companionship, and so compelled to adapt to each other's foibles and become more social, less selfish beings.

Clothes have also undergone a complete change, in styles and materials, even in purpose, for children as well as adults, while hairstyles for both sexes express the alteration in the balance of power between men and women, parents and children. Children no longer dress as children, but as miniature adults, with their own scaled-down adult fashions, underlining the truth that they actually owe more loyalty to their peers than to their parents. The alteration has even changed the streetscape, leading to the disappearance of hats and the decline of coats, the rise of the trainer and the near-disappearance of the leather shoe. Uniforms, too, serve a much less layered, deferential society, and a more violent and unsupervised one. Policemen have tossed aside their formal, restrained tunics and their helmets, and now waddle about, hung with weaponry and radios, in militaristic pullovers and flat caps. Thanks to the years of terrorism, servicemen and women long ago gave up appearing on the streets in uniform, and there are now so few of them anyway that a planned change in the rules is unlikely to have much effect.

How have we been persuaded to make and accept these changes, not all welcome or helpful or needed or much desired? Scores of different pressures led to them, many of them rooted in the destruction and disruption of the Second World War, the austerity and chaos after that war and the manic suburbanization of the country that came with the new prosperity. In this time of unsettled change and constant uncertainty in superficial things, it was easier than ever for people to be persuaded that more significant parts of their lives should be altered for ever.

Other physical changes have propelled and exaggerated these new ways of thinking. The atomization of society by new types of housing has broken up the old sense of belonging. The crazed over-use of private cars and the triumph of the supermarket over the personal service grocery have kept us from meeting our fellow-creatures as effectively as any strict regime prison, and often reduced us to the level of objects rolling along someone else's production line. Greater than all these things is television, which has replaced individual imagination with images provided and selected by others, but also, and perhaps more importantly, destroyed the old forms of social sanction, a fear of the neighbours' opinion or the even greater fear of upsetting the family. Television provided new judges of our behaviour, who were wittier, cleverer and more open-minded than anyone we knew in person. It also transformed child-rearing and narrowed the horizons of childhood itself.

Once, programmes for children had some reference to the outside world, to the old traditions of story-telling. Now, programme-makers devise Teletubbies who are living televisions, with little screens in their stomachs, a simple reflection of the fact that children learn to live their lives through the screen.

Closely linked to this takeover of our brains by TV studios has been the rebuilding of our towns, cities and villages. Life in isolated boxes, next to neighbours with whom we have nothing in common except a postcode, has pushed people into the arms of the new electronic culture. With the deportation of people from crowded city centres to remote estates, the whole shape of our urban life has been altered. Streets are wider, roads straighter, a highly literate cityscape of ornate shopsigns and wordy advertisements has given way to a post-literate one of pictograms, posters and logos. Detail has vanished, replaced by sweeping (and windswept) prospects. Smelly but characteristic features of town life, such as breweries and cattlemarkets, have been uprooted, as have most small urban industries, so that few of us can see any connection between what we consume and its real origins in the field, farmyard or slaughterhouse. Specifically local or specifically British styles of architecture have given way to the international blandness of concrete and glass, fresh air to air conditioning, actually needless in our temperate climate but forced on us by the strange style of buildings which we have chosen. The universal conscription of women into paid work has emptied the suburbs, rich and poor, so that streets, parks and gardens are depopulated during the day. Distances between home and work, home and school, and extended families have grown far greater.

Lonely and self-reliant, much of our social life concentrated in the workplace rather than the home, we have become a people dependent on television for a simulation of social contact in our leisured hours. Yet few seem to realize the power of a medium which stole into our lives while we were not paying attention. Early television was nothing like the modern force which has now displaced all other forms of culture and entertainment. Its effect on the imagination has been the motor of the new morality and the new conformism.

The age of books allowed each individual to form his own picture of the world. Each of us had his own deeply personal idea of what the great characters of fiction and history were really like, from Henry VIII and Richard III to Oliver Twist and Sherlock Holmes. We were able to imagine ourselves facing their problems and dilemmas, our thoughts enriched but not taken over by the things which we had read. But the arrival of cinema, and then of television, imposed on all of us the imagination of one director or one actor. However brilliant and apposite their portrayal may have been, it drove out our own. It made each one of us more like the other, it narrowed the gaps between us and made us simultaneously less alone and more conformist. We have all noticed the way in which mass culture has flattened out accents and made us dress and even walk in standardized fashions. The smaller, milder regional dialects of southern England have begun to vanish, replaced by the Estuary English used by many broadcasters. Even the stronger dialects of the north of England have accepted many terms and forms which are southern or American in origin.

This regimentation has also affected our thinking, and our ability to choose. In a society of stable values and unchanging tradition, this would not be specially important, and the cinema had far less impact on 1930s Britain than television was to have fifty or sixty years later. The effect of television, especially colour television, on a society whose values were all open to question and whose morals were dissolving was explosive, and continues to be.

The condition of 1960s Britain was rather like the huge scrapyards of the time full of the steam engines which had been such a characteristic part of the urban and rural landscape for the previous century. Those cemeteries of rusting iron monsters were a melancholy metaphor for the state of the nation. Britain had been living on her Victorian inheritance, an elderly but rather grand steam locomotive, hiding her leaky valves behind shiny paint and well-polished brass, obsolete but magnificent. Now the truth could not be concealed any more. In a matter of a few months, a whole way of life was condemned to be cut up with blowtorches and turned into lawn-mowers and tumble-driers.

I myself clearly remember standing on the Portsmouth shore on the sultry August day in 1960 when the Royal Navy's last battleship, HMS *Vanguard,* was towed to the breakers' yard. The great 44,000-ton sea monster had been a relic when she was completed in 1946, too late for the war in which she was meant to fight. She had been built for a world that no longer existed, and had spent the last few years of her life as a hulk, unable to move under her own power. Yet with her beautiful lines and enormous guns (dating from 1916 and rarely if ever fired) she was one of the most impressive and evocative sights of her times. It was typical of those times that, as she was dragged to her last resting place, she ran aground on a mud-bank. Nothing, it seemed, could go right for us any more.

For as a people, we were already rather unsure of ourselves, privately aware that much of our grandeur was empty and obsolete, unable, like *Vanguard,* to move under our own power. In some ways, there are painful similarities between the state of 1960s Britain and that of the Soviet Union just before the fall of communism. Both lived on and in the past, sustained by a more or less mythical view of the Second World War. Even twenty years after the war, the cultural shadow of it still lay across the country. In films, in literature, even in children's comics, the war against Hitler was the main scene of drama. Newspapers quarried their metaphors from it, language was heavily influenced by it. The armed services, normally a closed world at least twenty years behind the times in modes of speech and morality, were given a far greater role in national life than at any other time before or since. The clipped accent of the officer class had its life prolonged way beyond its rightful span. Our image of ourselves as a people was lifted up into heroism by our honourable and solitary defiance of Hitler in 1940, and we liked to see ourselves as the inheritors of Henry V and the imitators of the Greeks and Romans.

Of course, these ideas had been quietly subverted for years by the Left, and were secretly despised by a small but influential part of the educated middle class. George Orwell had rightly pointed out in the early months of the war that Britain was unique in having an intelligentsia that despised patriotism. That current in national thought had been suppressed by many things: Russia's entry into the war had allowed even the extreme Left to appear patriotic; the discovery of the extermination camps had transformed a defensive 'imperialist' war into a Just War, even if only with hindsight; and the powerful myth that the Tories had all been appeasers, whilst the Left had been keen to fight the Nazis (though largely false), had allowed the intellectuals to claim the war as their own. The Suez catastrophe and humiliation, imperial withdrawal from Asia and Africa, and the simple passage of time eventually permitted open mockery of the war years to emerge, round about the time of Churchill's death.

Another, quite separate influence also undermined and belittled Britain's image of herself, and the British people's view of themselves. The influence of American culture on this country has turned out to be one of the great paradoxes of modern history—the arsenal of conservatism and capitalism has done more to eat away at British self-confidence and British institutions than the Soviet Union or the Communist Party ever did. One reason for this is that high-octane American ways of behaving and speaking are simply too powerful for this much smaller and narrower country. The other is that the growing realization that the USA was the true victor of 1945, and not we ourselves, has shaken our self-confidence more deeply than most of us care to admit. Patriotism, deprived of a home country that it can happily love and respect, has a nasty habit of turning into an angry rejection of the motherland, combined with a purblind admiration of some other nation. This was probably the explanation for the outbreak of pro-Soviet treachery among an educated élite sixty years ago. It is also part of the explanation for the admiration of all things American which became such a strong feature of British life in the years after Churchill.

How else can we explain our rapid conversion to things the older élite did not much like and often despised, from commercial television to the basing of all transport policy upon the car, to the increasing use of American terms in language? Even our criminals and our police began to behave like Americans, and our very different racial problems began to take on American characteristics, while observers used American terminology to describe them. It cannot just be the backwash of wartime American wealth. We became affluent ourselves long ago. The unspeakable truth was that by 1941 we were a defeated nation, whose conquerors had neglected to invade us. Impoverished, beaten in battle in Flanders and Malaya, condemned as it seemed to grey years of sacrifice with no certain end, we were invaded by *our allies* instead. The old power of British traditions, the magic of British uniforms and the authority of British upper-class voices, the power of British ceremony, began to crumble from within at this point. It simply could not compete with the vigorous, wealthy, well-fed, sheer success of the Americans who were suddenly mixing with us, and whose influence was deep and swift because of the common language and the natural friendliness which almost always springs up between these two peoples.

The Americanization of our sex lives was probably more important than all these put together. American attitudes towards divorce and adultery, the collapse of American puritanism (so well described by David Halberstam in his extraordinary book *The Fifties*) under the blows of Kinsey and the contraceptive pill, fanned out across this country like an infectious disease. The ground had been prepared by the wartime experience of the American way of life. Now, hurried along by Marshall Aid, Hollywood, TV, popular music and the return of American servicemen to fight the Cold War, America's supposed 'classlessness', actually a fiction, mocked our minutely graded caste system. The triumph of Elvis Presley, whose influence was rightly seen as revolutionary by American conservatives, brought an entirely new thing into our lives—the sexualization of the young, combined with the narcotic emotional power of modern rock music. Even in the vast and flexible society that is the modern USA, Presley was the cultural equivalent of a 100-megaton explosion. In Britain's narrow, restrained atmosphere, the charge was more powerful still. Presley dug beneath the fortifications of British sexual reserve, leaving them so weakened that John Lennon and Mick Jagger could knock them down completely.

The vastness of the USA, combined with its great social mobility, has always encouraged people to uproot themselves from failed lives and start out again somewhere else. In the past, Britain's smallness and its settled class system have compelled us to be polite, restrained and repressed, or face chaos. Japan's elaborate manners and customs are a similar response to living at close quarters on cramped islands. Until the war, British people were probably more inclined to accept adultery than divorce—which is actually a licence to remarry rather than (as so often portrayed) a permit to leave a failed or troubled marriage. Hollywood's culture of serial divorce, followed soon afterwards by the pulsing sexuality of rock and roll, were unleashed on a Britain whose whole family structure was already seriously undermined by the prolonged separation and disruption of conflict, and by the wartime conscription of millions of women into the workplace, and its false message that women—even married women—could be as independent as men. In fact, this could only be achieved with the support of an impossibly expensive welfare system of nurseries and state canteens, whose disappearance in the late 1940s and 1950s seems to have given the British family a brief respite from attack. However, instead of women adapting to cope with the absence of a wartime welfare state, governments decided to rebuild that welfare state, even though there was no war to justify it.

This was because the damage to the foundations of the traditional family was permanent. As a result, the arrival of North American feminism led to one of the highest rates of female employment in any of the West's advanced nations. This was at least in part because it came just as industry and business were discovering that women made ideal and compliant employees.

It would be very wrong to blame the Americans for everything. All these things took place as part of an epic struggle between state and family, a struggle with its roots in the war, intensified by the creation of the welfare state and brought to the highest pitch of intensity by the moral chaos and dependency culture which came into being in the Thatcher years—paradoxically the years when the Left believed that they were actually losing the battle to a right-wing counter-revolution. One of my main contentions is that Thatcherism was a miserable failure on its own terms, and actually speeded up the triumph of the state.

Margaret Thatcher fought two great battles, the Cold War abroad and the battle against militant trade unionism at home. She was successful in both, and exhausted her moral energy in them. But, like her victory in the Falklands conflict, her triumphs actually concealed deeper failures. The defeat of the USSR only cleared the ground for a new battle against German domination of Europe, advancing behind the smokescreen of European Union and armed with the weapons of supranational statism. Her victory over relics such as Arthur Scargill left intact the monstrous new growth of public sector unionism, whose main purpose was not to hold the nation to ransom through costly strikes, but to act as a gigantic lobby for the endless expansion of the tax-financed employment sector. In this battle, the cultural institutions—the BBC, the universities, the education establishment and the (tax-funded) artistic élite—were bound to be the allies of the state and so of the statist European ideal.

The two Britains which faced each other in April 1997 were utterly alien to one another and unfairly matched. One was old and dying, treasuring values and ideas which stretched back into a misty past. One was new and hardly born, clinging just as fiercely to its own values of classlessness, anti-racism, sexual inclusiveness and licence, contempt for the nation state, dislike of deference, scorn for restraint and incomprehension for the web of traditions and prejudices which were revered by the other side. Culturally, Labour had been in power for years and, as a result, its leaders and supporters always seemed enraged that they were not also in control of the government. The final years of the Tories were marked by an almost fanatical fury among Leftists against the rather pitiful figures of the Tory leadership. Cartoons in left-wing papers portrayed John Major as a decomposing corpse. One particular Labour election broadcast, which would have warmed the heart of Josef Goebbels, showed speeded-up footage of some of the uglier Tory leaders, cruelly edited and set to mocking music. The broadcast, which also contained a blatant lie about Tory pension plans, was filled with the righteous hatred which revolutionaries feel towards those they plan to overthrow. If anybody had been in doubt that the new government viewed the Tories as enemies rather than as opponents, that broadcast would have warned them of what was coming.

We were seeing something much more than a change of government. There was the air of a putsch about the way in which stage-managed platoons of Labour Party employees pretended to be a cheering crowd in Downing Street, each issued by commissars with Union Jacks which they privately despised and which they intended to render obsolete in the coming months. This was how the modern men, the men who had grown up with colour TV and the Beatles, stormed Britain's gates.

ONE

The Warrior and the Victim

THE FINAL DAYS OF IMPERIAL BRITAIN are bracketed—appropriately enough—by the funerals of an old man and of a beautiful young woman. The first, of Sir Winston Churchill, reached into a past of grandeur and certainty, while the second, of Diana, Princess of Wales, foreshadowed a future of doubt and decline. The two events were different in every possible way, except that both were unmistakably British. The dead warrior was almost ninety, full of years and ready to die. He represented the virtues of courage, fortitude and endurance; he was picturesque rather than glamorous; and his death was expected. The lost princess was snatched from life in the midst of youth, beauty and glamour. Her disputed virtues were founded on suffering (real or imagined) and appealed more to the outcasts and the wounded than to the dutiful plain heart of England. Yet the funerals of such people, however different they may be from each other, are specially good moments at which to take the temperature of the nation, far better than general elections. If Britain was a little frigid according to the Fahrenheit thermometer of 1965, she was seriously feverish by the Celsius measure in the late summer of 1997.

Had Winston Churchill's cortège rolled through the London of 1997, it would have been met by puzzlement and even indifference by millions who were almost completely ignorant of his life and his era. If, by some magic process, the British people of 1965 had been shown the events surrounding the Princess's death, they would have been shocked and—in many cases—actually disgusted. There is no clearer measure of the change which has overtaken the culture of this country in a matter of thirty-five years, the sort of change which in past times might have come about over a matter of centuries.

Imagine for a moment that a young woman, tearfully placing flowers against the gates of Kensington Palace in the autumn of 1997, has been plucked out of her time and allowed to wander at will through the London of thirty-two years before. Imagine how much would amaze her, and how little she would find that was well known to her by sight, touch, sound, taste or smell. Joining the shuffling line of mourners waiting to file past Churchill's coffin in Westminster Hall, she would be astonished by how strongly men outnumbered women, and by the dowdy and conservative fashions they wore. She would be surprised to see so many overcoats and hats and headscarves, so many carefully polished and much-mended leather shoes, so many tightly tied ties on the men, so many schoolboys wearing shorts and caps. Overhearing their conversation, she would notice the absence of swear-words, the edgy, plummy accents of the middle-class and the earthy tongue of the working-class Londoner, much richer, slower and gamier than the thin Estuary English of her own time.

She would be pulled up short to find public lavatories labelled Ladies and Gentlemen, by the absence of heavy traffic, the smallness of lorries, the cumbersome designs of vans, by the slowness and the bulbous shape of most cars, by the speed and frequency of buses, which would seem unnaturally red because of the general absence of bright colour from the streetscape. The conductors with their buttoned-up uniforms, peaked caps and hand-cranked ticket machines would seem to be escapees from a folklore museum. She would be puzzled to find large, irregular paving stones at her feet even in the suburbs, instead of tarmac. She would be pleased to find the walls clear of the scribblings of graffiti artists. The streetlamps would appear oddly small, infrequent and dim. There would be less litter, less dog-muck and much less chewing gum stuck to the pavement than she was used to.

She would turn up her nose at the number of people smoking, and at the amazing variety of places where they were allowed to do it. She might be shocked to hear homosexuals openly referred to as 'queers', though she would be unlikely to experience any indelicate conversations except by accident, unless she wandered into very avant-garde circles. She would find the newspapers grey, thin and mostly stodgy, many of them still using double- and triple-decker headlines. *The Times,* with advertisements on its front page, would baffle her, as would the *Sun,* a rather grave left-leaning newspaper. The *Express* and the *Mail* would remind her of today's *Daily Telegraph,* while the high seriousness of the *Daily Mirror* would leave her wondering what had happened to taste and education in the lost years between. The banknotes would seem oddly large, the coinage heavy and complicated, with many pennies old and worn, dating back to the last century and claiming imperial ownership of India in their long Latin inscriptions. Yet shopkeepers and their assistants would manipulate their heavy, ringing, mechanical cash registers with confidence, perfectly able to make the complicated calculations in their heads without the aid of calculators.

She would find the generally accepted level of hygiene rather low, the slogans on the advertising billboards blatant and naïve, the policemen astonishingly numerous yet far less menacing, without their modern armoury of billy-club, dangling handcuffs and squawking radio, but buttoned into dull-but-disciplined tunics. She would search long and hard for a public telephone, and be amused by its whirring black boxes, chrome buttons marked A and B and its dial. She would be wonderfully surprised to discover a complete rack of telephone directories containing, in four not-very-thick volumes, the name and number of every subscriber in London. She would be confused by the purr of the dialling tone, and surprised to find that she needed the operator to call her home town, a mere forty miles away, if, that is, her home town even existed. She might find that it was as yet unbuilt, a stretch of brambly heath, fields, hedges and woods, perhaps of elm trees destined to die in the approaching epidemic.

London itself would seem extraordinarily dark and dirty even by daylight, with Nelson's Column, the great frontages of Whitehall and Westminster Abbey, not to mention the Houses of Parliament, all sombre black, and most of the rest dingily brown or grey. The colour brown, in fact, would seem to crop up in almost every aspect of urban life, from food to furniture. If she had time to venture into the provinces, she would perhaps feel oppressed by the survival of so many Victorian buildings, so much Gothic architecture, perhaps cheered by the absence of inner ring-roads, one-way systems, pedestrian precincts and multistorey carparks. The sight, sound and smell of steam engines pulling regular scheduled trains, and of racks of milk churns awaiting collection at wayside stations (in defiance of yet-to-be-invented health regulations) would convince her that she had wandered back further in time than she actually had done. She would rapidly notice that the past was smellier than the present, the air often reeking of breweries, cattlemarkets, cabbage and hot grease.

She would feel entirely safe as she travelled late at night on the London Underground, but irritated by the way that male travellers automatically offered her their seats and made way for her. Yet she would be pleased to see dozens of uniformed staff, wearing peaked caps like the conductors on the buses. Changing onto a suburban train, she would grapple with many unfamiliar sights—concertina steel barriers barring her way to the platform unless she showed a ticket, the ticket itself, a thick but tiny piece of pasteboard, the unfamiliar livery of the carriages and the compartments marked Ladies Only which offended her feminist instincts with their name, while soothing them with their sensible purpose. Placing her feet upon the seat opposite, she would be hurt and chastened when her shocked travelling companions—with one voice—urged her to take them down again. She would marvel at the flimsy locks on people's front doors.

After a while, she would observe that drivers in cars were not wearing seat belts, and did not even seem to have them fitted, while few motorcyclists wore helmets. She might be perturbed to see that most drivers, and most people working in jobs above the level of secretary, cleaner and shop assistant, were male. She would be struck by the numbers of people walking. She would be puzzled at the large numbers of women accompanying their own children. At her hotel, she would be struck by the way the staff had never heard of credit cards, by the fact that her room lacked its own bathroom or television, and by the strange radio, slow to warm up and apparently broadcasting through a screen of blankets, that seemed capable of receiving only three stations, none of them transmitting anything recognizable as popular music to her. If she visited anyone at home, she would be very likely to shiver at the absence of central heating, and to toss and turn beneath the unfamiliar weight of sheets and blankets instead of a familiar duvet.

Wherever she stayed, she would gape in disappointment at the tiny black-and-white television set, wobbling on its stalky legs, and equipped with but two—possibly three—channels. Turning it on during the afternoon, she would experience the test card rather than a talk show. Later, she would be slightly outraged to see several commercials for cigarettes, and terse news programmes entirely anchored by men. She would realize that she had hardly seen a black or brown face all day. Those she did see had been dressed, if anything, more conventionally than everyone else. Her travels would be undisturbed by the one-sided braying conversations of mobile phone users, or the leaking whisper of personal stereo players. She would, however, have been surprised by the number of people whistling as they walked. She would see no joggers. Cyclists, though more numerous, would be wearing trouser-clips rather than crash helmets or lycra shorts.

If she went out in search of food, she would look in vain for a late-night supermarket or even a corner shop, though she might be able to buy milk in an awkward waxy carton from a machine. An off-licence would surprise her with its small selection of beer, cider (sweet or dry, in a thick brown bottle corked with a rubber stopper), uninspiring wine, gin and whisky. The pub it was usually attached to would not be welcoming, and its range of tepid bitter ales would seem drearily narrow. Lager, as recently as this, was a fairly exotic drink brewed abroad and served in special tall glasses, if at all. Pepsi Cola and Coca-Cola might be available, but usually in bottles. Children still drank ginger beer or dandelion and burdock as a treat. Sandwiches, in pubs and cafes, would be unwrapped. Bread would usually be white and sliced. In grocers' shops she would see white hen's eggs on sale, bearing the Lion stamp of the Egg Marketing Board. If she tried to buy beer in a can rather than a bottle, she would discover that she needed to use a special tool to punch holes in it. Restaurants would listen in polite incomprehension to her requests for a pizza or a hamburger. If she entered one of the rare Wimpy Bars, she would wince in disappointment at the tasteless brown disc clamped between two slices of unfresh bun. Perhaps moving on to a café, she would gag at the thick gravy, push aside the watery murdered vegetables, refuse the stodgy pudding and reject the washy unrecognizable coffee in favour of strong brown tea thickened with copious white sugar, and full of leaves that clung to her gums. She would notice that older people often had bad teeth of their own or ill-fitting, obviously false ones, and that she was strikingly taller than them.

As she made her way back to her hotel, she would be disturbed by the silence and emptiness of the streets after the pubs closed at 10.30, and the absence of traffic. She would notice for the first time the unfamiliar, literate traffic signs 'Halt at Major Road Ahead' or 'Children Crossing', with their red cast-iron triangles and discs. She would hesitate at zebra crossings, protected by nothing more than stripes in the road and yellow Belisha beacons.* And she would think how different the shopping streets looked without yellow lines painted along every gutter, and how pleasant the side streets looked without cars parked nose to tail along them. She might observe that many more houses had little front gardens instead of concrete car-parking bays. The clanging bell of a passing ambulance would make her jump, as no siren ever could have done. If she found herself trapped in the past during a Sunday, she would fully understand the despairing comment of the French visitor Hyppolite Taine, who said of Victorian London that on the sabbath it resembled nothing so much as a 'large and well-ordered cemetery.' The British Sunday was still very much in force, and almost everything would have been closed very firmly indeed.

On the morning of Churchill's funeral, the crowds, friendly and considerate, united by a common loss, would reassure her that the world had not changed quite as much as she feared. Or had it? For the family feeling that genuinely united Britain on 31 January 1965 was entirely different from the largely manufactured and partly stage-managed sentiment that bewitched it on 6 September 1997. It was also much less dependent upon television for its atmosphere.

Churchill's death, at the age of ninety, was peaceful and came as no surprise. The grief, therefore, was the gentle sorrow of farewell, rather than the fierce and partisan mourning of sudden and seemingly unjust bereavement. Churchill was certainly not universally loved. In 1965 there were people, probably numbered in tens of thousands, for whom his long-ago role as a class warrior and Tory politician still seemed more important than his part in saving the whole world from tyranny. Yet they would have respected him, and acknowledged that national mourning was fitting and proper. But even these mild malcontents were a minority of a minority.

In 1997 there were uncounted millions who felt that the mourning for Princess Diana was overblown and unjustified, and who feared that the crowds weeping for the Princess could easily have been turned into a republican mob. They did not welcome the unending coverage on TV and radio, they did not rejoice at the Prime Minister's role in the obsequies, they did not want to sign any book of condolence or take flowers to Kensington, they strongly disapproved of Earl Spencer's funeral speech, they had doubts about the taste of Elton John's performance in the Abbey, they disliked the applause and the flash of cameras which marked the passing of the Princess's coffin. Great numbers of such people, for the most part those who could remember 1965, were, however, silent.

The society they now lived in, where the word of television was law, suddenly allowed only one point of view to be expressed openly, and it was not theirs. They suspected that they were far from alone, but could not be sure, and as a result lacked confidence. Their feelings were not being expressed through the only medium that counted, and they were therefore reduced to mere individuals, powerless atoms. This dictatorship of grief, wielded by a powerful media élite, was an extreme version of what had been taking place for some time. More astute social conservatives realized that the lens of television was sending society a picture of itself that was simultaneously flattering, dishonest and designed to encourage only one set of ideas about what was good—in politics, humour, architecture, foreign affairs, charity, fashion, education and morals.

But the new conformists who had captured the cultural high ground needed—as they had from the first—the illusion that they were rebels against something, that they were in fact a brave guerrilla band still fighting for the cause in some remote sierra. Just as the Cuban dictator Fidel Castro still called his government-controlled radio station 'Rebel Radio', and dressed in beautifully tailored jungle fatigues long after he was past pensionable age, they liked to think they were still revolutionaries. So that they could believe this, they had invented the image of an all-powerful establishment, made up of hanging judges, public school headmasters, hereditary peers, biblical bishops, militarists, Fleet Street barons, Royal Academicians who still liked proper pictures, the Lord Chamberlain, poets who rhymed and scanned, and of course the monarchy. Most of these sorts of people were already trembling on the edge of the grave by the middle 1950s. In fact, it was just at the moment when their influence was turning to dust and ashes that they suddenly became famous. They were required, or at least their images were, to make the younger generation feel as if they were true, bold revolutionaries, marching against a wicked foe with bandoliers romantically slung across their manly (or womanly) chests. It is no wonder that the famous portrait of Ernesto 'Che' Guevara, beret atop untamed hair and beard, became a sort of religious icon for the suburban revolutionaries who protested in the 1960s and 1970s, but occupied the corner offices in the 1990s.

Thus, as the surviving representatives of the older way of life hobbled towards the obituary columns, their lives were artificially prolonged by the satire industry and the 'anti-establishment' tendencies in politics, academe, broadcasting and the press. Their supposed influence gave the glory of revolutionary struggle to what would otherwise have been little more than the triumph of ambition. Everyone needs an ethical justification for his or her life, and revolution is a better justification than most.

The convenient fiction of a stuffy and obstructive establishment was never more blatantly and falsely employed than during the miserable few days when the Queen and her family were urged to snivel in public over the death of Diana, and Buckingham Palace was forced to fly the wrong flag at half-mast to placate a supposedly enraged populace. How widely this enraged view was truly held it is now impossible to say. The education system and years of television had seriously reduced the ability of the British people to think for themselves, and television's conformist power had never been so strong. It is hard to believe that a real majority of British citizens were thirsting to humiliate their Queen in this fashion, but it appeared to be so on television. Many media people hoped that it was so, and by reflecting this—possibly false—image into people's homes, they brought it to life. Opinion on such things is extraordinarily hard to measure, and we may never know what views dominated in the British population at that time. What is well known now is that many people did feel they were somehow separated from the mainstream of thought, because they personally did not hold the views which were being trumpeted from the studios and the outside broadcast compounds at the gates of Buckingham Palace.

Those who queued to see Churchill lying in state were a loyal, restrained and self-controlled people, not much given to mass hysteria despite a sentimentality that today seems cloying. They were also better equipped, through experience and education, to think for themselves. Thanks to recent war, the fathers of millions of families had seen the face of battle. Thanks to the empire, every corner-boy had seen the Taj Mahal, or the Pyramids, or the jungles of Burma. In 1965, even the radicals were loyal patriots. Republicanism was a tiny strand of opinion in a nation which accepted that it was a monarchy in much the same way that it accepted that air was for breathing and water for drinking. Most unhesitatingly believed that British institutions and inventions were the best in the world. The throne represented not so much authority as continuity, respectability and the family, characteristics specially valued by the lower middle and working class, who also clung fiercely to good manners and proper behaviour. British soldiers, ships, aeroplanes, policemen and justice were all the best in the world. Hadn't we beaten the Germans? We knew how to behave, we were fair in our dealings and, if a thing was British-made, it was unrivalled.

This feeling had been beautifully expressed by the thriller writer Eric Ambler in a 1937 book, *Uncommon Danger*. These are the sentiments he places in the mouth of a travelling salesman:

> Fifteen years I've been trailing about this blasted Continent now, and I've hated every moment of it. I hate their grub. I hate their drinks, I hate their way of going on and I hate them. They say the British are all stuck up about foreigners, that we're all men and women just the same, and they've got a lot of good points that we haven't. It's all lies, and when you've been away from home as long as I have, you'll know it too. They're not like us, not at all. People come over here for a fortnight's holiday and see a lot of pretty chalets and chateaux and schloesser and say what a fine place it is to live in. They don't know what they're talking about. They only see the top coat. They don't see the real differences. They don't see behind the scenes. They don't see them when their blood's up. I've seen them all right. I was in sunny Italy when the fascisti went for the freemasons in twenty-five. Florence it was. Night after night of it with shooting and beating and screams, till you felt like vomiting. I was in Vienna in thirty-four when they turned the guns on the municipal flats with the women and children inside them. A lot of the men they strung up afterwards had to be lifted on to the gallows because of their wounds. I saw the Paris riots with the garde mobile shooting down the crowd like flies and everyone howling 'mort au vaches' like lunatics. I saw the Nazis in Frankfurt kick a man to death in his front garden. After the first he never made a sound. I was arrested

that night because I'd seen it but they had to let me go. In Spain, they tell me, they doused men with petrol and set light to them.

Nice chaps, aren't they? Picturesque, gay, cleverer, more logical than silly us.

This is a fair if rather politically aware summary of the prejudices (and postjudices) of an unexceptional and reasonably well-educated Englishman well into the post-war era. It is followed by some pretty scathing remarks on the business practices of our European partners-to-be, and on their attitudes towards trade unions. People brought up in post-cultural-revolution Britain would dismiss this passionate speech as right-wing, and typical of the so-called 'snobbery with violence' school of writing. This merely shows how little they know of the past. When he wrote this book, Ambler was flirting with the communist-inspired popular front. The most attractive characters in the story are a pair of Soviet agents, who manage to save stolen Kremlin secrets from falling into fascist hands, with the aid of a British journalist. In the 1950s and early 1960s, just as in the 1930s, almost all British people still mistrusted 'abroad' and felt superior to foreigners, whether they were of the Left or the Right. Communists did not care about racial or sexual politics. It was less than half a century since the South African Communist Party had tried to rally that nation's wageslaves with the cry 'Workers of the World Unite for a White South Africa!'

More modern divisions over social or sexual attitudes were simply not reflected in the left-right split. Working-class socialists were likely to be less sympathetic to homosexuality, more opposed to abortion, more likely to support stiff alcohol licensing laws (and even to have been brought up believing in temperance) than middle-class Conservatives. Two of the most dogged opponents of abortion law reform were the Mahon brothers, Labour MPs from Merseyside. Nobody saw anything strange about this. Labour's working-class base was also its conservative foundation. Working-class socialists of the time were at one with the middle class on the need for good behaviour. All were also intensely law abiding, orderly and respectable. They would have been dismayed by the casual clothing and habits of many of those who waited to sign books of condolence for the Princess on the long warm evenings before the funeral. In 1965, there were no picnics, no bottles of wine or cans of beer (eating in the street, except for a holiday ice cream or a homebound parcel of fish and chips, was practically unknown, and drinking in the street quite unthinkable for most people), no gaudy casual clothes to be seen as they waited to pass through Westminster Hall. Such things simply were not done.

Yet they were not an unemotional people, simply highly restrained in their emotion. Rene MacColl wrote in the *Daily Express* that 'for a British crowd, the tears were surprisingly copious. People dashed at their eyes with handkerchiefs, gripped by what was clearly a sharp and personal sense of grief.' Yet there was utter silence, so that 'even a whisper would have sounded shrill'.

It may have been because of the freezing, sleety weather, or because in 1965 people worked more rigid hours for less flexible employers, but the crowds were not so large as those who flowed through central London in the warm, relaxed days and nights of Diana Week. Yet at the time, the 321,360 who filed through Westminster Hall seemed to be an astonishingly large number. In those days, people had not been fed television images of gigantic crowds in turbulent foreign countries, and London was not used to large demonstrations of public feeling. There had been nothing like this since the Coronation, though that was a relatively recent event, only twelve years before. In any case, this was still the world capital of restraint. The habit of heaping flowers was as yet unborn. Lady Churchill had requested that there be no flowers, and had been obeyed by everyone except the schoolchildren of Sir Winston's old parliamentary seat at Woodford, who laid modest posies around the village cross.

The event was not experienced wholly through television. There was no rolling news service, and the broadcasters contented themselves with unearthing a few old episodes of Churchill's TV biography, *The Valiant Years*. Flags were flown at half-mast for only two days, theatres respectfully dimmed their outside lights and sporting events went ahead as normal, though footballers playing on the day of the burial were asked to wear black armbands. Many others did the same, or wore black ties. The traditions of mourning, including the doffing of hats and the drawing down of blinds, were still well-known parts of life. The idea of applause at a funeral, or the throwing of flowers at a hearse, would have caused amazement.

So would the suggestion that, say, Vera Lynn might sing a popular song in St Paul's Cathedral during the obsequies. It would just not have been done, and that would have been that. The language of the service was the sonorous and beautiful liturgy of the sixteenth century. New translations of the Bible were available, but nobody would have thought of using them in St Paul's Cathedral on such a day. 'Go-ahead' clergymen, as they were then humorously called, might have been practising modernized prayers and hymns in a few churches, and Anglicans were still trying to digest the 'South Bank' religion expressed in John Robinson's *Honest to God* two years before. But the language of faith was still the language of Thomas Cranmer. The hymns, 'Fight the Good Fight' and Bunyan's 'Who Would True Valour See' were still well known to almost everybody, and could be sung heartily without embarrassment or fear that the singer would be accused of militarism.

Most people of all classes were still familiar with the basic texts of the Christian faith, its words, music, traditions and seasons. They would have known what the Beatitudes were, known what was meant by the Sermon on the Mount, the

Good Samaritan, the Prodigal Son and the Eye of the Needle. The Church's terminology and its calendar were still part of normal speech. 'Whitsun' was a national spring holiday, a traditional time to get married, as recalled in Philip Larkin's poem 'The Whitsun Weddings', then modern, now an evocation of an England of steam engines and small fields that is impossibly distant from today. People went to 'Communion' or perhaps 'Mass', but seldom if ever to 'Eucharists'. The faithful of the Church of England and the Methodist Church, for the most part, went to services where communion was not taken. Children sang hymns in school, and would have been amazed to see, as we did in the aftermath of the Diana funeral, teachers singing them solo, while the school looked on in silence as if witnessing the performance of an obscure and forgotten folktune.

Yet even as Earl Attlee stumbled on the cathedral steps (he was attending his old rival's funeral in defiance of doctor's orders), many of the things which appeared set and secure that day were already ceasing to be. The vast and busy London docks, which had dipped their cranes as the ex–Prime Minister's coffin was borne past them by boat, were doomed to be put out of business by new container ports free of ancient union practices, and then to be turned into costly zones of new offices, apartment blocks and wine bars. The soldiers, sailors and airmen who escorted the procession all knew or suspected that their great imperial age was over. In less than two years, a pitiless series of spending cuts would abolish or merge ancient regiments, condemn dozens of ships to the scrapyard and close a string of hard-won (and recently recaptured) bases east of Suez.

As the Spitfires, survivors of the war, flew overhead in salute, the air marshals knew that Britain would never again build her own fighting aircraft. The TSR-2, a final attempt by the British aircraft industry to produce a home-grown strike plane, was about to be cancelled amid jeers that it was 'the world's first white elephant with folding wings'. The entire fleet of 1950s vintage Valiant nuclear bombers had just been grounded and scrapped because of metal fatigue. An approaching defence review would sink the Navy's hopes of a new aircraft carrier, dooming its ability to act as a global force, though it would still—just—be capable of mounting the Falklands operation seventeen years later. In one of the last colonial wars, British troops were fighting to keep Indonesia out of Malaya. Three decades later, we would be selling weapons to Malaysia and Indonesia.

For the observant there were many other signs and portents of change to come. The leaders who came from the old dominions, Menzies, Holyoake and Diefenbaker, were all themselves old and grey, survivors of the time when the people of these countries automatically thought of Britain as 'home', and saw it as their duty to defend her when she was in trouble. General de Gaulle was the last French leader to believe passionately in a 'Europe of Nations' rather than the federal superstate that was already taking shape.

In and around London, the old security and safety were passing. There was alarm at the increase in the number of burglaries in the capital. The Home Office had just revealed that 20,000 London homes had been broken into in 1964, compared with 5,500 in 1938. (The current total is something like 165,000 a year.) During the funeral, robbers ransacked the home of Churchill's private secretary, Montague Brown, demolishing the illusions of those who believed that there was honour among British thieves.

The last hangings in Britain had recently taken place, and criminals had stopped searching each other for weapons before setting off on bank raids, for they no longer feared being executed as accomplices to murder. Something called 'Beat Music' was being broadcast by 'pirate' offshore radio stations, by people known as disc jockeys, who spoke a new, slangy, informal and Americanized version of English, quite unlike the BBC, whose 'popular' programmes owed much more to the Britain of the 1940s than to the America of the 1950s. The new, disturbing sound and the first stirrings of a new crime wave seemed to be linked in some way. As Churchill lay dying, there had been a fatal stabbing in Southend after a 'Beat' dance. Two policemen were shot during a car chase in the London outskirts. A 'Beat' star's brother was tried for the crime of loitering with intent, since abolished.

A play called *Divorce Me, Darling* respectfully delayed its West End opening until the funeral was over. The subject was a little daring at a time when 93 per cent of marriages, including Churchill's own, endured to the grave. Few anticipated then how swiftly that would change, and how much. The entire sexual revolution, outside a small and supposedly educated élite, had yet to begin. As late as 1965, the child of divorced parents was an exception at any school, illegitimate children were a shameful rarity, homosexual acts were illegal, and contraception and abortion were taboo subjects in most homes, though 'avant-garde' broadcasters were already pushing hard at the limits of public taste, especially on the newly opened BBC2 channel, available only in limited areas, and also in the then-famous Wednesday Plays on BBC1, and on the original satire programme *That Was The Week That Was (TW3)*. There was resistance. Mrs Mary Whitehouse had already founded her campaign to clean up television at a meeting in Birmingham which was far bigger than she—or the BBC—had expected.*

Though many changes had begun to gather pace in 1963, the year of Philip Larkin's great divide, when sexual intercourse began, just after the *Lady Chatterley* trial and the issue of the Beatles' first LP, they had not gone deep or reached into the lives of the cautious suburban millions. Just as a time-traveller from 1997 would have found 1965 London alien and unfamiliar, a similar voyager from 1937 would have felt very much at home. As George Orwell wrote in his lyrical *The Lion and the Unicorn* in 1941, it would take more than a mere world war to change the deep character of Britain:

> Nor need we fear that as the pattern changes life in England will lose its peculiar flavour. The new red cities of Greater London are crude enough, but these things are only the rash that accompanies a change. In whatever shape England emerges from the war it will be deeply tinged with the characteristics that I have spoken of earlier. The intellectuals who hope to see it Russianized or Germanized will be disappointed. The gentleness, the hypocrisy, the thoughtlessness, the reverence for law and the hatred of uniforms will remain, along with the suet puddings and the misty skies. It needs some very great disaster, such as prolonged subjugation by a foreign enemy, to destroy a national culture. The Stock Exchange will be pulled down, the horse plough will give way to the tractor, the country houses will be turned into children's holiday camps, the Eton and Harrow match will be forgotten, but England will still be England, an everlasting animal stretching into the future and the past and, like all living things, having the power to change out of recognition and yet remain the same.

However, Orwell had not reckoned with a change still more shocking than any of these (and his predictions were uncannily accurate, though he did not foresee the death of the suet pudding, an item of diet which came close to an obsession for him). In the same essay, he derided the English intelligentsia for their isolation from the common people:

> In intention, at any rate, the English intelligentsia are Europeanized. They take their cookery from Paris and their opinions from Moscow. In the general patriotism of the country they form a sort of island of dissident thought. England is perhaps the only great country whose intellectuals are ashamed of their own nationality. In left-wing circles it is

always felt that there is something slightly disgraceful in being an Englishman and that it is a duty to snigger at every English institution, from horse racing to suet puddings. It is a strange fact, but it is unquestionably true that almost any English intellectual would feel more ashamed of standing to attention during 'God Save the King' than of stealing from a poor box.

To a great extent this, too, was still true in 1965. But within two or three years, this once-laughable strand of thought and feeling would break out of its little bookish world and storm the cultural centres of the country, making patriotism, monarchy and Englishness in general unfashionable and—worst of all—comical. Intellectual London, in George Orwell's use of the world, had already seen and laughed at Alan Bennett's *Beyond the Fringe*. This play's little jokes about the war now seem incredibly mild, but they truly shocked those who heard them—even those who took pleasure in the debunking of war-worship—when it was first staged. The much bolder mockery of *Forty Years On* would not follow until 1968, though the satire of *That Was The Week That Was* was already a cult among the southern middle class.

However, this sort of humour, political, deliberately subversive of common beliefs and institutions, would take many years to force out the other kinds, mildly bawdy, affectionate, a little camp but essentially non-political. But it would triumph. When the well-loved comedy writer Frank Muir died in 1997, his friend and collaborator Denis Norden sadly remarked that Muir's humour had been rooted in a rich British shared culture, as had that of the incomparable P. G. Wodehouse. He damned what had replaced it as being based on nothing more than 'lager, football and bodily functions'.

Those words might be the epitaph for the three decades between the two funerals. In 1965, the people of Britain may have been poorer, smaller, shabbier, dirtier, colder, narrower, more set in their ways, ignorant of olive oil, polenta and—even—lager. But they knew what united them, they shared a complicated web of beliefs, attitudes, prejudices, loyalties and dislikes. By 1997 they were unsure and at sea. Those over forty no longer felt they were living in the country where they had grown up, and while they may secretly have held to older views and customs, they publicly accepted the new arrangements with a tolerant smile. Those under forty, for the most part, had only the sketchiest notion of who they were and of how or when their surroundings had come to be as they were, had little common language with either parents or grandparents, and despised much of what the previous generation had admired. Like the radical pioneers of the 1960s, they still believed themselves to be rebels against heavy-handed authority. But they had little idea of what they were rebelling against or even why, only that rebellion was almost always the right attitude, that the ideas of the past were invariably wrong, that putting the clock back was a sin, while progress and change were both inevitable and right.

The seeds of this crop had been sown long before Churchill's death in January 1965. Many of the years since the Second World War had been rackety and uncertain, shabby and farcical. The family inheritance was mortgaged to pay for a war which we had shamefully sought to avoid until the last possible moment. The new generation, still deeply affected by the fearful loss and destruction of the 1914–18 war, lacked the confidence, or if you prefer, the arrogance of the old. A brief and intense effort to recreate the safe and stable world of the 1930s middle class had obviously failed. Higher taxes and the decay of deference had made it impossible for them to find or hire willing servants any more. The great national common effort of 1939–45 had mortally wounded a class system based on deference and background. It had replaced it with a mixture of snobbery and meritocracy which was, if anything, more puzzling and illogical than what had gone before. When a return of affluence and a fall in taxes allowed the wealthier professionals to have servants once more, they tended to come from abroad or from former colonies. Few if any British people would now be prepared to serve in a fellow-citizen's house.

The last truly aristocratic Conservative government, whose ministers spent August upon the grouse moors like characters in a John Buchan shilling shocker, had perished just over a year before, partly because it had ceased to be respectable. It is quite amazing to reflect that the infidelity of John Profumo with Christine Keeler had led to a wild, flapping scandal and an inquiry chaired by a High Court judge, when only thirty-two years later Robin Cook could house his mistress in Carlton Gardens and the nation either shrugged or giggled. The Profumo affair had reinforced the dismal lessons of Suez, seven years before—that Britain was no longer a serious country. The Suez episode, while still mourned by many as a great opportunity lost through American interference, had upset the idea that the Soldier of the Queen always won his battles. Even those—and they were probably in the great majority—who never questioned its rightness understood that withdrawal meant defeat and a diminished standing in the world.

India had been independent for almost twenty years, and the colonies of Africa were throwing off British rule as fast as new flags could be designed and new national anthems written. The old struggle between Afrikaner and British settlers in South Africa had ended in the triumph of the Nationalist Party, the building of grand apartheid and the founding of a Boer republic outside the Commonwealth. Though atlases still showed the remaining Commonwealth countries in reassuring pink, the rest of the Empire was all but gone. There was no longer the slightest doubt that the United States had become by far the richer and the more powerful of the two great English-speaking powers, which a generation ago had seen themselves as equals and rivals.

Yet the survival of the fabled Victorian, Sir Winston, into the modern age somehow postponed a final recognition of the

truth about Britain. As young men are restrained by the survival of a once-feared father, and liberated by his death, so the
new, less majestic England could not properly be born until
this symbol of lost times was safely out of the way. Just as President Kennedy's murder signalled the end of the USA's era of
white-bread suburban innocence, Churchill's death compelled
those living in his shadow to grow up, very quickly, in ways
which he would not much have liked. It is a sad truth that
young men often go to old men's obsequies mainly to make
sure that they are dead, and many young men in the Britain
of 1965 were relieved and liberated once the elegiac ceremonies
were over. Or at least they felt they were.

There is another quite simple reason for the restlessness of
the time: the fact that the great 'bulge' of children born in the
years immediately after the war were about to come of age, at
twenty-one as they still did then, and so had started to anticipate the new freedoms of adult life. Those who had matured
before this date had all grown up in the deep shadow of the
war generation, whose heroes and footsoldiers were still in
their full vigour. Now, with their leader dead, these veterans
were suddenly middle-aged, and knew that they too must eventually step aside.

In some ways like the USSR until Gorbachev, the peoples
of the United Kingdom had been living in the enjoyable but
stifling fug of wartime myth. Schoolboys growing up in 1950s
Britain could see the evidence of recent violent struggle all
around them. Cities were still pitted with bomb sites, glaring
evidence of a destructive but honourable war (the last of these,
off Ludgate Hill in the City of London, was only developed in
1999). In this atmosphere of lingering national solidarity, all
schoolchildren still lived very much under the joint authority
of the wartime generation, with parents and teachers forming
an impenetrable barrier of power.

Comprehensive schools were beginning to replace grammar
schools and secondary moderns.* One specially adventurous

comprehensive—Risinghill in London—had abolished caning, still in daily use in most private and state schools. However, this radical academy was still patrolled by prefects, who politely asked the headmaster's permission before taking part in a protest march. Teachers were still imparting an unchanged view of the world, more or less patriotic, centred upon the history of England and its literature. The world of *Grange Hill,* of mass truancy, of middle-class flight from big-city state schools, was still in the unknown future. If deference between the classes was vanishing, deference between the generations was still strong.

The young, of course, knew that Britain was always right in every conflict she undertook. As for the older people who had lived in the years before 1939, the discovery of the death camps during the liberation of Germany had simply driven away memories of the low morale, division and doubt which had afflicted much of the country in 1938 and 1939, when Conservatives had seen war as avoidable, and left-wingers had believed it would be a base imperialist conflict which did not deserve their support. Once victory was possible, and once the battle had been given a clear moral purpose by the opening of the camp gates, both Left and Right had invented fables to prove that they—and only they—had truly understood the evil of Nazism, and sought to combat it at the earliest possible moment. Those fables still lay behind much political debate in 1965, but Left and Right were equally able to respect Churchill, who had been the only politician with a consistent record of hostility to appeasement and understanding of the German threat.

The Left liked to claim that it had fought the first battles against fascism in Spain, and had pioneered the idea of collective security against the dictators. It conveniently forgot that it had opposed British rearmament on the grounds that the weapons would be used for imperialist purposes. The Labour-supporting *Daily Herald* had called the very modest Defence

White Paper of 1934 (which began the rebuilding of the RAF) an 'insult to Germany'. Labour in Parliament had voted against RAF expansion long after the nature of the Nazi regime became clear, and opposed military conscription even after Hitler had marched into Prague in 1939. The Right, just as falsely, maintained that it had been playing for time during the appeasement period, and pretended that the policy had worked, delivering the Spitfires just in time to fight the Battle of Britain. The truth was that the Tories had been scared of rearming because they thought it would be unpopular, and that—as so often—they had been frightened away from the wiser course by the Treasury.

It is probably because these comforting but dishonest fables were so potent that Britain had still to confront the fact that her principal European ally of necessity, the USSR, was a tyranny as gory and revolting as Hitler's. To admit this would be to accept that the suffering, the deaths and the destruction had been a desperate battle for survival first, brought about by unreadiness and parsimony, and a crusade second. The treatment of the Dunkirk retreat as a triumph was a significant part of this. A film which drew attention to the darker, gloomier side of Dunkirk, was a box-office failure, and it would be some time yet before the real nature of the event could be openly discussed in Nicholas Harman's well-titled *Dunkirk: The Necessary Myth*.

This was specially important because of the huge scale of the war effort and the breadth and depth of the destruction it had caused not just to the physical fabric of the country but to its social fabric. Few now recall that the immediate postwar years were a time when many were alarmed by a rapid increase in crime, an atmosphere of purposeless rebellion among the young and a great deal of family breakdown because of the number of marriages which failed to survive the long partings of war. There are some surprisingly frank descriptions of a working-class marriage wrecked by war in Nicholas

Monsarrat's *The Cruel Sea,* almost certainly drawn from the lives of sailors with whom he had served.

The cosiness and the myths, like a warm, lighted house amid a winter landscape, continued to have a strong appeal as long as the memories of war were kept alive by our surroundings. Even in 1965, some walls still bore the urgently painted signs pointing to air-raid shelters or emergency fire hydrants, faded but clearly visible. Some roads still carried the traces of anti-invasion tank traps. The atmosphere of war persisted in all kinds of telling ways. Children's games were about battles with the Germans; story-books for boys had bomber pilots as their heroes. Without embarrassment, adults wrote and children read books with titles such as *Men of Glory.* Young and old believed that 'we' had won the war, with a little help from the Americans and the Russians, though we knew far more about purely British victories like the Battle of Britain, El Alamein and the sinking of the Nazi battleship *Bismarck* than we did about the decisive tank clashes of Kursk or the sea battles at Guadalcanal and Midway.

The important truth at the heart of this was that British determination *had* turned the hinge of fate in 1940, but this truth was surrounded by illusions and self-deceptions. Perhaps most important of all, the sweet glow of shared adversity and distant but real danger was preserved by the new conflict in the East. Our troops were still in Germany, more or less where they had finished up in May 1945. Their task was different, and yet the same—rescuing a chaotic and wilful Europe from strange foreign tyrants. A sprawling grey navy, physically similar to the one that had sunk the U-boats, still patrolled the cold northern seas, and the RAF, whose senior officers were survivors of the last war, still watched the skies for approaching danger with radar which we believed we had invented, though now the planes were powered with jets, which, again, we believed were a purely British idea.

Even our nuclear bombs, born out of fearful memories of our defenceless state after Dunkirk, had a sort of anti-Nazi flavour to them, even though they were aimed at the USSR. We had changed enemies almost as smoothly as the people of Orwell's Airstrip One had swapped Eastasia for Eurasia, while fighting the same war. It was this continuity, of mood, of manners, of surroundings, of language, of daily habit, which was about to be broken. Every familiar pathway was about to be ploughed up, every feature of the landscape about to be changed.

Now, for one last time, we were preparing to parade this benevolent and heartwarming mixture of noble truth and decent myth. The myth was decent because—unlike the USSR—Britain's good deeds in war flowed from a society that was profoundly civilized, gentle and humane. Russia's anti-Nazi valour arose from the need to defend a noxious regime against the treacherous attack of a temporary ally. Britain's was the generous fulfilment of an obligation, an obligation made only after she had been provoked beyond endurance. Yet the many good things about pre-war Britain, and the nation's ethical and responsible behaviour in 1939, were already beginning to be forgotten or overlaid by the time of Churchill's death. Those who recalled that Britain had any sort of welfare state before 1945, or who had experienced the prosperity and full employment of the south-east before the war, were growing fewer and less influential. The Left's picture of the 1920s and 1930s as a time of unrelieved depression, Jarrow marches, callousness and more or less pro-Nazi appeasement was already becoming the generally believed version.*

The remnants of Edwardian confidence and Victorian religious faith were losing their power to influence the British people. Routine, tradition and unchanging surroundings keep habits and ways of thought alive. Disruption, demolition, novelty and innovation destroy custom and certainty. For the very young, the ambitious and especially for those whose deep desires are frustrated by the invisible chains of an ordered society, change is always healthy and good and desirable. But for those with painfully earned skills, for those who seek security in an ordered way of life, change is a mixed curse, bringing confusion and even fear along with novelty and freshness. Whether the British people liked it or not, they were destined to spend the next three decades dancing and twitching and leaping to the beat of rapid and unstoppable change, a beat that was to grow faster and wilder with each passing year.

'Who controls the past,' ran the Party slogan, 'controls the future; who controls the present controls the past.'
—George Orwell, *Nineteen Eighty-Four*

If I forget thee, O Jerusalem, may my right hand forget its cunning.
—Psalm 137

I wasn't born yesterday.
—English saying

TWO

Born Yesterday

MOST OF US WERE BORN YESTERDAY, to all intents and purposes. The lore of our tribe, the stories of our ancestors, the memories which our parents held in common, have simply ceased to be. Thirty or forty years ago, we might all have known the stories of Alfred and the cakes, of Canute and the waves, of Caractacus and Boadicea, Hereward the Wake and Thomas à Becket. The titles of the parables—the Sower, the Prodigal Son, the Talents—would have instantly conjured up a picture in the rich colours of a stained-glass window. Phrases such as 'all sorts and conditions of men' and 'when two or three are gathered together', 'the fatted calf' and 'he passed by on the other side' would have meant the same thing to everyone who heard them. Now these things are as meaningless to millions as the forgotten myths of Greece.

We drive past ancient churches, Victorian town halls, abandoned grammar schools and guano-spattered statues, quite unaware of the forces that brought them into being, the struggles they commemorate or the sort of people who built them. A modern child, shown Sellar and Yeatman's *1066 and All That,* simply wouldn't get the joke. You cannot laugh at this satire on forgetfulness and confusion unless you, too, share the experience of misunderstanding and mixing up the Wars of the Roses, Lambert Simnel and Perkin Warbeck and the rest. You cannot even be enjoyably confused or forgetful about something which you never even knew in the first place. The young have not only been deprived of a good laugh, they have lost a common frame of reference with their forefathers, and the bridges which once linked them to the past have been fenced off, blocked or even blown up.

In the summer of 1998, in a last dying twitch of remembrance, elderly survivors of Japanese prison camps held silent protests along the processional route of Emperor Akihito of Japan, in London for a largely pointless state visit during which he was invested with the Order of the Garter, itself a decoration almost as incomprehensible to most modern Britons as Japanese music. A young woman called Alison Roberts perfectly summed up the feelings of her generation in an article for the London *Evening Standard* (27/05/98). She wrote:

> I represent the post-war 'blissfully ignorant generation'. People in their twenties (I was born in 1970) know about the Second World War as they might know about some vague, terrible history, taught at school and seen on the television but without even the solidity of indirect experience—my parents were born as the war ended, and had only tales of ration books and exotic bananas.

Miss Roberts went on to complain that the attacks on Japan by demonstrators and others were 'deeply racist'. Arguing that Britain was still unhealthily obsessed by the war, she asserted with some justice:

> Of course our national character has changed, profoundly and not least in our attitude towards war. Culturally, the very notion of willing sacrifice for King and country is anathema to most of my generation. It's class-ridden, mawkish, the stuff of costume drama and GCSE level poetry. I can't imagine any of my male friends accepting the kind of 'duty' which our grandfathers once accepted without protest.

We should be grateful to Miss Roberts for this unusually articulate statement, as she showed a rare perception of the fact that she was not equipped to understand her own country's recent past. Few of her age, and fewer still born in the twenty-five years after her, will ever be able to express their position so clearly. Most will not be aware of it, dwelling in a void of unknowing.

Into this void, all kinds of rubbish are blown by the wayward winds of modern education and popular 'culture'. A nation is the sum of its memories, and when those memories are allowed to die, it is less of a nation. However, when a people cease to believe their national myths, and cease to know or respect their history, it does not follow that they become blandly smiling internationalists. Far from it. In many cases they become fervent local patriots, fanatical supporters of a football team and imbued with a truly xenophobic hatred of people and football supporters from another town. Unmoved by national poetry or song, they instead allow themselves to be moved, or manipulated, by the fashionable pieties of 'protest' music. Deprived of older loyalties, they seek tribal sensations by being part of a supposed 'generation', with its special fashions in clothes, hair, entertainment, drugs and thought. The nation-state, as many people forget, is one of the most reliable engines of unselfishness and human solidarity. If it breaks down, the feelings which would have found their home in it seek other places where they are welcome.

It is hard to see why any society should have tried so hard to wipe out its own memory, as Britain has done in the past three decades. If this were Germany, Russia or Japan, there would at least be an excuse for voluntary amnesia, though there would also be very good reasons for making sure that it did not take hold. But the history of Britain, though far from perfect, is not shameful.

What is it about our past that has led to its being reformed out of existence? Like so much of what took place in the thirty years of upheaval, this change began long, long ago, part of the great unfinished, frustrated English revolution which, having been turned back by the Restoration of 1660, has sought ever since to break out in other ways. The revolutionaries' lowest point was the high point of the United Kingdom, of Protestantism and of Empire, all of which strengthened the throne, the aristocracy, the class system and the petty, infuriating illogicalities of the British class system. Thanks to this identification of conservatism with patriotism and with naval and military success, the link between radical or liberal views and anti-nationalist, anti-military sentiment has always been strong, helped along by post-colonial guilt. What is more, in our island nation, centuries of safety behind the shields of sea and navy have created the illusion that the world is a much kinder place than it truly is and so allowed the arguments of idealists to flourish, arguments which would have shrivelled in no time among the frequently conquered peoples and portable frontiers of the continent.

Kipling chided the pacifists of his time for 'making mock of uniforms that guard you while you sleep', and the witty reactionary Saki (H. H. Munro) made fun of some very early political correctness in his short story 'The Toys of Peace'. It quoted from a newspaper of March 1914, which reported that

> in the view of the National Peace Council there are grave objections to presenting our boys with regiments of fighting men, batteries of guns and squadrons of 'Dreadnoughts'. Boys, the Council admits, naturally love fighting and all the panoply of war, but that is no reason for encouraging, and perhaps giving permanent form to, their primitive instincts.

The story recounts the comic attempts of liberal parents to interest their sons in 'peace toys', including a model of John Stuart Mill, a ballot-box and a municipal bathhouse. After the beautifully described fiasco reveals that the boys have a vast and detailed knowledge of Europe's blood-soaked past, the father

retreated to the library and spent some thirty or forty minutes in wondering whether it would be possible to compile
a history for use in elementary schools, in which there should
be no prominent mention of battles, massacres, murderous
intrigues and violent deaths. The York and Lancaster period
and the Napoleonic era would, he admitted to himself, present considerable difficulties, and the Thirty Years War would
entail something of a gap if you left it out altogether. Still,
it would be something gained if, at a highly impressionable
age, children got to fix their attention on the invention of
calico printing instead of the Spanish Armada or the Battle
of Waterloo.

Saki did not live to see, as other reactionary satirists have done,
that it is impossible to invent anything so ludicrous that liberals will not eventually make it come true.

The arguments of the National Peace Council and everybody like them were buried by the German aggression of August
1914, an aggression which Saki had warned of in his novel
When William Came and had sought to prevent, by arguing
for universal military service. He and others who urged a proper
British Army in the Edwardian era are now mainly forgotten
because of the widely accepted version of history which suggests that 1914 Europe was a crate of dynamite waiting for a
detonator to set it off and that the war was brought about by
an 'arms race' and 'Nationalism'—not that Europe was destabilized by a serious imbalance of power, which the arms race
sadly failed to overcome. The liberal intelligentsia of the 1920s
and early 1930s took advantage of the universal revulsion
against the 1914–18 slaughter to put forward the very pacifist arguments which the war ought to have discredited for
good. Such was the disillusionment of the times, and so strong
the desire to end war for ever, that they had an audience wider
than ever before. It may also be true that many of the most
conservative and sceptical leaders of society had been ground

to fragments in the Flanders mud, since they had been the earliest to rally to the colours. Anyone who doubts the scale of the loss to thought, literature, the arts and politics should study the heartbreaking war memorials in every Oxford and Cambridge college, where the long, long lists of the dead prove that Britain's élite did not shirk its duties, any more than the middle class or the working class did.

So it was that—just as most Germans came to believe that their armies had been 'stabbed in the back' by socialism in 1918—almost everyone in Britain would come to blame the first Great War on 'militarism and the arms race'. The 'arms race' argument suffered a temporary setback when it was precisely Britain's failure to take part in the renewed arms race which led directly to a new imbalance of power, and therefore to the Second World War. The great paradox is that it was during the unprecedented armed peace of the 1950s and 1960s that a new and still more potent anti-nationalist, pacifist strain grew up in our culture.

The very success of NATO, together with the invincible strength of the USA, provided the conditions for Europeans to argue that war and nationhood were obsolete. The countries whose quarrel had divided Western Europe, France and Germany, embarked on a huge project to abolish war through economic and ultimately political union, a project that would later come to be known as the European Union, and to dominate the debate on the future of Europe. At the core of this scheme was a desire to return to a past which predated the nation-state. After all, the quarrel between France and Germany had really been a creation of the nineteenth century. The idea that they are fundamentally hostile to each other is a very recent one, and the real conflict in Europe has been between Britain, uniquely suited to be a nation-state because of its island position and its maritime tradition, and the continental urge towards some sort of unity, either imposed or agreed. The idea of a nation-state has never been particularly popular in Europe outside France, and even there, since Verdun and Vichy, it has been weakened by bloodletting, defeat and occupation.

Few in England, at this stage at least, grasped the significance of this rejection of the nation-state. But, partly under the auspices of the Council of Europe, the idea of using history to weaken the ties of nationhood and increase understanding began to spread among some historians. One of them was a man called E. H. Dance, a successful author of school histories with a passionate dislike of nationalist versions of the British past. By 1960, in a fascinating essay by Dance, we find the old arguments surfacing again. Like the peace-loving parents in Saki's story, he was clearly grieved by what he called 'drum and trumpet' history, seeing it as narrowly nationalistic and the likely cause of future war.

In *History the Betrayer,* Dance regrets that tradition and custom are keeping old ideas alive (precisely what they are supposed to do, of course) and urges action to change this.

'A generation of teachers teach what they learned when they were young; generations of scholars learn what they will teach to others; and therefore the history taught in schools and universities lags far behind the new world for which it is supposed to prepare its citizens.' The new world, not really specified, seems to be a Europe with all its old borders and conflicts smoothed over. 'So long as every people remains ignorant of the basic ideals and cultures of other peoples, disaster will always be, as now, just around the corner.'

Dance argues for a sort of world culture, in which nobody is taught that his own country's history comes first. 'Can anyone pretend we have no time for Aknathon or Buddha or Asoka or Al Hazen while we are finding time for Caractacus and Gaveston and Lambert Simnel and Titus Oates, and dozens of others as insignificant?' he asks, obviously outraged by the triviality of standard English history. After all, 'The rejection of trifles would make room for a good deal of vital significance in world history which at present is ignored.'

But Dance was not simply arguing for a different selection of facts because they would be more rewarding, nor for an expansion of the syllabus, though that is the most attractive part of his plan.

'It will not be enough to discard merely the unnecessary or the wrong. There is so much for which we ought to find room that we shall have to get rid of a good deal which is undoubtedly valuable—merely because to retain it will involve excluding things more valuable still.'

He has a much deeper purpose: 'Rejecting the non-essential is comparatively easy; what has to be tackled is the far harder task of rejecting what we have always thought it important to teach. We need a revolutionary "self-denying ordinance" followed by a "new model" which will cause offence to all but the least conservative.'

The new internationalism has a domestic agenda, too. These are 'modern pupils', so they will have to get used to a different order of things in Britain as well as in Europe and the world: 'Hardly any of them need to learn the traditions and duties of an upper class. All of them are going to live in a world where the working classes have powers and obligations inconceivable to the employees of Tom Brown and his contemporaries;* a world in which England counts for less than it did, and the US, Russia, India and China for far more.'

And let's not have too much about the 'Mother of Parliaments' and the cradle of democracy, either. 'There is less need to know how and why parliamentary democracy has succeeded in England than how and why it has failed nearly everywhere else.'

I had never heard of Mr Dance before I set out to write this book, and I doubt whether many outside the inner circles of the education industry have heard of him either. It was only when I asked experts for some pointers to the origins of the new history that I tracked him down. His arguments obviously seeped deep into the colleges of education and then into the schools. It was extraordinary, reading his words, to realize how long ago they were written. It is almost forty years since he urged: 'There is great value, not merely in getting prejudices removed from the school-books, but in persuading public opinion in general, at the present moment, that corrections are needed in the school-books.'

And he urged it with a passion and energy which it is hard not to admire, given the huge task which it must have seemed back then, to overturn the entire world of history teaching. 'History books and history teaching, and indeed all education, are at present vitiated by prejudices of many different kinds. They will continue to be so vitiated unless the prejudices are removed, not merely now but constantly.'

Dance was back again eleven years later, speaking with a good deal more confidence, in *History for a United World*. By this time, the tide of ideas was plainly flowing his way, and he was down to practicalities:

> What we still lack is textbooks, elementary and advanced, for schools. No doubt this is because too few certificate candidates take anything but old conventional topics and periods, and this is largely the fault of the examiners who set the syllabuses. Until they change their habits it will not pay publishers to produce enough school textbooks on the new topics and periods; until the textbooks are produced, teachers will find it very difficult to switch over from what is conventional to what is still novel.

Proclaiming that this vicious circle has to be broken, Dance demands a storming of the Winter Palace:

> It cannot be broken without a completely revolutionary attitude on the part of history teachers in schools and colleges and universities. This revolution in attitude has to be both negative and positive: negative, in the shape of a ruthless rejection of all the old history which has become less

important than the new; and positive, in the shape of a determined adoption of the new history which has become more important than the old. In both cases there is need for revolution; and it needs to be really revolutionary.

Like most such radicals, Dance could never have imagined that his revolution would go so far, or that it would destroy the rigour, discipline and language which he took for granted. It probably could not have happened at all without the reconstruction of Britain's entire education system which began with the comprehensive project and then moved on into new types of exams and a breathtaking expansion of the universities.

One man who experienced the revolution painfully and directly was Christopher McGovern, a history teacher who believed strongly in the old syllabus. His loyalty to older ideas of history eventually cost him his job, one of the very few instances of a teacher in the British state sector being forced out of his classroom. After a period of internal exile when he was not allowed to do what he did best, he found a position at a private school, where parents pay readily for his traditional approach. But even Mr McGovern did not understand the scale of the planned change when it first began to affect the schools.

He still remembers the slow and innocent-seeming beginning of the history upheaval:

> I started teaching in 1975. In 1974 there was something called the Schools Council History Project. This was a revolution in history teaching because it focused on skills rather than knowledge. One had to look at the skills which the subject taught. They looked at how historians taught and how to evaluate evidence. They looked at themes such as causation and change. They wanted to distil causation from history. For instance, they chose books on the history of medicine because it is one of the few areas which actually does allow you to distil the idea of continuity.

They also felt that one of the key skills was the ability to empathise. They wanted to assess the child's ability to empathise. But there was a problem. They had to find material which would allow these things to be taught. They decided it didn't matter what content you taught. What you were emphasising were skills and themes.

McGovern says the modern course is designed to aid empathy between the pupil and the people of the past, and so is quite naturally dominated by social history. But the effect of this is to drive out traditional political history. Current courses typically include 'Mid-Victorian Britain' and 'Elizabethan England' plus 'a problem of the modern world', for example Ireland, the Common Market, Palestine or China. This is half the course, chosen more or less at random. The other half is purely 'skills' and unseen historical evidence.

The old exam emphasized essay writing—five essays related to a period of history, with plenty of scope for political history. A 1980 (i.e. before the new ideas had taken hold) Oxford local O (Ordinary) level paper offers questions on four periods between 1066 and 1951.* Typical questions include 'What were the Constitutions of Clarendon? Why did they lead to conflict between Henry II and Thomas Becket?' or 'Explain how the Scots successfully resisted the English attempts at conquest under Edward I, and won recognition of their independence in 1328', or 'Write an account of the First Civil War, showing why Charles I lost', or 'Describe the importance of either a) price inflation or b) enclosure during the sixteenth century'. These questions would themselves be baffling to most modern school students, who would on the other hand be well-versed in the diseases suffered by Civil War soldiers or the poor diet of nineteenth-century Londoners.

McGovern says that the advocates of the new history argued that children were bored by the old methods. He points out that the numbers taking history have declined since the reforms, which effectively demolishes that argument. He suspects that many teachers supported the new history because they thought they were aiding the creation of a multicultural society. Like Dance, only more so because of the arrival of many new Britons from Asia and the Caribbean, they felt that the traditional history of Britain was not just irrelevant but actually divisive and damaging. Some may have seen this as an opportunity to put forward a new image of the British past. Others plainly saw it as a chance to dismantle the old ideas. One astonishing feature of history teaching in British schools today is that it is consciously designed to sow doubt, and to undermine the idea that there can be any certainty about the past.

The idea that the child is an explorer, finding out for himself, is relentlessly stressed in the scriptures of the new history. Writing in 1984 (in *Empathy and History in the Classroom*), Denis Shemilt says, 'A secondary aim, shared with all other parts of the project course, is to reinforce the idea that history is an enquiry into the evidence, rather than a series of established truths.' Why should the new historians have been so keen to do this? Could it have been because they wished to tear down the existing ideas? In the introduction to their *History Teaching and Historical Understanding,* two lecturers in education, A. K. Dickinson and P. J. Lee, complain that old-fashioned methods 'had two very undesirable characteristics': they concentrated excessively on introducing pupils to their national heritage, and on treating history as a body of received information to be accepted and memorized.

As the new history took root, the reformers were hugely helped by the destruction of the old GCE (General Certificate of Education)* O level examinations, which were straightforward tests of knowledge and understanding, marked independently and therefore immune to the personal prejudices of teachers. In *Teaching GCSE History,* Booth and Brown point out: 'The national criteria make it mandatory on GCSE

[General Certificate of Secondary Education] committees to examine proposed syllabuses for sexism and discrimination in any form; history has a crucial role to play in multicultural education with its insistence on understanding and tolerance of points of view alien to one's own culture, society and time.' They continue:

> The GCSE marks a radical change in our examination sys-
> tem and a great extension in the involvement of teachers in
> the examining process.... For history teachers in particular
> it presents a challenge and an opportunity to demonstrate
> that history is a crucial element in the curriculum of a dem-
> ocratic society and that it is useful and relevant as well as
> enjoyable when properly understood and taught.

The sort of topics recommended in these and other books of this type have a weary familiarity for anyone acquainted with the Marxist interpretation of the twentieth century: 'the working classes', 'women in society', 'imperialism' and so on. Florence Nightingale, the heroine of the Crimean War and founder of modern nursing, is often displaced or rivalled by a black role model, Mary Seacole. A few last-ditchers did try to struggle against the new history, though few even noticed what was going on. In 'The Wayward Curriculum', an attack on the new exams produced by the Social Affairs Unit, Denis Shemilt is quoted still more tellingly as having said: 'Nobody will confuse history with "learning stories"; nobody will think it is only about the past; nobody will think that history books or newspapers are "true". We have, I think, gained a great deal.'

Whether we have gained or lost, the change is certainly huge. It is shocking to compare the last edition of the standard English O level text with the GCSE textbooks which have replaced it. *An Illustrated History of Modern Britain* by Richards and Hunt was published by Longman in 1950 and went into three editions, the last in 1983, taking the story up to 1980. Anyone educated before the deluge will be perfectly familiar with it. It is a clear and concise narrative of events at home and abroad, mildly opinionated, brightly illustrated and literate.

It is not uncritical of Britain's role in the world, or complacent about social problems at home. In fact a rigid conservative would find much to complain about in its view of the industrial revolution, and a keen socialist might be unhappy with its treatment of the 1945 Labour government. Neither would really be able to say that it gives a false picture, and it is a great shame that such an excellent, clear manual of recent British history should now be out of print and practically impossible to obtain. It is especially sad when it is set beside the works of the new history.

Even the best of these textbooks have a horrible common feature: they are not really books, but elaborate lists and catalogues. In many cases, it would be quite impossible to sit down and read them without developing attention deficit hyperactivity disorder. The Cambridge History Project's series, actually designed for A level studies,* should be more stimulating and advanced than Richards and Hunt, and in parts they certainly are. But instead of narrative chapters, they are divided up into modules and units, and these are in turn broken up into charts, brief biographies of major characters, and long strings of so-called 'sources'. In *Was There a Mid-17th-century English Revolution?* by Robert Ellis, a typical unit contains forty-eight such sources. These can range from extracts from Cromwell's letters to bits of articles from *History Today* and (of course) books by the Marxist Christopher Hill. Any student who gets as far as this book will be interested in history anyway, and is bound to learn some. But the purpose of the book is much more to teach him the nature of the subject, rather than any actual history. These are not real sources, consulted by him in their originals as he follows a course of inquiry, just selected snippets picked for another purpose, by someone else.

The problem is far, far, worse at the lower levels—and these are much more important, for they are as close as a moderately intelligent child is likely to get to history in an English school nowadays.

Not only are the textbooks scrappy and episodic, without a proper narrative, but the authors seem to have selected their so-called sources to serve a particular view of Britain's recent past, one which is not exactly Marxist (for that would be paying it a compliment) but drearily left-wing, and focused upon suffering and deprivation rather than upon achievement or heroism. They are also notably more forgiving of the misdeeds of communist totalitarianism than of fascist totalitarianism.

Take *The Twentieth Century World* by Neil DeMarco and Richard Radway. It opens with a description of communism that is entirely uncritical: 'Communists believed that colonies should overthrow their European rulers. They believed that workers should control the factories and the peasants should own the land—an idea that was especially popular in the poorer, mainly agricultural parts of the world.' Perhaps for 'balance', it goes on: 'Communist ideas did not go down well with factory owners and rich landowners.' Well, they wouldn't, would they? On the opposite page, the book illustrates India's attitude to Britain with what is actually a Japanese propaganda cartoon showing the cringing British being driven out of India by stern Indians, but this is not information the book thinks it worthwhile to pass on to the reader. The next few pages jump back to 1914, and are a determined attempt to cast doubt on the widely held belief that Germany started the First World War.

The 'oppressed vs. oppressors' version of the past extends much further back than this. In *From Workshop to Empire*, by Hamish Macdonald, two pages (32–33) are given over to the living conditions of Nelson's sailors and Wellington's soldiers. They concentrate upon 'dangerous working conditions'— tall masts, rope ladders, wet weather, high winds, danger of falling to deck or overboard, and the way of life below decks with 'no privacy, dark and very crowded, no proper furniture', as compared to the Admiral's cabin, which is 'private, light and spacious, comfortably furnished'. The text complains, in the tones of a social worker of the late twentieth century, that 'Sailors worked in all weathers with no safety net to protect them should they fall from the rigging.' It adds, 'a sea battle must have been terrifying'—as indeed it must.

How can any child, reading this shop steward's version of history, possibly empathize with people whose moral, patriotic and cultural background has not been explained? Men underwent these conditions, or something like them, it is true. But they were unlike us in many ways and better than us in many ways, an idea which simply cannot be tolerated by people who believe that change is always a forward movement and who are so determined to judge history by the standards of the present. If our ancestors had been like us, they would have lost at Trafalgar and Waterloo, and given up on the attempt to colonize North America, because of the absence of safety nets, sexual equality and proper child care. These are interesting subjects for discussion, but are they really the point of teaching national history?

As for the description of the army—all harsh punishments, low pay and bought commissions, illustrated (of course) with a flogging and an unflattering cartoon—it is quite impossible to work out how this dismal rabble fought its way up through Spain to defeat the armies of the greatest military genius the world has ever seen.

While being so harsh to British institutions, these books are oddly fair to others. *The Twentieth Century World* speaks of Wilhelmine Germany's apparently aggressive policies and excuses Germany's naval expansion as a response to encirclement by Britain, France and Russia. 'Remember,' it says bluntly, 'the war was caused by the diplomatic game being played by the Great Powers.' And then: 'Remember. Germany was not the only country responsible for starting the war'. On the basis of five skimpy pages, clearly biased, pupils are then invited to weigh the 'evidence' and decide whether it was fair to blame Germany for starting the war, a question which has consumed oceans of ink and forests of trees over more than eighty years.

What sort of history does this new attitude replace? Go back to the 1940s and you will find that the assumptions of historians are far from conservative. *This England* by Isidore Tenen was a successful and popular textbook for more than two decades. Its 1944 introduction is charmingly dated, as it earnestly begs girls 'not to shirk those parts of the book which might seem more suitable for boys'. But it is shot through with idealistic soppy liberalism, hoping piously for a peaceful solution to the problems of Northern Ireland, and calling for United Nations armed forces. It is frank about the Empire, accepting that 'it has shrunk considerably. It was bound to happen, sooner or later. All over the world, men have come to resent the rule of privileged foreigners.' Paradoxically, this does not affect its fundamental patriotism, then a shared property of both Left and Right. It declares: 'As long as freedom, justice, toleration and self-discipline are respected among mankind, we shall have good reason to be proud of "This England".'

Yet this, perhaps the part of British history which provides the ultimate justification and vindication of this country's existence, its heroic and solitary battle against Nazi tyranny, is now passed over almost in silence. Winston Churchill is now an optional subject in the history syllabus. At the celebration of the 50th anniversary of VE-day in 1995, a 45-minute videotape sent to schools mentioned Churchill only for a few seconds, and then to say that he lost the 1945 election.

This belittling of the Second World War is the most striking and unforgivable feature of the new non-history history. For it was the continuing memory of that unique war which held the national patriotic consensus together. After describing the Nazi regime, Isidore Tenen expressed feelings which would now be unspeakable: 'In view of what you have just read, the Allied soldiers who began the attack by storming the beaches on ... D-day ... were crusaders in as holy a war as any in history.... We were fighting to save not only ourselves but all Europe, nay, the whole world, from a ghastly slavery of body and mind.'

But if we seek a little further back, we find that this is just a revival of an older feeling, a revival made acceptable to the socialist and Labour-supporting part of the nation because of the nature of the Nazi regime, but not a new thing at all. Many British children grew up with the clear and simple sentiments of *Our Island Story*, H. E. Marshall's innocent classic, now glimpsed on the shelves of second-hand bookstores but unknown to the unsentimental and uninterested young. Far from being the one-sided propaganda imagined by modern liberals, this book contains such sentiments as 'Napoleon Bonaparte was one of the most wonderful men who ever lived. Beginning life as a poor unknown soldier, he soon rose to be leader of the French army. He rose and rose until his people made him Emperor of France.'

Even those who can vaguely remember reading this book as children would be surprised by its more or less liberal tone, its willingness to admit that there are blots on the British record, and especially its sharp criticism of the more tyrannical English kings. In the days when British children were brought up to be proud of their country and its past, they were encouraged to do so 'warts and all', another quotation once understood by everyone but now a mystery to millions.

There is no doubt that the arrival of a large number of immigrants from former imperial colonies has helped to confuse the teaching of history. Yet there is no reason why it should have made us so coy. The West Indian immigrants who arrived first were in many cases more British than the British, having been taught the history and poetry of Britain in highly traditional schools modelled on the old British system. The other new arrivals, though less aware of Anglo-Saxon culture, came here very much of their own free will, partly because of a British obligation to take them in and partly because—in the case of the East African Asians—they rightly expected fairer treatment from Britain than they were receiving under Jomo Kenyatta or Idi Amin. A confident nation, whose teachers believed in their own country, would have seen history as a chance to make the new arrivals more fully British. Instead, apologetically and shamefacedly, those teachers saw our history as an embarrassment. Even though the immigrants had actually come here to share in British traditions formed over centuries of experience, leading to growing wisdom and tolerance, it was assumed that they would find the study of those traditions offensive or racist. And thus was born the idea of multicultural education, yet another excuse to denigrate the nation-state, apologize for the Empire and abolish the lore of the British tribe. It could not have come at a worse time.

The serious decline in standards which resulted from the abolition of grammar schools, the watering down of examinations to help cover up this decline, the growing power of individual teachers over what was to be examined, all helped to destroy the traditional history syllabus. Alternative sources of information, particularly the powerful new form of the TV documentary, began to popularize views of the recent past which had previously been held only by a radical minority. Any of these things by itself would have shaken the foundations of traditional history. All together, and combined with the rush to apologize to our new multicultural citizens, they demolished an entire discipline in a matter of years. In an incredibly short time, we have been turned into a nation without heroes, without pride in our past or knowledge of either our past triumphs or our past follies and disasters. We are like an amnesia patient, waking up in the hospital ward, with both past and future great blank spaces stretching behind and before us, doomed to repeat mistakes we do not even know we have already made.

THREE

Class War

SOMEWHERE IN BRITAIN at this very moment, an otherwise intelligent couple are gazing at their son or daughter and saying, 'It goes against our principles, but, reluctantly, we will have to go private.' They are not talking about some complex surgery, but about schools. Their dilemma sums up the curious attitude of the cultural revolutionaries towards education. They believe, in most cases with some passion, that education should be used to eradicate privilege and élitism, to spread the gospel of the new society in which everyone (and everything) is equal, a sort of concrete embodiment of that hideous song 'Imagine', which has become the hymn of sixties boomers. However, when it threatens to eradicate their own privilege by turning their children into mannerless, uncultured ignoramuses, they are not so keen. They therefore either find a state school in an expensive area of town, which selects through wealth, so paying their fees through their mortgages, or they pay fees directly.

There is no moral difference between these two, but there is a political difference. Tony Blair could never have become or remained leader of the Labour Party if he had paid fees for a school like the London Oratory. But because it is a 'state' school, he is grudgingly allowed to use it, despite mutterings that it is selective and therefore élitist (which of course it is).

All socialist governing élites face this problem, and generally solve it by creating special enclaves of state provision which are open in theory to all, but in practice only to them and their families. In Soviet Moscow, everyone knew which the élite schools were, but they also knew that they could not get their children into them unless they could pull the right political strings. Oddly enough, the schools for the ordinary Soviet citizens were far better than their equivalents in Britain, as long as you did not object to the lies told about history, or to the Marxist indoctrination and the anti-religious propaganda. Because the Soviet schools were the wholehearted servants of the state and the Communist Party, they were disciplined, ordered places. Teachers had power, there were right and wrong answers, there was an accepted body of knowledge which had to be learned, and poor work earned bad grades. Young Russians are immensely better educated than their Western counterparts. It will be interesting to see if this survives the collapse of Soviet power.

In this country, the problem is that education is one of the bitterly contested barricades in the unfinished British Revolution, which began in the seventeenth century, was frustrated in the eighteenth century and was diverted into state socialism for much of the twentieth century. The private school system, with some exceptions, still represents the patriotic Britain of the Hanoverian dynasty. Most of its foundations are more or less religious in a traditional way, instinctively monarchist and based upon tradition and deference. They are also quite unapologetic about privilege, they sustain élites and foster their growth, and they encourage competition in work and sport. They are deeply conservative institutions. But then, schools in stable societies always are conservative. They need to be. Unless there is agreement about what is to be taught, and who is to teach it, and how it is to be measured, there can be no education.

In the days when Britain was still clearly dominated by religious, aristocratic and monarchist ideals, this created few problems for the state schools. There were arguments about whether the churches or the town halls should run them—and about the rights of nonconformists and Roman Catholics. It was hard to define the position of many grammar schools, which were neither private nor state-run, but their ethos, timetable and shape were modelled on the successful nineteenth-century public schools, organized in houses, patrolled by prefects, housed in panelled, crenellated, vaguely baronial or churchy buildings.

But in the post-war decades, when the old élite had clearly lost all their nerve and much of their power, this conservative ethos was one of the main targets of the Left. They rightly saw the eleven-plus examination* and the grammar schools as obstacles to the equality and the 'democratic' or levelled society which they sought to build. They disliked the downward thrust of authority, the power of tradition and of course the continued teaching of religion. They even disliked the buildings, which they quite rightly saw as solidified propaganda for the *ancien régime*. This dislike may help to explain the strange truth that so many of the 1980s and 1990s Labour élite were educated at grammar schools and owe their advancement to their excellent teaching, but that none of them has ever lifted a finger to save a grammar school from closure, let alone resurrect one that has been destroyed. They were glad of the education and the advantages, but they loathed, and continue to loathe, the culture of such schools.

They were delighted to see the old buildings demolished or turned into resource centres. They were pleased to see the old links broken, the dragooning of children into great education factories in modern glass cubes, usually designed so that religious worship or even assembly wasn't physically possible—assuming anyone on the staff wanted such things. They were glad to see the end of hymn singing, honours boards, blazers, prize days and prefects. They were unmoved by the near-disappearance of sports from the state curriculum. What they did not understand was that, without all these things, the education of the children would suffer so badly. The new anti-authoritarian schools had, as their implied purpose, the destabilization of the old system. However, because the British Revolution remained unfinished, they could only teach chaos. They could not return to proper conservative methods until they had finally wiped out the old culture. This they still have not done.

It is possible to prove that the cultural revolutionaries never meant to wreck the schools, and in fact that they solemnly promised that they would not do so. Yet they were so mistaken that the disaster they caused has led to one of the worst crises of Labour. After a long struggle, even the mainstream of the party have given up their long-sustained pretence that standards are as high as they used to be, and it is only a matter of time before the wretched decline of the university sector—obvious to all but politicians—also becomes an accepted truth. However, in neither case has the grudging confession of waste and failure compelled those responsible to change their ways. Why ever not? The explanation lies in politics and the cultural wars of the last forty years.

The education reformers who declared, in Education Secretary Anthony Crosland's justly famous words, that they would 'shut down every ****ing grammar school in the country' were not even thinking about education. They were thinking about class and hierarchy, authority, permanence, deference and about that favourite, almost unhinged obsession of the progressive milieu: 'change'. From the start, their purpose was social engineering, and the consolidation of the semi-revolution which had begun during the war, continued in the Labour years which followed, and had not been seriously reversed in the Tory 1950s. You might think nowadays that there had been some great discovery in the field of education in the 1930s and 1940s, a discovery which somehow led all teachers to the conclusion that rigour in exams, selection and

discipline were counter-productive. No such discovery was
made, yet the education experts were entirely convinced, by
the early 1960s, that all these things had to go. Why, if not for
educational reasons?

If you look now at prophetic documents of the comprehensive revolution, such as Margaret (Postgate) Cole's pamphlet 'What Is a Comprehensive School?' you will find them
filled with the kind of 'onwards and upwards' atmosphere
that—yet again—dates back to the wild optimism of Edwardian Fabianism. The cover of this little squib shows a model of
Kidbrooke comprehensive school, which it would be interesting to compare with the actual building today. It is all sweeping lawns and white concrete, like a set from a 1930s science
fiction movie, a rejection of both Gothic and Classic traditions
in favour of an unadorned, brutal modernity where there are
no shadowed corners—the place where there is no darkness,
perhaps. This, as we shall see later, is an important part of the
reform project.

'While the [1944 Education] Act was still in the making,
the Labour London County Council made up its mind that all
London children should have the right to go to any county
school of their choice, without any question of test or examination,' it declares. It then quotes R. McKinnon Wood, chair-
man of the LCC education committee: 'The Tories fight this
great democratic plan [my italics] for secondary education by
all possible means.' Miss Cole herself then refers to the *Education Green Book* of 1943 and its call for a 'more closely knit
society' in which 'conditions in all different types of schools
must be broadly equivalent'. Contemporary Tory opposition
to this was obviously more forceful and confident than in recent
years, and plainly stung Miss Cole and her friends. She quotes
Tory accusations that comprehensives would lead to 'free medi-
ocrity for all' and 'a mass factory of so-called education', along
with warnings that 'the clever child's progress will be held up
by the gropings of the sub-educated'. These rather accurate

predictions have worn a good deal better than Miss Cole's worthless pledge that 'Comprehensive schools are not to be all the same size, nor for the same sex. There will be boys' schools, girls' schools and mixed schools'—let alone her promise that 'grammar school education' will be fully provided in comprehensive schools for those who need it.

What she is really concerned about is actually nothing to do with education, and all to do with class and society. 'No child,' she declares, 'will enter upon its secondary school career with the stigma of failure attached to it.' Yet this will be done without any cost to education. For she asserts: 'Those who write and speak as though a comprehensive school implied comprehensive classes with children of all ranges of ability taught wholesale by despairing teachers, either have not taken the trouble to inform themselves correctly, or (more probably) are being deliberately dishonest propagandists.' Quick learners and slow learners, she assures us, will not be put to work together. She then denounces an alleged obsession with grammar schools, which puts such a high premium on learning. Her real purpose is revealed in bold type:

> We believe strongly that in a modern democratic community it is important, both socially and educationally, that children of all types shall learn to live with one another in youth; we believe that the advocates of 'segregated education', who would separate one, two or even five per cent of the nation's cleverest children at eleven years and educate them apart from their fellows to become 'leaders' are making a great educational mistake.

Much of the rest of the pamphlet would be worthy of a guidebook to 1950s Moscow or East Berlin, issued to credulous fellow-travellers, speaking as it does of 'the glories of our new schools of Kidbrooke, Woodberry Down, Sydenham or the Strand' and describing the purpose-designed buildings of a comprehensive as 'a place newer, more beautiful, more full of space and colour than any he [the pupil] has worked in before.'

But there are plenty more hostages to fortune, including a confession that this is a 'statement of hope and not of present achievement. Unlike our opponents, we do not claim to know exactly what they will be like.' Perhaps richest of all for any London parent, and many London teachers of the present era, is this bold piece of prose: 'It is an insult to the London [teaching] profession to suggest that it cannot maintain its standard of teaching because boys and girls of differing capacities are associated on the same premises.'

'We believe,' she summarises, 'that this is the road of educational and social progress.'

Seldom has the comprehensive ideal's real purpose, a revolutionary social one, been so neatly and combatively set out. Now, after more than half a century of experience, its supporters would be hard put to deny that its Tory critics saw the future far more clearly than they did. And yet, interestingly enough, there has been no retreat from the comprehensive fetish in any significant part of the education industry. Defying Miss Cole's predictions with their almost universal mixing of the sexes and their unavoidable and uniform huge scale, most of these places are lamentable failures on their own terms, let alone set beside the few remaining grammar schools, and so far behind the performance of most independent schools that they cannot really be measured fairly against each other any more. The most cogent critic of the new non-schooling, the journalist Melanie Phillips, has condemned the 'all must have prizes' ethos of the modern system, and is utterly unconvinced by the Blair government's alleged educational reforms, describing them witheringly as 'a hologram'.

In fact, two of the most effective measures launched by David Blunkett, Secretary of State for Education, have been: triggering ballots which will extinguish many of the remaining grammar schools, by a vote of parents who do *not* send their children to them; and crushing the Assisted Places Scheme, which gave state scholarships to a few promising poor children so they could attend private schools. Much of the rest of the legislation introduced by Mr Blunkett restores powers to local education authorities, which had been removed or weakened by the Tories. It also removes the powers of church-run grant-maintained schools to select their pupils on merit, yet again putting social levelling first and education second. Interestingly, when he ran schools in his home city of Sheffield, Mr Blunkett abolished uniforms—in defiance of a ballot he had himself organized—and corporal punishment. In a barely coherent defence of the uniform decision, he seemed to link the idea of school blazers with repressive and reactionary forms of government such as apartheid South Africa and Augusto Pinochet's Chile. (Many years later, as a consumer of schooling rather than a council leader, he would vote for the reintroduction of uniforms at his own son's school.) He also rezoned catchment areas to prevent schools in middle-class suburbs from becoming 'secret grammar schools', whose entry was controlled by the price of houses in their areas rather than by an eleven-plus test.

In private discussions in his ministry, Mr Blunkett recently said that 'parents who send their children to private schools should be whipped', an alleged joke which perhaps reveals more than some of his more serious pronouncements. Much as he may deplore the miserable standards imposed on working-class children, including his own sons, he is still wedded to the social policies which make poor schooling inevitable.

Proper education is a fundamentally conservative activity, based on the assumption that a body of knowledge exists, is in the hands of the adult and educated, and can be passed on in measurable ways, by disciplined learning reinforced with authority. Since the Left in Britain have never reconciled themselves to authority—monarchical, aristocratic, religious, traditional and ancient, their attitude towards the inherited education system remains instinctively, automatically revolutionary. Only once they consider their social revolution to be complete will they reimpose the necessary order and discipline, something which happens in all post-revolutionary societies once the new masters are firmly in power and the subversive morality and ethos of the revolutionary period become a threat to the new order, just as they were a danger to the old one. Britain's ruined education system is in many ways the victim of a long and unfinished civil war, and will not be left in peace until one side or the other triumphs for good.

The existence and expansion of the private schools has—for now at least—frustrated the ultimate levelling purpose of the comprehensive system, and provided an inconvenient outside measure by which the comprehensive failure can be judged. The most telling proof of this is that pupils from independent schools gain far more places at Oxford and Cambridge, as a proportion of their numbers, than do those from the state schools. A sign of the timorous and self-deceiving attitude of the education establishment is that Oxford and Cambridge are being made to feel ashamed of this, and some colleges are widely believed to discriminate in favour of state school applicants, obviously on political rather than academic grounds. This is despite a general lowering of Oxbridge standards, the dropping of language requirements and the abolition of special entrance exams, all changes plainly designed to appease the comprehensive lobby.

The Blair government has been sharply hostile to the ancient universities, not exactly because they are good at what they do but very nearly for this reason. The troubles of Oxford and Cambridge have come upon them entirely because they have tried to maintain some standards. This has happened, despite the fact that they are in general run and staffed by people with left-wing sympathies. These same people, failing to understand that their principles clash with their professionalism, have resisted some of the destructive anti-élitism which has pulled the rest of the system down. For those Oxford dons who spite-fully denied an honorary degree to Margaret Thatcher when she was Prime Minister, the behaviour of the 1997 Labour government must have come as a nasty shock. Far from being rewarded for their politics, they were immediately penalized with damaging attacks on their funds and their tutorial system, and with cutting words in a Labour conference speech from the Chancellor, Gordon Brown. It is hard to imagine any other advanced country in which votes could be won and political reputations made through attacks on that nation's finest universities, but there are few better illustrations of the way in which education symbolizes the unfinished English revolution which the Left now wishes to complete.

Further evidence of the political, anti-hierarchy attitudes behind education reform can be found in the tragic *Plowden Report* of 1967, which gave its blessing to self-styled 'progressive' methods in the primary schools, transforming them from an important trend to a near-universal force. As the enemy of the grammar schools, Anthony Crosland, wrote in the report's introduction, and as many experienced teachers believe, 'Primary education is the base on which all other education has to be built. Its importance cannot be overestimated.' In the years since Bridget Plowden's report encouraged the spread of discovery learning and began a bonfire of old-fashioned desks and blackboards, children in this country have changed completely. Many cannot read, write, or count. Many more can only do these things badly. Standards of behaviour, of self-control, of ability to respond to authority or concentrate on any task, have sunk. Other forces, such as television or the decline of the family, can also be blamed for this. However, the schools, which could have put a brake on the decline, have speeded it up.

It is painful now to read Plowden's soppy, Pollyanna words. She and her committee, just like Margaret Cole, had a purpose that they believed was more important than education.

After all, there was nothing really wrong with the nation's primary schools when her committee began their work, except in the small minority which had already adopted progressive methods. As Plowden herself says, 'English primary education has long had a high reputation. We heard repeatedly that English infant schools are the admiration of the world.' Who could say that now? They were able to deceive themselves that education would not suffer through the changes they urged in discipline, organization and methods, though it must have seemed a considerable risk. Was the truth that they did not care enough?

Take their attitude towards smacking, or corporal punishment as it is so grandly known. In a section which will surprise anyone used to modern teaching attitudes, the report admitted that: 'a) the overwhelming majority (between 80 and 90 per cent) of the teaching profession were then against the abolition of corporal punishment, though few supported it except as a final sanction; b) public opinion appeared to be in favour of its retention and a considerable majority of parents agreed to its occasional use.' It went on to point out that 'local authority regulations reflect public opinion and the lack of any pressure for change', and it hinted strongly that it was not much used except as a last resort, accepting that it was mainly employed against older boys, not against infants or girls. It sensibly rejected the idea of making it an offence for a teacher to inflict any sort of corporal punishment because of the danger of malicious prosecution.

But then it lurched into revolutionary near-hysteria. After the sweet reason of what had gone before, the tone suddenly changed into a tight-lipped determination to get rid of the hated thing. While almost nobody in Britain could be found who was discontented with the current arrangements, what did *they* know? Psychologists—those stand-by experts who can always be counted on to decry common sense, defy public opinion and loathe hallowed tradition—were cited as saying that the advantages of corporal punishment were outweighed by its disadvantages. (Things have, of course, moved on since then. It would be impossible nowadays to find a psychologist who accepted that corporal punishment had any advantages at all.) But perhaps the thoughts of the psychologists are not convincing enough? In that case, how about a generalization about all those civilized foreigners, with their pavement cafés and their artistic nature. For of course this liberal committee must be suspicious of contentment with British methods among British people. We must compare ourselves with foreign countries, who are assumed automatically to do things so much better than we do. And wouldn't you know that corporal punishment has been 'almost universally outlawed in other Western countries. It can be associated with psychological perversion affecting both beater and beaten and it is ineffective in precisely those cases in which its use is most hotly defended.'

The committee here draw themselves up to their full height and pronounce, with all the weight and power of unsupported but deeply held liberal prejudice: 'We think the time has come to drop it. After full consideration, we recommend that the infliction of physical pain as a recognised method of punishment in primary schools must be forbidden.'

Having generously accepted that teachers and parents, and the public, are happy with things as they are, and that the thing is little used anyway, the reformers simply decided to do what they had been going to do all along. Their justification for this was almost as breathtaking as their *non sequitur* arguments. In paragraph 750 they admitted:

> Our recommendations are likely to meet with some opposition. We may be accused of encouraging softness and of encouraging the evil doer. The majority of teachers sincerely believe that corporal punishment may be necessary as a constraint. Indeed, a lack of corporal punishment in school will often contrast sharply with what happens in the child's home.

We believe, however, that the primary schools, as in so much else, should *lead* [my italics] public opinion, rather than follow it.

This is the joy of being a progressive. Whenever your views are rejected by experience, common sense and tradition, it is because you are *ahead* of the rest of the population, never because you are eccentric or wrong or just plain arrogant, or because they are not convinced by your arguments. They will catch up, and if not, so much the worse for them.

The same attitude is revealed in the report's tell-tale description of how its plan, to turn perfectly good if stern schools into picturesque nurseries of ignorance, should be implemented. Paragraphs 734 to 740 describe, in tones of nauseating naïvety, a visitor's impressions on a tour of an ideal progressive primary school:

When the bell rang, *if there was a bell* [my italics], no very obvious change took place ... during all this time he would hear few commands and few raised voices. Children would be asked to do things more often than told. They would move freely about the school, fetching what they needed, books or material, without formality or interference. Teachers would be among the children, taking part in their activities, helping and advising and discussing much more frequently than standing before a class, teaching. ... It is clear that to change a school run on traditional lines to one run on free lines requires faith and courage. The fact that a substantial number of schools have made the change is evidence that these qualities have not been wanting. They are certainly the first requirements in a reforming head, but they are not the only ones. It is not a question of saying 'freedom is in, discipline is out', an attitude which could lead to instant disaster. The change involves the total life of the school, and the staff, or a substantial proportion of it, must at least be ready for change and must understand something of the philosophy underlying it.

Here there follows a brief and almost unbearably painful description of one tiny educational putsch—painful, that is, to anyone with an imagination and a liking for the old ways of doing things: 'A small country school which had been run on traditional lines was able to make the change quickly because the staff of two retired simultaneously, and were replaced by a man and his wife who knew what they wanted to do and were able to set about it without delay. The children responded and, in less than a year, the school closely resembled that described at the beginning of this chapter.'

You can tell that they knew they were right.

But, of course, it will sometimes be harder than this. Plowden actually admitted that many schools would have serious problems with the liberated approach, though she at least partly blamed the timidity of staffs:

> Not all reforming heads are in the fortunate position of the one described earlier. They may have staff who cannot 'take it' and may feel it would be unwise as well as unjust to the staff to force the pace. They will have to move slowly and wait patiently for favourable signs and developments.
>
> In addition there are certainly schools and even whole areas where the difficulties involved in freedom are very grave. If a large proportion of children come from insecure or unloving homes, they will be disturbed and, although they may need freedom more desperately than children from good homes, the transition may be too perilous to face.

This was wise caution, justified over and again by what was to follow. But, apart from some vague remarks about guidance and the rejection of corporal punishment already dealt with, the report has little to say about how the new system could operate in such conditions. Just as MPs were quite unable to think of an effective substitute for capital punishment, Plowden and her colleagues could not come up with a realistic substitute for the ruler across the knuckles. They rejected sarcasm—a weapon that they said should never be employed—and urged punishments that were understood by children and seen to be just by them, but ended by saying feebly: 'the conclusion seems to be that in the matter of how to punish as well as in that of whether to punish, the judgement of the teacher must be respected, although, in the most difficult cases, expert advice on problems of behaviour should be sought from school doctors and child guidance clinics.' They then said that the judgement of the teacher should *not* be respected if he or she believed that corporal punishment was justified.

This is not just a matter of cruelty to children, but a far deeper issue too little thought about. The rebuking smack or slap, or even the blow of the ruler on the hand, are all symbols of authority imposed from above, unquestioned and unquestionable. They define the limit of a child's behaviour and they make it plain that the child is subject to the adult, who acts in the place of the parent. The doctor and psychologist, the use of pseudo-scientific discipline, are symbols of an entirely different form of government. If the child needs a smack, he is a free individual who has overstepped the line. If he needs a child guidance clinic, there is something wrong with him which must be cured. The conservative society accepts that rebellion and bad behaviour are natural and must be curbed. The liberal society requires all its citizens to be perfectly balanced, conforming to its ideals and aims with a happy heart and a willing mind—a rather sickening thought for the reactionary who does not care what is in his neighbour's heart provided he obeys the law. The same war between different principles lies behind the different ways of dealing with criminals, punishment versus rehabilitation, which have confronted each other throughout the century. This is revolutionary stuff, presented as kindness, undoubtedly the best way to present it, though not necessarily the most truthful way.

Plowden was also enjoyably frank about her underlying social purpose, and made an interesting comparison between British and American schools, rightly pointing out that the U.S. education system is an unashamed work of social engineering, aimed at creating Americans out of a diverse army of aliens and immigrants. As for Britain, 'Our society is in a state of transition and there is controversy about the relative rights of society and the individual.'

Plowden made a telling prediction about the kind of society in which the products of her report would grow up: 'It will certainly be one marked by rapid and far-reaching economic and social *change* [my italics]. It is likely to be richer than now, with even more choice of goods, with tastes dominated by majorities and with more leisure for all; more people will be called upon to change their occupation.' She emphatically rejected the mainly religious purpose for which primary schools were founded in the first place: 'The old English elementary school derived, in part at least, from the National Society for the Education of the Poorer Classes in the Principles of the Established Church, founded in 1811, the aim of which was to provide for what were then thought to be the educational needs of the working class. The effects of the hierarchical view of society which this title implied persisted long after the view itself became unacceptable and out of date.'

Unacceptable to whom? And out of date by what standard? The liberal revolution invariably assumes that time is on its side, and that ideas which it does not like are unacceptable to the world in general. That is how it proceeds. For example, in her discussion of religious education Plowden described as 'these two extremes' those who want no religious teaching at all and those who think that faith and worship should influence the entire curriculum and set the tone for the entire school, as if the latter view were a fringe eccentricity (as it has now become). Those in the middle, resolute for retreat and firm for compromise, are by implication the rational mainstream, even if their attitudes lead, as they have done, to the almost complete triumph of the other 'extreme', which endlessly seeks to push religion out of the schools.

One of the other most obvious changes in primary schools and, though not quite so dramatically, in secondary schools has been the alteration of buildings and furniture. In the *Economist* of 20 June 1998, the magazine's education correspondent recalls:

> One day, almost 30 years ago, when *The Economist*'s current education correspondent was a primary-school pupil, he walked into his classroom to find that it had changed. Instead of facing the front in rows, the desks had been bunched together in groups. From then on, the teacher spent less time talking to the whole class and pupils spent more time, alone or in groups, pursuing projects such as 'communication through the ages' at their own pace.

The writer was one of hundreds of thousands who must have experienced this early morning classroom coup d'etat, and we are lucky that he remembers it so clearly. For many, it must just have been a semi-conscious blur in the confused years of their unformed youth. But there was serious thought behind it. The reformers knew that architecture, lay-out and furniture were as influential as language and timetable, perhaps more so.

Plowden gave an impressive amount of space, including detailed floor plans and illustrative photographs, to what she wanted to see: 'Until recently primary schools were designed merely [merely?] as a collection of classrooms and a hall. Thirty years ago they were furnished in such a way as to make class instruction easy, group and individual work difficult.... Experiment in buildings has reinforced experiments in teaching.'

The revolutionary new buildings, by contrast, were to be designed to make class instruction difficult, group and individual work easy. Plowden praised a 1956 school built in Amersham, Buckinghamshire: 'The architects had observed a new relationship between teachers and children and a blurring of division between one subject and another, between theoretical and practical work and between one lesson period and the next.

'The "teaching area" was conceived as the whole school environment, rather than as a series of individual rooms.' And what was this environment to be used for? 'Inside there are small working areas each with a degree of privacy and a character of its own, opening on to a larger space sufficiently uncluttered to allow children to climb and jump, dance and engage in drama.'

The high-windowed, formal, severe designs of nineteenth-century village schools or their urban equivalents were obviously unsuited to this sort of world. But this formula works both ways. The new informal design was hostile to the old, hierarchical methods which frankly handed down knowledge from on high, often in the form of rules and truths learned by heart. In the new child-centred world of discovery, there was no room for this. Laurie Lee in *Cider with Rosie* recalled how 'unhearing, unquestioning, we rocked to our chanting, hammering the gold nails home'. Those golden nails were not just the times tables, but the lovely, elaborate, illogical pattern of the old imperial measurements—chains, furlongs, hundredweights, acres and the rest—too complicated for the liberated schoolrooms of the late twentieth century. (In fact, it is an odd truth that this sort of measure, highly practical and tested as it is, rarely survives any sort of revolution. It requires deference and tradition to survive. Without it, the toe-counting simplicity of decimal and metric systems is all that is left.)

Plowden did not openly denounce learning by heart, always dismissed as 'learning by rote' by those who loathe it. Instead she praised a so-called 'new approach':

It was not until a mathematical rather than a purely arith-
metical approach began to be made, that the whole subject
began to take on a new look. The various kinds of number
apparatus for the use of infant schools, none of which was
perhaps essential to the change that has taken place, have
helped teachers to think in a fresh way about number....
Even more important was the work of many infant teachers and their advisers who realized that learning in school
and out of school went on all the time and who directed
children's attention to the mathematical aspects of their environment and of their play. Many of these teachers came to
realize the contribution of experience to the formation of
concepts and the [my italics] *limited value of processes learnt
by rote.*

This is, of course, the most arrant drivel. Children were
never interested in knowing *why* seven sevens are forty-nine,
only in learning that they are so. Mathematical concepts, number and so forth are matters for professors. Yet this high-minded
piffle is accompanied by a statement of faith in children's ability to learn by 'experience' and 'out of school' the very things
that their teachers were now too proud to pass on to them.
Teachers objected with increasing fury to the idea that they
were mere engines for handing on the knowledge of others,
partly on the grounds that this was authoritarian. But they did
not hesitate to use their own authority to prevent such reactionary knowledge reaching their charges. Any parent investigating schools—state or private—for their young children is
likely to come up against a curious evasiveness if he or she asks
whether the school teaches times tables. A small minority actually do this, but most will only *test* them, relying on parents
to do the work of chanting them, or playing tapes in the car.

The modern primary school, its classrooms abolished and
its desks burnt, simply has nowhere to drive in the 'golden
nails', and its teachers would mostly think it élitist to drive

them in anyway, and 'authoritarian' to rely on the child's natural ability to learn in the 'unhearing, unquestioning' way described by Laurie Lee. In fact, they do not want unhearing and unquestioning pupils in the first place. They would, in a strange way, be happier with badly behaved, undisciplined, innumerate illiterates than with infants in disciplined rows who nonetheless knew enough to move on to secondary school or even to get jobs. The teachers themselves were never taught their tables by heart and never sat in rows facing a blackboard, and so find the idea of imposing this on others alien and embarrassing. As for grammar, spelling and poetry that rhymes and scans, which also rely on authority and agreement about what is worth learning, they have died in the state sector even more completely than times tables, though some private primary schools still attempt to teach them.

History and geography are dealt with elsewhere in this book. But in primary schools they now hardly feature at all, especially since the recognition of the reading crisis gave them the excuse to abandon almost all other subjects. Of course, if they restored the old rigid methods, and even the hated corporal punishment and the rigid if not so twee arrangement of classrooms, they might have time for all the subjects their grandparents managed to study so much more effectively in pre-revolutionary times. But to do so would be to put the clock back, one thing we are never allowed to do. It would restore order not merely to the classroom, but to the relationship between adult and child, inside and outside the family, the fundamental hierarchical link that challenges the supremacy of the modern state and its servants. And that would never do, even if the cost is a generation which can barely read the *Sun* newspaper or write its own name, let alone find Africa on a map or understand its place in the order of the centuries, or any reason why it might be proud or even moderately pleased to be there.

FOUR

The Pink Bits

IN JOHN BOORMAN'S SILLY but enjoyable film *Hope and Glory,* a Second World War teacher tries to explain to the children why bombs are falling on their houses and why their fathers have vanished for years, perhaps for ever. Pointing to a map of the world, she squawks 'The pink bits! They're fighting and dying for the pink bits!'

Anyone brought up before about 1965 will know what she means. I own a *Philips Universal Atlas* of 1939, from which the street maps of London have been censored in case the invading German panzers use them to find and crush resistance. Its two-page map of the world with 'British Empire Coloured Red' would warm any colonialist heart. Though right at the centre of the chart, Britain itself is tiny, which only emphasizes the enormous influence our cramped and soggy island has had over the globe, and it is perhaps because there is no room for two colours in such a small space that the then Irish Free State is also doused in pinkish-red ink. A great red highway spreads up the eastern side of Africa from the Cape of Good Hope to the Egyptian border—Egypt itself being tactfully shaded in a sort of khaki, perhaps to symbolize its status as a possession in all but name. Southern Asia is British from the Persian frontier to the tip of Singapore. Hundreds of tiny islands have their names underlined in imperial scarlet. Australia, New Zealand and Canada are red as well and the enormous size of Canada on Mercator's projection manages to make the USA look rather insignificant. Turn to the map of the Mediterranean, and the two letters Br in brackets stand beside Gibraltar and Malta— two letters which mean that the great harbours of these bare and stony places are filled with the majestic ships of the British Mediterranean Fleet, a little older and slower than they should be, but a warning to any aggressor that this artery of empire cannot easily be cut.

In war and peace, these places were the British world. A professional middle-class man in his fifties might never have been to France, Germany or Italy in his life, but in every factory, in every low, grey terraced street, there was a veteran of Army or Navy who had seen Bombay or Hong Kong or Alexandria, who had put down a riot in Haifa or put into Buenos Aires on the way to the Falklands. As for the British middle military classes, those hard, knowing, humorous men with faces like teak and voices like fine sandpaper, and memories of adventure, violence and heat, many of them were happier in the great waste places of the earth than they were under the narrow, damp skies of home. Travel, almost always by sea and often in hardship, was a national characteristic—but a special kind of travel where the destination was presumed to be less civilized, where the journey was for duty and not for pleasure, and where for the most part there was no point in learning the language.

This is not to say they were all scornful of the people and places they saw. Many came to love India and the Indians, learned their tongues, studied their cultures and religions and made friends with their people. Low or lofty or in between, there is no doubt that they understood the world in a different way from us. They were far less continental. My father, who spoke Spanish, travelled widely in South America, visited (in rather rough circumstances) Murmansk and Archangel, lived in Ceylon, Malta and the now-forgotten Chinese treaty port of

Wei Hai Wei, rarely set foot upon the European continent, never went to the USA and never visited Germany, even though that nation twice threw his entire life into utter turmoil. In the same way as many Americans never leave the territory of their nation, which is also an empire, pre-war Britons lived within the pink bits. Post-war Britons, before the great prosperity of the 1960s, still lived under the influence of the pink bits. Out of reluctance or economy, the map-makers continued to mark the former imperial territories in red or pink long after power had changed hands. School atlases of the 1950s had more in common with those of the 1930s than those of the 1990s.

The disappearance of the pink bits left us with nowhere to go in our former confident role, of proconsul and bringer of civilization, hymns and electricity. It compelled us to look more closely at our immediate neighbours, and to recognize that the USA was actually rather more significant than it had looked on the map next to Canada. It also made the sea much less important, both as a highway and as a moat. For we knew from the previous few decades that we could be attacked by air, and that a military power with enough preparation could send a successful invasion across the Channel—after all, if we could invade Normandy in 1944, anyone in full control of continental Europe could repeat the operation in reverse.

Yet it took some time for these ideas to penetrate the national imagination. In a typical geography textbook of the 1950s, you can almost hear the waves crashing on to the cliffs: 'Ever since the days of Queen Elizabeth the sea has meant life to Britain. Her sea-captains led the way to the lands that make her Empire. Sea-ways bring our food and materials for our factories. ... In our greatest danger, the sea has protected us.' This book, by the way, also assumes a common knowledge of British culture that would leave a 1990s teenager staring blankly. It casually quotes Longfellow, Hardy and Kipling, and refers to Tennyson's great 'Ballad of the Fleet' as if 'every school-boy knew' these now-neglected verses.

It also reveals a web of attitudes towards foreign parts and peoples which is strikingly different from today's, though far from the ignorant and defamatory caricature of crude jack-booted superiority which many now seem to believe to have been usual. There certainly is some superiority, though it is restrained by benevolence and a fair amount of modesty. Admittedly, there is a little discreet boasting: 'Britain's great overseas empire must be reckoned the reward of her qualities.' There is also a fair amount of mild racial and cultural prejudice, though those who try to confuse this with Nazi master race theories merely reveal their own ignorance of those theories and the deeds which were closely modelled on them. True, it displays pictures of 'Australian natives', backward aborigines, and comments in now unspeakable words, 'Both the (American) redskins and the (Australian) blackfellows in their distant continents had lost touch with the rest of the world and its ideas.' It accompanies a picture of two Eskimo children with the caption: 'Faces are broad and flat with narrow eyes. Hair is coarse, straight and black. They are talking to a Canadian missionary and, like most Eskimos, seem very cheerful.' In discussing the Eskimo way of life, it comments, 'But the white man is changing all this,' with the clear suggestion that he is changing it for the better. However, this arrogance is balanced by an understanding that Europe has brought other things apart from benefits to the people it has conquered and colonized. It refers to what it calls 'White men's diseases' (smallpox and measles).

When it ventures into continental Europe, there is also a distinct suggestion that these countries and peoples are different from us, less fortunate, less prosperous, much less secure. There is also some enjoyable national stereotyping, as we would now call it, though it is not as blatant as it would have been forty years before. George Orwell (in 'Boys' Weeklies', 1939) satirically summed up the British attitude to foreigners:

FRENCHMAN: Excitable. Wears beard, gesticulates wildly.
SPANIARD, MEXICAN, ETC.: Sinister, treacherous.
ARAB, AFGHAN, ETC.: Sinister, treacherous.
CHINESE: Sinister, treacherous, wears pigtail.

'As a rule,' he writes, 'it is assumed that foreigners of any one race are all alike and will conform more or less exactly to these patterns.' Of course, he is talking about comic books for lower-middle-class boys of limited education, but there are refined hints of a similar view in many more adult and learned places. He himself later wrote elsewhere that some stereotypes were true and that, for instance, Italians could do nothing without making a deafening noise.

The troubles of foreigners, their poverty, their lack of a steady history or maritime tradition, their hot climates, lack of coal and iron, their Roman Catholicism and their peculiar history, are seen as setting them apart. This is shown in the curious view of the Irish, both British and independent. In the early 1950s, our geographers could write as neutral fact: 'The population of Northern Ireland is largely descended from English and Scottish settlers planted there by James I. These people were not only keener businessmen than most Irishmen, they were also Protestants, whereas the Irish in general are strong Roman Catholics.' There is an unstated but implied view that, if Britain were not an island, and a Protestant island at that, she might just share their unhappy fate.

You can hear it faintly in these comments from *Man the World Over*:

> Money is scarce in Spain, and farming suffers not only from drought but from backward methods.... Many labourers cannot read or write and most are very poor.
>
> Many of Spain's troubles are due to her history. For 700 years she was busy fighting Moorish conquerors from Africa. Then for 300 years she lived on the wealth of her American

empire. When that was lost, the Spaniards were quite unfitted to make their living, as others did, by trade.

Italy also gets a poor review: 'Except for its cities, Southern Italy makes slow progress.' As for another European partner, Greece: 'Fate has been unkind. Her soil is poor, her min-
erals are few, and she has little to export but currants and
tobacco. The government in Athens finds it hard to make ends
meet—either in money matters or in politics.'

France is more generously treated, but might feel a little
patronized by the verdict of the geographers: 'All Frenchwomen
are careful housekeepers, which is the secret of their success. . . .
The French excel in small manufactures needing cleverness and
good taste, such as toys, jewellery and the ever-changing articles of fashion.' All this, very much pre-dating the age of Papa
and Nicole and the Eurostar,* is illustrated with drawings of
Breton peasants in colourful national dress, and a photograph
of a Basque boy with some oxen. 'France,' Carter and Brentnall opine, is 'first and foremost a farming country'. They do
mention her role as a great colonial power, but make kind
excuses for the failure of French-run areas ('hardly developed
at all') to advance as much as British possessions by pointing
out that the French have, in their rash and foolish Gallic fashion, acquired the wrong parts of the world. 'In tropical Africa
and Indo-China, the climate is too unhealthy for white settlement,' they explain. The Netherlands also are thoroughly
patronized. 'For all her trading, Holland is mainly a country
of peasants who own, as in France, their little farms.'

I am sure it is no accident that this series is comparatively
reticent about the Germans, about whom it could say so much.
Given its willingness to pass judgements on the characteristics
of the other nations, it is interesting in itself that there are
almost no comparable remarks about Europe's greatest military, industrial, musical and literary nation. The only hint of
an attitude comes in a description of the people of the north

German plain: 'The Germans are hard-working and, with the help of science, grow great quantities of rye and potatoes and breed many pigs in this unpromising region.' Hard-working and scientific, eh? That had certainly been proved quite recently, to the satisfaction of all involved. But best leave it at that—a fine example of the old British restraint that now seems to have disappeared so completely.

But those who would simply dismiss these books, and this era, as dominated by a crude and lofty racialism are missing the mark entirely. In the same series, the old British superiority over the USA is demonstrated in a way which completely upsets such modern prejudice. British people of this period were extraordinarily free of racial prejudice (a point well illustrated in fiction, particularly the unsettling film *Yanks,* which deals intelligently with the many strains between the declining British superpower and the rising American one, and in Nevil Shute's fascinating novel *The Chequer Board,* where working-class and rural Britons come into hard conflict with American southerners over the treatment of black soldiers); and they were surprised by the level of bitterness between blacks and whites in the USA. *Man the World Over* describes conditions in the American South: 'The feeling between the races is often very strong particularly where, as in some districts of the south, there are more negroes than whites.'

There is, on the other hand, a sort of realistic understanding for the Southern whites which could certainly not be expressed now: 'When the land-owners in the South bought negro slaves from West Africa, it was not considered a wrong thing to do. It seemed the simplest way of finding people to work for them under a hot sun,' which is harshly true and, while unpleasant, something many modern writers on this subject might bear in mind. But they simply could not say it.

In another book of the same era, *North America* by Thomas Pickles, there is active condemnation of the American racial division: 'For a hundred years and more in the "black belt" of the "deep south" the Negroes have been denied the equal rights which are theirs by the law of the land.' The same author, writing as long ago as 1932, warns: 'The almost worldwide domination of the white man does not mean that our way of life is the only right way, or that peoples of other races are necessarily inferior; indeed the study of geography shows us that "coloured" peoples have a great deal to contribute to the well-being of the world.'

No doubt this sort of sentiment would be completely unacceptable to those who police the language and thoughts of modern schoolbooks, but that is not the point. The crude belief that our grandfathers were all filled with a callous racial prejudice and felt themselves superior to other races is not justified by the facts. The truth is far more complicated, and—given the circumstances of the times—far more creditable. They were better than we think they were, and our blithe assumption of moral superiority is not justified. And since much of our condemnation of the past is designed to make current generations feel good about themselves and to prevent fair and serious consideration of older ways of behaving and thinking, this is no small thing.

The belief that pre-revolutionary Britons scorned abroad and foreigners is linked with a similar prejudice against their patriotism, almost always decried as 'flag-waving' and an inability to see the faults of their own country. The whole population are viewed as if they were a sort of vast and deluded audience at the Last Night of the Proms, thoughtlessly extolling the land of hope and glory and its ever-wider bounds,* when they should really have been worrying about slums, rickets and factory conditions.

It is perfectly true that an unashamed love of country was part of British thought until very recently. But what form did it take? It was very much linked to the geography and landscape of these islands, rather than to military or even naval glory. A complete outsider, the Spanish-American philosopher

George Santayana may have understood it better than most liberal Britons, to whom patriotism is a constant bafflement.

> Instinctively the Englishman is no missionary, no conqueror. He prefers the country to the town, and home to foreign parts. He is rather glad and relieved if only natives will remain natives and strangers strangers. Yet outwardly he is most hospitable and accepts almost anybody for the time being; he travels and conquers without a settled design, because he has the instinct of exploration. His adventures are all external; they change him so little that he is not afraid of them. He carries his English weather in his heart wherever he goes, and it becomes a cool spot in the desert, and a steady and sane oracle amongst all the deliriums of mankind. Never since the heroic days of Greece has the world had such a sweet, just, boyish master. It will be a black day for the human race when scientific blackguards, conspirators, churls and fanatics manage to supplant him.

Santayana links patriotism with weather and landscape, rather than marching bands and flapping banners. The poet Rupert Brooke described an old friend's similar response on hearing of the outbreak of war in 1914:

> His astonishment grew as the full flood of 'England' swept him on from thought to thought. He felt the triumphant helplessness of a lover. Grey, uneven little fields, and small, ancient hedges rushed before him, wild flowers, elms and beeches, gentleness, sedate houses of red brick, proudly unassuming, a countryside of rambling hills and friendly copses. He seemed to be raised high, looking down on a landscape, compounded of the western view from the Cotswolds, and the Weald, and the high land in Wiltshire, and the Midlands seen from the hills above Prince's Risborough. And all this to the accompaniment of tunes heard long ago, an intolerable number of them being hymns.

But this beloved landscape, just like the pink patches on the map, was destined to disappear. Oddly enough, so was its dark twin, the filthy, close-packed, diseased slumscape of the great industrial belt of the north, that 'smudge of smoke and misery, hidden by the curve of the earth's surface', described as late as the 1930s by George Orwell and J. B. Priestley.

But in the years immediately before the cultural revolution, both rural and urban Britain would still have been completely familiar to a Victorian. In our 1952 geography textbook (Carter and Brentnall), a chapter on the English countryside is illustrated by a photograph of a delightful sylvan view in Wiltshire, taken on a rainy day, with an endless soft prospect of hedgerows and elms. A few pages on, the book turns to the Black Country of the West Midlands, 'a dreary scene of tall chimneys, black smoke, old slag heaps, railway lines and neglected waste'.

It moves further north, attaching this harsh caption to a picture of a Lancashire streetscape: 'A sea of roofs ... a cotton town of close-packed streets and monotonous rows of ugly workers' houses round the mills. Apparently the houses have small backyards, but no bright gardens for health-giving spare-time enjoyment. It is very ugly,' editorialize the geographers, 'and an example of how things should *not* be done.'

The hard tone continues in a description of Tyneside: 'This great industrial region, like that of South Wales, has known great hardships from which it has taken long to recover.'

This anger follows in a direct descent from the socialist writers of the 1920s and 1930s, who described the miserable lives of the northern poor to the educated middle class of the south, and made them feel rightly ashamed. Books such as Priestley's *English Journey* and Orwell's *Road to Wigan Pier* lived on in the minds of all who had read them. Who could forget this passage of Orwell's?

As we moved slowly through the outskirts of the town we passed row after row of little grey slum houses running at right angles to the embankment. At the back of one of the houses a young woman was kneeling on the stones, poking a stick up the leaden waste-pipe, which ran from the sink inside and which I suppose was blocked. I had time to see everything about her—her sacking apron, her clumsy clogs, her arms reddened by the cold. She looked up as the train passed, and I was almost near enough to catch her eye. She had a round pale face, the usual exhausted face of the slum-girl who is twenty-five and looks forty, thanks to miscarriages and drudgery; and it wore, for the second in which I saw it, the most desolate, hopeless expression I have ever seen.... She knew well enough what was happening to her— understood as well as I did how dreadful a destiny it was to be kneeling there in the bitter cold, on the slimy stones of a slum backyard, poking a stick up a foul drain-pipe.

Moved by this and similar depictions of the fate of their fellow creatures, the British middle class resolved to change that destiny and abolish that fate. Quite reasonably, they imagined that this could most easily be done by sweeping away the festering dumps in which the poor lived their desperate lives. This unfortunately meant that developers and planners could rebuild our cities without any real restraint. And they did. But even before the madness of the tower blocks, there were serious doubts about the policy of large-scale rehousing. Alongside his denunciation of the slums, Orwell makes some prophetic but less-well-remembered points about council housing, then largely admired uncritically as the solution to squalor. Remember that Orwell had seen at first hand the foulest and most overcrowded houses in the lowest and most diseased quarters of the most depressing cities in the kingdom. Yet he has the honesty to point out that the new estates have many disadvantages—higher costs of travel and heating, more expensive shops. The simplest solution to this is of course the continental one of flats—but Orwell again notes that people do not like them, and refer to them scornfully as 'tenements'. So it is the new housing estates or nothing.

But long before most people had understood the problems of these places, Orwell had seen them:

> It is not that slum-dwellers want dirt and congestion for their own sakes, as the fat-bellied bourgeoisie love to believe.... Give people a decent house and they soon learn to keep it decent. Moreover, with a smart-looking house to live up to, they improve in self-respect and cleanliness, and their children start life with better chances. Nevertheless, in a Corporation estate there is an uncomfortable, almost prison-like atmosphere, and the people who live there are perfectly well aware of it.
>
> And it is here that one comes on the central difficulty of the housing problem. When you walk through the smoke-dim slums of Manchester you think that nothing is needed except to tear down these abominations and build decent houses in their place. But the trouble is that in destroying the slum you destroy other things as well.... There is something ruthless and soulless about the whole business.... There are some Corporation estates in which new tenants are systematically deloused before being allowed into their houses. All their possessions except what they stand up in are taken away from them, fumigated and sent on to their new house. This procedure has its points ... but it is the kind of thing that makes you wish that the word 'hygiene' could be dropped out of the dictionary. Bugs are bad, but the state of affairs in which men will allow themselves to be dipped like sheep is worse.

Orwell also makes the far-sighted point that, by clearing and rehousing an area, you destroy local shops and pubs, on which a whole society depends for its networks and links. Even without the war which demolished much that was shameful and left us with a clean page on which to write, even without the tower blocks and the inner ring-roads, the landscape of the British poor was being swept away by well-meaning but dictatorial social engineers, whose ruthlessly optimistic idea of the future was both ugly and mistaken, and had other purposes behind it apart from health, space and cleanliness, as John Betjeman argued in these unusually bitter lines from 'The Planster's Vision':

> I have a Vision of the Future, chum,
> The workers' flats in fields of soya beans,
> Tower up like silver pencils, score on score,
> And surging millions hear the challenge come
> From microphones in communal canteens,
> 'No Right! No Wrong! All's perfect, evermore.'

And we all know now what the reality turned out to be, a reality which has given the explosive demolition experts plenty of work for decades to come, as they expensively knock down many of the towers which turned out to look more like rotting teeth or broken bones than like silver pencils. Betjeman rightly grasped that the city of towers was not just a project to clear the nineteenth-century stews and slums, but a vain expression of the egos of the planners and politicians who had laid their rulers and protractors across the map, and decreed these huge monuments to themselves and their ideas like some modern Ozymandias. Because the vast, cold estates and the tower blocks were planned in the minds of politicians and reformers, they were largely forced on people who were in no position to argue. They were slum-dwellers, weren't they? So they were bound to be grateful. Like most planned things, their failure was easily foreseeable if anyone had wanted to foresee it. Orwell would have spotted instantly the un-English nature of the things, their hostility to the love of flowers and gardens and having your own front door. But the desire to build a new world, to act as if Britain were starting again from year one, was too strong—and the mean, dingy houses of the first industrial revolution were a purely British failure, which gave added power to the sweeping, sunlit concrete visions of the continental architects and their disciples among the planners. Just as important, perhaps more so, were the *unplanned* and often accidental things which would transform the urban and rural landscapes of the middle classes.

The post-war housing shortage affected almost everyone. Middle-class couples lived with their parents or in ramshackle converted flats in the centres of cities. The 1920s and 1930s suburbs were not big enough to contain the middle class which increasingly wanted to live in them, because it was finally safe to have children again after the years of war and separation, and because they could now afford the cars which made such remoteness possible and desirable. While the councils threw up new estates and raised their first tower blocks, private builders were concreting over great tracts of farmland for new estates of semis and detached houses.* These were significantly smaller than many of the pre-war estate houses, the first to be built in the sure knowledge that there would not even be one servant, that the lady of the house would work in her own kitchen, the first to be all-electric, or at least coal-free, as clean air laws discouraged the open fire. It is incredible to think that, as late as the early 1960s, many people still kept a coal fire burning all the year round, with a hob on which a kettle permanently sang. They were already part of a disappearing world. A few miles away, in the new suburbs, the only hobs were electric ones.

By the mid-1960s, new suburbs and—in some cases—whole new towns were where most people lived. Distances were greater, isolation from shops and neighbours sharper, though not as great or sharp as they were to become. It seems likely that the more dramatic isolation of North America's young mothers in suburbs was one of the main reasons for the feminist explosion of the late 1960s and early 1970s. Something similar was almost certainly going on in much of Britain, as families paid the price for the space and sweet air of the suburbs, in remoteness from the beating heart of city life.

While this was happening, other changes were devastating the countryside which so many Britons had seen as the symbol of their country's unchanging, rural core. Look now at the reconnaissance pictures taken by the Luftwaffe, or from the Nazi airship Hindenburg in the 1930s, and you will see the English countryside as millions still see it in their imagination. The fields are tiny and irregular, the villages small, the towns compact, the roads narrow and winding. Only in a few prosperous parts of the South were the new ribbons of factories and semi-detached houses common. In the world thus pictured, which continued into the late 1950s, telephone directories for most urban districts were still thin volumes, growing thinner as you went further north. Hospitals, schools, shops, libraries, churches, town halls, telephone exchanges, postal sorting offices, police stations and newspapers were overwhelmingly local, and generations still tended to live not far from each other. Goods which were not available close by were often delivered, including bread and meat, an astonishing thing to those who have grown up in the supermarket age. Laundry was collected from middle-class homes in strange suitcase-shaped boxes made of a kind of pressed cardboard, and delivered back to them, starched and clean, a week later.

But fifteen years after the end of the war, air travellers would already have seen the skeleton of an entirely new Britain. Instead of 1930s ribbons, the suburbs reached out in blobs and branches, whole new towns but without the compactness and the reliance on a centre. As the population swelled and the desire for green space and fresh air grew, the infection spread to smaller and smaller towns, each acquiring their own mini-suburbs until, by the 1990s, the villages of south-east England actually had suburbs too, 'urbages' of new, neat streets.

In the last few years, many of these developments were built to house the second and third marriages brought about by the relaxation of divorce laws. One development company is said to have christened a particular style of small house the 'Exe', as a punning joke on the kind of people most likely to buy it.

A complete agricultural revolution, begun during the war, was meanwhile tearing up the hedges and bringing ancient pasture under the plough. The original, and creditable, excuse for intensive farming was that Britain might need to feed herself, and could never again risk being starved into submission. Later, subsidies and profit took over. In any case, small fields were no longer profitable. Even if they had been, many of them were enclosed by hedges which depended on elm trees to hold them together. When Dutch Elm Disease arrived in England in the late 1960s it was as if a curse had descended on the countryside. The elms had given the countryside much of its shape. Not merely did these huge, friendly vegetables give a wooded aspect to every distant view, they were an essential part of the hedgerows themselves. When they died or were cut down, they left gaps which could often only be filled with man-made fences. That meant there was little incentive to maintain the rest of the hedge, which in many cases was allowed to grow thin and weak before being grubbed up or replaced with yet more wire. As all this happened, the most environmentally friendly rural transport system imaginable, the dense network of railway branches, was being torn up in the name of 'economy', compelling country-dwellers to travel by car. Industrial farming was hugely reducing the number of labourers, which in turn destroyed the need for many trades and services in villages and small towns. Ronald Blythe's elegiac *Akenfield* records the last of these trades, the end of an established village life which had lasted for centuries until now, the century when suddenly we knew better.

Everyone from country parsons to shopkeepers and pub landlords was affected by this depopulation, a depopulation concealed by the reverse invasion of townspeople seeking the very thing that was now being destroyed for good, rural serenity. They could, of course, buy the houses, but they did not truly live in them and so unintentionally destroyed what they had hoped to find. They made it impossible for the local poor to afford property, but contributed nothing to the real job-creating economy, often bringing their own middle-class groceries or eating in costly restaurants. It was also difficult for them, even with the best will in the world, to take a full part in the remaining social activities of a place they only visited for relaxation. How many of them appreciated the irony of the fact that they lived in 'The Old Rectory', 'The Old Forge' or 'The Old Schoolhouse'?

New, faster roads and bypasses were built to relieve the pressure of traffic on small towns and to ease the flow of workers between the towns where everyone had to work and the villages where everyone wanted to live. But these roads—wide, straight, designed for ease and speed, often lined with new developments themselves—changed the character of the countryside more than almost anything. Just forty years ago, a road journey across Britain would never rise above thirty miles an hour. It would be a matter of winding curves, dangerous bends, bottlenecks and crossroads. But it also respected the landscape. The traveller saw the towns and the people, experienced the curve and heave of the earth's surface. Nowadays he sweeps past and sees nothing except roundabouts, Little Chefs, filling stations and edge-of-town do-it-yourself stores, furniture warehouses, multiplex cinemas and hypermarkets, rather like the exurbs of Atlanta, Georgia, but without the tang of true novelty and spaciousness that such places have in their native America. The towns themselves, prettily preserved in the parts where they have not been wholly demolished or overwhelmed by lumpish modernity, are concealed from him in the midst of one-way systems or pedestrian precincts. The hills and woods have been bulldozed to one side to ease his passage.

How much smoother and simpler it is to go from place to place, yet how much more pointless also—for the true characters of British towns have always been expressed in local building materials: flint here, diagonal brick and timber pattern here, chequerboard brickwork here, hanging tiles here, red sandstone here, dark liverish brick here, pargetted plaster here. And now those materials have been superseded by industrial building, and the crafts which grew up around them are dead. It has happened, finally and for ever, in the course of a generation, and we have not yet begun to mourn it.

To explore the scale of the change, it is worth looking at one English town, not exactly typical because it is unusually ancient and handsome, not poor, but affected in a normal way by the tidal wave of new houses, cars and roads which has engulfed so much of this island.

Murray's *Blue Guide to England* for 1920 is nowadays a handbook to an entirely foreign country, unbombed, undeveloped, its travellers' routes built around the railway network rather than along little-used roads. Abingdon is here described as 'a pleasant old agricultural town' of 6,809 inhabitants. Ordnance Survey maps of the same period show close-packed houses built along a few main roads converging on a church and a market square. There are a smithy, a brewery and a mill, a clothing factory and a Sunday school. Many of the surrounding fields are marked 'liable to floods'. The road plan is haphazard and medieval, with some large villas built in an obviously planned semicircle around a park which commemorates Prince Albert. What industry there is, including a gasworks, is mostly grouped near the railway terminus. It is easy to imagine a slumbering place of corn merchants, horse-troughs, brewers' drays piled with wooden barrels, beadle-infested churches, and some dirty and diseased poverty in the narrow streets down by the river and the gaol. There are some minor new outskirts, again obvious from their straight lines. Near them, in common exile from the mainstream of town life, stand the Roman Catholic church and the grim hexagon of the Union Workhouse.

Move on to 1938, and the suburbs have grown, but only slightly. The workhouse has disappeared, replaced by some neat new streets. The MG motor works and a leather factory have appeared between the cemetery and the isolation hospital. But the ancient centre is still obviously the dominant quarter of the town, the thing any visitor or resident would mean by the word Abingdon. In 1959, the picture is more or less the same.

But turn now to the 1995 edition of the *Blue Guide,* distant successor of the 1920 book. In a touching echo of the past, Abingdon is now described as 'a pleasant old town' (note the disappearance of that 'agricultural'). It now has 22,700 inhabitants. The old town hall has become a museum and the gaol is a leisure centre. Those who know what the words signify are rightly warned that 'a shopping precinct runs NW', though the guide tactfully omits any description of the horror, similar to dozens which disfigure lovely towns from one end of the kingdom to the other.

But now look at the Ordnance Survey map. It is as if interplanetary invaders have landed from a distant galaxy. The ancient patterns of the old town can still be detected at the heart of a wholly alien street-plan, whose shape and scale are quite foreign to the place onto which they have been grafted. Semi-circles, ellipses and long, straight, broad prospects, lined with houses with long narrow strips of garden behind them, sprawl to the north-east, the north-west and to the south of the ancient settlement. The railway terminus is closed (and the railway itself has been pulled up). Every outlying village has its own allocation of suburb, or urbage, and it is easy to see that it will need a very strong political will to prevent all these settlements from joining together into one megalopolis in the next few decades. Bounding the new Abingdon to the west, and cutting it off from most of its ancient Common, runs one of Britain's unofficial motorways, the A34 trunk road which connects the industrial Midlands and north with Southampton and the continental markets. Bounding it to the south-east lie enormous gravel pits, where the very surface of the earth has been gobbled up to feed the road-building industry, leaving a strange unnatural landscape of sinister deep lakes, fenced off lest children fall into their man-made depths and drown. On the edges of the new town sit the usual superstores and sports centres. Down the road at Didcot looms a monstrous power station, built here so that it could use rail-borne coal from South Wales but now fired by gas, one of dozens of new cathedrals built to serve the electric deities of consumerism, but unusual in being so close to the comfortable, post-industrial landscape where those gods are most keenly worshipped.

It is a world transformed. No Act of Parliament, not even thirty of them, could possibly have as much effect on human behaviour as this upheaval in our physical surroundings, mostly concentrated into two or three frenzied decades. The urban poor have been uprooted and displaced as thoroughly as if they were refugees, the networks of family, trade, friendship and habit bulldozed away. The better-off have suburbanized themselves, devouring the countryside on whose edges they hoped to live, and exchanging crowds, dirt and old, down-at-heel housing for the clean solitude of the outer city and the tyranny of commuting. Most of the places where people met each other on equal terms have been destroyed or removed, leaving the supermarket and the garden centre as the only places where we encounter strangers, apart from when we are in our cars. The countryside, from which British people of all classes have drawn much of their national identity, and to which they have looked for solace and reassurance, has largely disappeared, digested by urban sprawl, levelled by new roads and denuded by the natural disaster of elm disease.

The face of Britain has undergone radical plastic surgery so that it can no longer recognize itself in the mirror. Yet this transformation has never been seriously debated. We were not asked if we wanted this change, though many of us wanted our own little portion of it. Now that we have it, it is surely reasonable to suggest that it has helped to uproot us, to cut the ties which once bound us to a past which was crucially different. And so it has sped the revolution, a revolution founded upon ugliness, upon bypassing history and preserving a little of it beneath a kind of bell-jar, while constructing a new world which owed almost nothing to what had gone before.

FIVE

Hell Freezes Over

H ELL WAS ABOLISHED AROUND the same time that abortion was legalized and the death penalty was done away with. It would not be surprising to peer into an old Hansard* from the middle 1960s and find that the House of Commons had quietly passed the Infernal Regions (Closure) Act one unseasonably hot Friday afternoon when the Scottish MPs were all away. A beaming Roy Jenkins would have found parliamentary time for it, as part of his efforts to make Britain a more 'civilized' society.* Like so many similar reforms, making Satan redundant was or appeared to be a change whose time had come. After all, nobody went to Hell any more, did they? For by the 1960s, eternal damnation, like most of the more worrying aspects of the Christian religion, had apparently fallen into disuse. Bishops, notably the 'South Bank' group headed by John Robinson of Woolwich, had begun to admit, rather coyly to start with, that they were not sure about the existence of God or the truth of their religion's central beliefs.

It would take some years before the Bishop of Durham, Dr David Jenkins, would speak of the resurrection as 'conjuring tricks with bones', but by the time he said these words few Anglican clergy found them shocking. The idea that one had to *believe* to be a parson or even a bishop was by then all but dead, and there was a group of Anglican clergy, known perhaps humorously as the 'Sea of Faith', who appeared to all intents and purposes to be atheists. The South Bank Bishops had done the necessary pioneering for all this, and it was only the poor believers, huddling together for warmth in the near-empty pews, who were distressed. Dr Robinson had also distinguished himself at the trial for obscenity of D. H. Lawrence's second-rate novel *Lady Chatterley's Lover.* He attained temporary fame by comparing sexual intercourse to Holy Communion 'in a real sense', and suggesting that this was a book which every Christian ought to read.

By the time the Bishop gave his evidence, change was already far advanced, though not obvious to outsiders. The Ten Commandments, once blazoned behind every altar in the kingdom, were frequently left out of the Church of England's Communion service (in those days an austere and forbidding experience strikingly unlike sexual intercourse). The King James version of the Bible, with its majestic but sometimes frightening language, was rejected by modernizers who sought to make it more 'accessible', replaced by new versions which nonetheless somehow lacked the old scriptures' force.

This force may well have been the reason for the change, for it is hard to see what is meant by 'accessible' when large parts of it, including such phrases as 'by the skin of your teeth', 'the parting of the ways' and 'the last gasp' have entered the living language of the entire English-speaking world.

But in the Church as almost everywhere else, the slow crumbling and rotting of the institution from within gave those who wanted change a perfect opportunity.

Two world wars had done terrible things to English Christianity. The established church was part of the old order, rural, aristocratic, hierarchical, which was smashed to pieces at the Battle of the Somme on 1 July 1916. With some brave exceptions it had not had much to say to the common soldiers as they fought and died. Many of them would not have listened with any great enthusiasm anyway. The industrial revolution had already taken most people away from the country parishes where the Church's ancient roots were strong. The Church had never really succeeded in planting itself in the giant new cities, or in the suburbs. Its most reliable urban supporters, the educated middle class, were assailed by doubt. Charles Darwin's theory of evolution had provided a popular scientific theory which allowed millions to expel God from the universe.

A world without God meant no punishment for sin, and therefore no sin. This was an attractive idea to many, in an age where man appeared to be able to do everything and overcome anything. If the physical world had limitless possibilities, why should human behaviour be limited by dusty and unwelcome prescriptions from ancient times? While the Church absorbed this blow, the Bishops lost their grip on the schools, one of their few strongholds, as the state began its long, catastrophic takeover of education. The castration of the House of Lords by the Asquith government had snatched away much of the bishops' political influence, just when they needed it. Most laws began life in the other place, and most important ministers now made their statements and answered questions in the Commons, where no Anglican divines were even allowed to sit.

The clergy themselves were divided between would-be Roman Catholics and defensive Protestants, whose party differences, ever-present in the Church of England, were sharper than at any time for centuries. The new age made all these things more important, and so more dangerous. The Second World War—by splitting so many working-class and middle-class couples for good—had democratized divorce, previously a mainly middle- and upper-class habit. Those six years undid all the good achieved by the great struggle to prevent King Edward VIII from marrying the divorced Wallis Simpson, a struggle which had ended with the apparent victory of tradition, loyalty and constancy. When the tragedy came to be repeated, and Princess Margaret nobly chose duty instead of self by deciding not to marry the divorced Group Captain Peter Townsend, her gesture was too late. The fortress she sacrificed herself to defend had already fallen. In time, she would find that the rest of the country laughed at her rather than followed her good example, and her life since then is a sad example of the moral and marital confusion of the British people which has existed ever since, from palace to high-rise.

Like many of the other great British or English institutions, the Church had good reason to feel that it was no longer as 'relevant' as it had been. It depended upon stable families and lasting marriages to pass on its faith and traditions, which few would learn outside the home, or without parental pressure and guidance. However, unlike some of the other threatened institutions, it was difficult for it to modernize itself—for by its nature it was supposed to be a timeless thing, based upon the eternal rather than on the worldly. How was it to become 'relevant' to the new age without becoming completely irrelevant to its purpose of saving souls? Two main answers seem to have occurred to leading Christians. The first was an increasingly social theology, suited to the new social democracy, in which Christian charity to your neighbour was expressed through political action at home and abroad, rather than in your own conduct. This was especially attractive to the British because the Church's old missionary links with the former colonies now gave it a potent voice in places such as South Africa, where it was to play an often creditable role in resisting the stupidities of Grand Apartheid. At home, the new social gospel was also a way of getting its voice heard in the irreligious, clangorous new world of suburbs and motor cars.

As it sought to be 'relevant' and forward-looking, the Church of England found its Bible, its Prayer Book and its buildings something of an embarrassment. All spoke a wholly different language—not just in vocabulary, grammar and cadence, but in thought and in the goals and rules they regarded as important. The language of both Prayer Book and Bible had been deliberately archaic when they were first written. Like most religions, the sixteenth-century Anglicans recognized that the ordinary spoken tongue of street, shop and kitchen was not suited to dealing with the eternal. Apart from anything else, much of it is designed to be sung rather than said, and it was allied from the start with some of the most beautiful music written in Britain.

Thomas Cranmer and the great translators also consciously built their books to last, just as the architects of church buildings had done, and continued to do. They believed that some ideas lay outside normal time and could therefore be expressed in a way that defied passing fashion. This belief survived until the late twentieth century, the first era in history which consciously preferred the temporary to the lasting, the modish to the classical. It affected many other things apart from language: Christopher Wren's church buildings are quite unlike his other architecture, though obviously by the same hand. Cardinal John Henry Newman's prayers and poetry are written in a style quite unlike his prose, and so on.

Some of those who set out to revise the great texts of English religion knew this very well. Others were merely carried forward on the slopping tide of change, that odd feeling which gripped Western societies in the 1950s and 1960s that humanity had reached some new high, sunlit plateau of achievement and was uniquely fitted to modernize its surroundings. One of the innovators in the Church of England was Ronald Jasper, the Dean of York, whose own history of prayer-book revision is flavoured with the breezy self-assurance which infected architects, educationalists, town planners and artists. He and many others took advantage of the complicated bureaucracy which took over the running of the Church in the years after the Second World War. This structure, based on the new General Synod, acquired the powers which parliament no longer wanted to exercise. Through a system of indirect elections it allowed a small number of committed activists to have a powerful influence over decisions, often acting in concert with the growing number of liberal clergymen by now emerging from the theological colleges.

Jasper sat on the Anglican Church's Liturgical Commission for a quarter of a century. In his book *The Development of the Anglican Liturgy 1662–1980*, he describes with barely hidden glee the rout of the traditionalists, few of whom seem to have understood what was going on until much later, when a rearguard resistance was founded.

The approach of the revisers was crabwise and cunning. They never set out openly to destroy, and their new prayer book *The Alternative Service Book 1980* was always presented as just that, an alternative. The truth was that it very quickly became the dominant service book, with the strong backing of senior clergy, theological colleges and church bureaucrats. It could not have succeeded half so well if it had been more straightforwardly launched.

As Ronald Jasper says,

> 1662 had a long history; and many generations of worshippers had found it a source of inspiration and spiritual enrichment. Clearly it still had many devotees and it could continue to serve the Church for a long time to come. But to put it to death and drive it out of existence by some legal fiat would be unkind and unnecessary. If it were to die, it must die a natural death, simply because people did not want it any longer. What was needed was a series of alternative services to place beside it. Public worship would ultimately find its own level; and whatever survived would do so because that was what met people's needs; and new services would have to win their way on their own merits.

This is an amazing passage. At the heart of it is a strange gap. The old book, he admits is much-loved and by no means dead. So *why* put it to death at all, let alone in an unkind and needless fashion? The unspoken reason for murdering Cranmer's book must explain the curious, pointless 'But' which appears in the middle of this paragraph. *Why* were alternative services needed? What were 'people's needs' if they were not being met by the beloved and beautiful, inspiring and enriching Book of Common Prayer? The truth is that the desire for change came from the Church's *nomenklatura,* the apparatus men in the theological colleges and the universities, twentieth-century liberals increasingly embarrassed by the uneducated, unreconstructed, unfashionable faith of the lay people.

After all, how many churchgoers know or care what an epiclesis is, or give a second's thought to the shape or order of services which they have been attending since they were children, and which their parents, grandparents and great-grandparents knew by heart? However, in an irreligious age, where fewer and fewer such people existed, the Church, like the railways or the government, was more and more being run for the benefit of its own employees rather than for the mere churchgoers or the nation itself. During this period it acquired its own governing body, the General Synod, whose lay members were picked from among activists in a procedure which might have been designed to exclude the ordinary. And the employees—the priests and bishops—were in turmoil.

The true reason for that turmoil was that the Anglican Church was not the Tory Party at prayer, as is so often claimed, but something far more important. It was at the heart of England's—and so Britain's—separation from the Roman Catholic, supranational Continent. It was an important symbol of the restoration of monarchy after a brief and unhappy period of Republicanism under Cromwell, and so part of the structure which resisted the ideas of the French Revolution. It was the core of the United Kingdom, Catholic *and* Reformed, open-minded yet governed by rules, intensely English, rooted in the distant past. Its version of the divine order was a mirror of the English state at the end of the seventeenth century. Its paradoxical birth, thanks to a broken royal marriage, had been followed by a troubled childhood and adolescence. It had never been fully Catholic or Protestant, and had shrouded its beliefs in elegant vagueness. Did the bread and wine at Holy Communion become Christ's body and blood, or not? Er, you decide, or, as Queen Elizabeth I more gracefully put it: 'Twas God the word that spake it, He took the bread and brake it; and what the word did make it; That I believe, and take it.'

Though it would quickly become a much-loved home for tradition and beauty, Anglicanism had risen out of another cultural revolution, as brutal and destructive as our own, poignantly described by Eamon Duffy in his history of the end of English Roman Catholicism, *The Stripping of the Altars*. It was held together mainly by its foolish and passionate enemies, given its only true identity by the noble martyrdoms it suffered under Queen Mary, reinforced by its untypically brave resistance to James II in 1688, and blessed by its identification with the countryside, the true symbol of English patriotism, and with national independence. Its fearsome state services, commemorating the crushing of the Gunpowder Plot and the Restoration of the Stuarts, linked it likewise with throne and flag, as did the Royal Arms displayed in every church to emphasize that 'The Bishop of Rome hath no jurisdiction in this Realm of England' (The XXXIX Articles, Article XXXVII) and the battle flags of victorious regiments and naval squadrons, which hung proudly in the side aisles.

Like so much of British culture, the Church's pitiful collapse in the twentieth century really began in the nineteenth. Foreign threats to British security had lessened, so much so that Catholic emancipation was possible at last, even in Ireland. The great and shockingly Protestant and patriotic state services were quietly dropped as the events they remembered ceased to be politics and became history. Much of the Protestant fervour of the common people leaked away into Methodism and the other more openly reformed churches. The Church seemed shambling, lazy, complacent and purposeless. So it was that the long, unresolved argument about what sort of Church it was broke out again, and the great Anglo-Catholic revival opened a chasm which has never since been closed. It also began a period of furious navel-gazing, disputes which mattered intensely to those involved, but baffled or repelled ordinary backsliding churchgoers as they raged on into the twentieth century and our own time.

What did they care about copes and aumbrys and whether the priest faced the altar? How much did the order of the various parts of the service trouble them? Among the clergy, the works of clever critics such as Dom Gregory Dix were well known and much discussed. Among the people in the pew, they were unknown. The more recent quarrel about women priests is merely the same argument in a new form, deeply and rightly important to the people involved as individuals, but baffling and off-putting to millions of others. Again and again—above all in the battle for a new Prayer Book in 1928—the two sides failed to compromise. The 1928 episode was the last time that Parliament felt qualified to intervene in Church affairs, by forbidding it flatly to change. MPs after the Second World War were mostly irreligious or indifferent, and so inclined to let the Church get on with whatever it wanted to do. This of course meant abandoning it to its own fanatics and extremists, and leaving the mass of Anglicans with no one to defend them. The unspoken solution, if it can be called a solution, was to dissolve the Church while pretending that it still existed.

Anyone who went to an Anglican Church fifty years ago could be fairly certain of what he would get. There were a few rather eccentric 'high' establishments, full of bells and smells, but usually well known as such. Otherwise there would be an eight o'clock service of Holy Communion, which the faithful would attend monthly, a mid-morning Matins or Morning Prayer, the main service of the day, and Evensong. Ward Lock's guidebooks used to list the type of hymnbook used to give visitors a clue as to what to expect in the way of Catholic vs.

Protestant. If the mid-morning service was some sort of Communion, they would mention it as something unusual. This pattern showed that the Church of England, though it said so nowhere in its prayers or statutes, was a Protestant and non-Continental church. Evensong was something of a survival from the days when the servants were too busy to go to morning service, yet it was one of the glories of the English Church, with a peculiar medieval beauty perfectly suited to the ancient buildings which are Anglicanism's other great (and embarrassing) treasure. Perhaps this is why it survives in rather soulless beauty as the one traditional ceremony still regularly dignified by choir and procession in the great cathedrals, though stripped of confession and absolution and really much more of a religious concert to be watched than a service to take part in. Laurie Lee, in a passage which would still have made sense to any churchgoing person in the 1950s, described in *Cider with Rosie* Evensong's special and specially English atmosphere compared with Matins:

> In the morning in the packed congregation solemnity ruled. There was power, lamentation, full-throated singing, heavy prayers and public repentance. No-one in the village stayed away without reason, and no-one yet wished to do so. We had come to the church because it was Sunday, just as we washed our clothes on Monday.... Later came Evensong, which was as different from Matins as a tryst from a Trafalgar Square rally.... The service was almost a reverie, our hymns nocturnal and quiet, the psalms traditional and never varying so that one could sing them without a book. The scattered faithful, half-obscured by darkness, sang them as though to themselves 'Lord, now lettest thou thy servant depart in peace....' It was sung, eyes closed, in trembling tones. It could not have been sung in the morning.

But this unchanging timetable was due to be wrenched to pieces and replaced. In more and more churches, Protestant

Matins was replaced by Catholic Parish Communion, a service all very well for the faithful and enthusiastic, but exclusive for the casual visitor or the ordinary sinner. Hymns were revised and modernized, old pews removed and replaced with chairs, churches themselves redecorated and cleaned, an increasing number with new central altars, in open competition with the ancient tables (Anglican churches aren't supposed to have altars) beneath the east window.

These changes, many of them presented as a return to the 'early church,' grew in number and speed after the war. A clergyman, Canon G. W. O. Addleshaw, and an architect, Frederick Etchells, wrote *The Architectural Setting of Anglican Worship* which—appearing during post-war rebuilding and suburban expansion—influenced many new and restored churches. It argued for a central altar. New translations of the Bible, often deliberately modern, were appearing throughout the English-speaking world, and appealed again to the initiates and the apparatus, rather than to the common people. Traditional music, too, came under attack from something calling itself the Twentieth Century Light Music Group, which urged 'familiar' idiom. Within a few years they would have idioms which were all too familiar.

By the early 1990s, all these movements had succeeded so well that the Anglican Church no longer had any recognized or familiar forms of service. Anything was possible. A worshipper moving from church to church even in the same city, would not have hoped or even expected to find anything more than a vague similarity in the services he encountered. Bibles, prayers, hymns, styles of music, arrangement of the building, the clothes worn by the worshippers would all have been entirely unpredictable. He might discover priests (or priestesses) in crumpled white linen, or draped in embroidered copes, flanked by candle-bearing acolytes. He might see people speaking 'in tongues' or rolling upon the floor, or confessing in public to having partaken of oral sex. He might hear traditional

Victorian hymns or a guitar. He might be choked by incense or urged to get up and down five times a minute and shout. The service might be run by a priest or a 'president'. Had he been in Sheffield in the early 1990s, he might have found his way into the services run by Chris Brain, described in *The Rise and Fall of the Nine o'Clock Service*: 'Druidic white-robed figures around an altar resembling a crescent moon ... hundreds of black-clad figures peer out of the darkness, swaying to swirling, strangely ethereal breaths of ambient techno.'

This, remember, is taking place in an Anglican church, heir to the monastic tradition and the poetry of Thomas Cranmer. But instead of the timeless comfort of beauty and order, the worshipper hears, 'The Lord is here ... his spirit is with us', and then listens to the 'first song, led by the band', followed by 'body prayer, a sort of Christianised yoga', and then a multi-decibel confession: 'Creator God, the source of all life, we confess our sin to you ... we confess that as we've wanted more and more we have dominated and exploited your creation ... we admit ... that we are complicit in destroying you by polluting the air and sea, by destroying the forest, by starving the people of the Third World.'

Then 'a rapper comes over the top, giving it all he's got, and gradually fades into a sample of an Eastern voice wailing.' Then Chris (Brain) says: 'God who knows the equality of all people, and the trap of false dreams, release and deliver you, Amen.' He then 'fades into the sound of running water and birdsong and then it is time for the sacrament'.

Chris Brain, of course, went too far even for the modern Anglican hierarchy, who were probably embarrassed because his services were far too *close* to their ideas, rather than because they were too distant from them. But in the anarchy of modern Anglicanism it is hard to blame him for thinking he could get away with it—the yoga, the halfwit Marxism, the pagan nature worship, the disorder and irreverence are not actually that much of a step beyond the boundaries.

Yet again, we were warned of this. In December 1974, Parliament directly debated this issue for what was almost certainly the last time in history. The recently formed General Synod of the Church, a body composed of activists and clergy, now wanted complete freedom to press ahead with its reforms. To do so, it had to get Parliament to repeal several ancient laws and hand over its powers to the Church hierarchy. Battle was most fiercely joined in the Lords on 14 November, when the future Archbishop of York, Dr John Habgood, denied that the Synod was 'hell-bent on a programme of thoughtless reform' and insisted that nothing was planned beyond the experimental 'series three' services, the first in which God was addressed as 'You' rather than 'Thou'. On 4 December, the Commons debated the issue. MPs assailed the new services as 'weak gibberish' and 'sterile bureaucratic words of modern usage'. Only two politicians seem really to have understood what was going on, both of them Tories. Eldon Griffiths said the Church wanted the freedom of disestablishment, of no longer being a state church, without wanting to pay the price in loss of status. Enoch Powell warned the Commons that they had to decide whether to give the church its freedom to act as it felt, whether 'we are able to remove that stamp and stability and replace them by the freedom of unlimited innovation in the future which this measure portends'. In the end, they voted for unlimited innovation by 145 votes to 45, though not even Enoch Powell can have imagined that the vote would lead to Chris Brain and his Nine o'Clock Service.

Did the revisers themselves know what they were doing? Was it part of their purpose to unsettle? Did they consciously use salami tactics of tiny change after tiny change to weaken and undermine the traditionalists? It is impossible to be sure, since so far nobody has revealed the details of their own internal discussions. All their published works about reform assume that it is both right and inevitable because the new Bibles and services will be better in some theological way. But Ronald Jasper gives a small clue to the truth in this passage:

As for the consumer level, it seemed to me that for severely practical purposes we should be aiming to cater for the members of the General Synod, since in the first instance they were the people who would decide by two-third majorities what was acceptable; and on the whole they were a middle-aged, middle-class, fairly well-educated group. It was a rough and ready principle, but as good a guide as any other. Furthermore, we should aim for a judicious blend of old and new, so that people would be reassured by the presence of familiar elements: it would be wise, for example, to start the rite with a virtually unchanged Collect for Purity. Series 2 had encouraged people to break with the 1662 structure while retaining the language; series 3 must now encourage people to break with the 1662 language; and I believed this would prove to be a much more difficult and lengthy task.

These do not appear to be the words or thoughts of a man reluctantly adapting an ancient church to irresistible outside forces of history. These are the words of an enthusiast and campaigner, not above a little public relations to coat his bitter pill in honey. What does he mean by 'the consumer level'? Why should people need to be reassured? Why 'must' series 3 encourage people to break with Cranmer's language?

There is no doubt that some sort of change was needed in the Church of England by the middle of the twentieth century. A Prayer Book mostly written in 1549 for a country-dwelling people would certainly have benefited from some sensible revisions and additions. There are obscure passages in the King James Bible (though they are often just as obscure in the modern versions if not more so). Some church buildings are dingy and ill-furnished and could do with repair and brightening. Some churches simply don't have enough of a congregation to survive, and must face the possibility of closure. But these are exactly the changes which have not been made.

The Prayer Book, whose language is so much part of

English speech and thought that excerpts from it occupy almost seventeen pages of the *Oxford Dictionary of Quotations* (Revised Fourth Edition, 1996), has virtually ceased to exist in the daily worship of the Church. The King James Bible (almost thirty-eight pages of the same *Dictionary of Quotations*) is rarely if ever read at its services, or taught in its schools. Meanwhile, many beautiful churches and cathedrals have been insensitively modernised: Chester Cathedral, for instance, among other barbarities, has television screens clamped to the pillars of its nave. Many others have been equipped with ugly new central altars and community-centre chairs. Wren's lovely St Stephen Walbrook in the city of London, built as a Protestant preaching house, now has a circular stone altar derided as The Camembert Cheese, ringed with the sort of canvas chairs used by Hollywood directors. Still others have been turned into pay-as-you-enter museums where some religion takes place. Some ugly new ones have been built, and many fine Victorian buildings closed down.

Congregations are undeniably far smaller than they were thirty or forty years ago, and while some churches are healthy it is often because they have gone over to charismatic forms of worship which have nothing to do with the broad church traditions of the Church of England. Almost all Anglican churches now seem to be for enthusiasts only. Few but the most determined dare enter, and many of these churches take the form of a club, unintentionally exclusive, utterly unconnected with the world outside, by tradition, language or anything else. Many young children entirely deprived of a tradition passed on without thinking by twenty previous generations have no idea at all of what goes on in churches, and it is noticeable that many of the new suburbs now springing up have no church buildings anywhere near them.

So, if the purpose of all this was to revive the Church and make it more part of the world, then it has not succeeded. Those who urged modernization claimed that their methods and measures would bring back the lost sheep; their complete failure to do so has not made them return to traditional services or rip out their new furniture, or to question in a fundamental way the basis of their reforms. So we must wonder if they have other, over-riding purposes.

The author was given a clue to what these might be when he made a small survey of the state of affairs in a medium-sized English provincial town in the mid-1980s. A superficial glance at church porches was reassuring. There were many traditional services still taking place. But in hardly any churches were they the *main* service. They were held for the benefit of a dwindling number of older people who would not accept the new forms of worship. Almost everywhere, the main, mid-morning service with choir and hymns and nursery and coffee afterwards was a modern-language Communion. There was another problem. The two different sorts of liturgy operated on two different calendars, so the Bible passages which were read were out of step and the seasons did not even chime. You could not alternate ancient and modern without losing continuity.

Types of music also varied, and churches seeking to attract the young could no longer rely on them knowing a basic repertory of hymns. As Roger Scruton, philosopher and village church organist, wrote in 1996 in an eloquent lament:

> Schoolchildren of my generation assembled each morning before classes in order to listen to much-needed admonitions and to sing from the great collection of Anglican music. . . . We absorbed one of the most impressive traditions of amateur music-making ever known, and most of us still hear in our heads tunes, words and harmonies which have focused the thoughts and feelings of English speakers for as long as the Anglican Church has represented the established religion of this country. . . .
>
> From relics of medieval plainsong, through Renaissance psalmody, the Lutheran and Calvinist hymnals, the great

flowering of the English hymn in the eighteenth century, and the mixture of all this with romantic harmony and patriotic sentiment in Victorian times, right down to the village organists and choirmasters who were my immediate predecessors, the chain of composition remained unbroken.

And then, without anybody noticing it, it came to an end. For composition must cease when performance ceases. A few old voices sing along as I play each Sunday; if children are present, however (and children in church are now a rarity), they have no knowledge of the tunes and no conception of singing in a solemn way. During the hymns they stand in awkward and undignified silence.

For miles around there are churches like ours, in which the organ too is silent—not because congregations have ceased to sing, but because nobody is able to play. ... The musical culture into which I was initiated and which has been the greatest source of joy to me and my contemporaries is now dormant, surfacing for a week or so each Christmas, but too feeble to stay awake beyond Boxing Day. (*The Times,* 1 December 1996)

This same thing was strikingly noticeable in television coverage of the response in British schools to the death of Princess Diana. A teacher was shown singing a hymn, not a specially complex or unfamiliar one, while the children looked on, tongue-tied and embarrassed, an audience rather than a congregation.

As I made my inquiries into the state of the liturgy, I met with some peculiar responses. One or two clergymen sympathized and were helpful. Several were cold and indifferent. One used subterfuge to obtain a copy of my survey, when he could have had it by asking. Two incidents were very striking. When I visited a great church, one of the most beautiful and magnificent for miles around, I asked one of its clergy if they ever used the 1662 Prayer Book. He made it clear that he knew all about my inquiry, said that they never used 1662 and then, almost hissing between clenched teeth, snapped: 'I *hate* Cranmer's theology of penitence.' Not long afterwards, one of the few churches in the district which used the old Prayer Book suddenly faced change. The incumbent vicar, much loved by his flock but despised by the pseudo-intellectual young clergymen in surrounding parishes, fell ill and had to retire. When his successor came to be installed, the Bishop, who knew this place to be a centre of tradition, insisted on a modern form of service and, worse still, demanded that the congregation underwent the 'Peace', the informal and intrusive rite of handshaking which had never been used there before. It was not just language these people were concerned about, and they were fiercely intolerant of those who would not join in their wave of change. It seemed unlikely that any parson who resisted would get preferment of any kind, and few if any younger priests were even being trained to use the old Book, even though it was by law and tradition the core of the whole church.

The truth was that the new services were not in any way comparable to the old ones. There were so many alternatives and let-out clauses that the clergy were free to use practically any forms that they wished. The Old Testament and the Psalms, with their harsher and more uncompromising approach, were relegated or eliminated. The Ten Commandments, already skipped by many clergy, practically disappeared from view. Prayers for the Royal Family tended to get left out, but lengthy pleas about the most fashionable international crisis would be inserted elsewhere.

The glories of the language were offensive to the modernizers because they reminded them of what they owed to the past, because they reinforced the bonds of tradition, but above all because they constantly reminded them of a view of religion which was not theirs. It did not offer salvation through the Overseas Development Agency, the Anti-Apartheid Movement, Amnesty International and the Social Security budget.

It offered it in an entirely non-political way, through the faith and deeds of the individual.

At the heart of any comparison between the two books lies the confession before Communion, as close as Anglicanism gets to penitence. In the Alternative Service Book Rite A (now the most commonly used), the worshipper says:

> Almighty God, our heavenly Father, we have sinned against you and against our fellow men, in thought and word and deed, through negligence, through weakness, through our own deliberate fault. We are truly sorry, and repent of all our sins. For the sake of your Son Jesus Christ, who died for us, forgive us all that is past; and grant that we may serve you in newness of life to the glory of your name. Amen. (ASB, Holy Communion Rite A, p. 127)

In the 1662 Book of Common Prayer, he says:

> Almighty God, Father of our Lord Jesus Christ, Maker of all things, Judge of all men; we acknowledge and bewail our manifold sins and wickedness, Which we, from time to time, most grievously have committed, By thought, word and deed, Against thy Divine Majesty, Provoking most justly thy wrath and indignation against us. We do earnestly repent, And are heartily sorry for these our misdoings; The remembrance of them is grievous unto us; the burden of them is intolerable. Have mercy upon us, Have mercy upon us, most merciful Father; For thy Son our Lord Jesus Christ's sake, Forgive us all that is past; And grant that we may ever hereafter Serve and please thee In newness of life, To the honour and glory of thy Name; Through Jesus Christ our Lord. Amen. (Original punctuation and capitalization, Book of Common Prayer, OUP, p. 270)

As if to prove that the modern version is not simply a setting of the old confession into modern language, the revisers also provide a modern confession in old language for the less-used Rite B alternative Communion. Worshippers are told to kneel, which is optional under the more democratic Rite A. Then they say:

> Almighty God, our heavenly Father, we have sinned against thee, through our own fault, in thought, and word, and deed, and in what we have left undone. We are heartily sorry, and repent of all our sins, For thy Son our Lord Jesus Christ's sake, forgive us all that is past; and grant that we may serve thee in newness of life, to the glory of thy name. Amen. (ASB, p. 187)

Both new versions are much shorter than the original, reducing the strength and importance of the confession as part of the service. The Rite A version introduces a whole new idea, that we sin against our fellow men. Is this important? Yes, for surely Christians have generally believed that sins are the deliberate defiance of the known will of God, not offences against other people. Also, neither new version admits that the burden of the sin is intolerable, or asks for mercy, although the priest immediately grants that mercy in his absolution.

But the main difference between them, though hard to measure, is that the 1662 version is extremely difficult to say without being forced into serious and painful thought, while both new versions are perfunctory and lack any real sense of, to be blunt, fear. They sound like the apologies offered by railway companies for late trains, or by hotels for bad service, hurried and weak, lacking any sense of the scale of what is being asked, and what could be granted in return, or of the consequences of insincerity or failure to live up to what is said.

The older version would no doubt be described as 'gloomy' and even 'dismal' by modernizers. Similar things are said about the Church of England's stony and uncompromising burial service, now largely abandoned except at the funerals of the very old indeed.

Study even the most modern Bible, and (as the latest Catholic catechism points out) there are several clear and uncompromising references to the existence of Hell. Souls are shown being dragged down to it in Michelangelo's great painting in the Sistine Chapel. The Bible story of Dives and Lazarus, the rich man who ignores the beggar at his gate and then, in the parching heat of Hell, asks for the beggar to be allowed to bring him a drop of water (the answer was no), went so powerfully into the English culture that it was the subject of a popular folk song and associated with one of the most memorable tunes rediscovered by Ralph Vaughan-Williams. The Church was always about death and judgement. Tombs are adorned with grinning, gap-toothed skulls (one, winged and crowned, leers across the nave of Oxford Cathedral). Rich men paid to have 'cadavers' displayed on their tombs—grisly and realistic representations of how they might be expected to look a few months after death. Many survive, and rather disturbing they are too. As you walk out of the West door of the seventeenth-century church of St James Garlickhythe in the City of London, the inscription on a tombstone beneath your feet ends with the dark words 'Prepare to Follow'. Churches were, in any case, surrounded by graveyards in constant use, though many have been rather prissily tidied up and landscaped in the last few decades, their tombstones pushed to one side to make the mowing easier.

Thanks to the *apparent* abolition of death in recent years, the fear of it, and of what lies beyond, have been shoved to the edges of our lives, and consideration of our eventual fate postponed until 'later', much like worrying about a pension in your twenties. People generally grow seriously old before they die, as they used not to do, and the deaths we notice— and are often outraged and angry over—are the deaths of the young and healthy. The old have usually become unpersons long before they die. Any visitor to the House of Lords can see this process in its purest form, since perfectly healthy, active and intelligent people can be found there in large numbers, who have effectively ceased to exist because they are no longer in active full-time work. Yet this mildly comic truth is only a slight caricature of society in general. After their final retirement from office or factory, people increasingly drop out of the consciousness of friends who only knew them because of what they did, rather than because of who they are. Weakened families, driven apart by serial divorce or geographic separation, likewise tend to ignore and neglect their older members, who generally face a long period of ill-health before death thanks to the 'advances' of modern medicine. This is why so many die in hospitals or nursing homes rather than in their own beds. Home death is becoming as rare as home birth.

The Church still goes through the motions, its priests and ministers officiating at abbreviated ceremonies in the production-line crematoria of the nation, at funerals where fewer and fewer of the younger mourners have any idea of how to behave, or dress, or speak, or of what to say. At the funerals of the young, entirely secular pop songs are often played as substitutes for hymns. In the last few years, mourners have taken to telling *jokes* during funeral eulogies, as if they were at a wedding. Decorum has disappeared not because people are consciously ill-mannered but because they have no idea that it is required. Children at a primary school in the Isle of Wight were spoken to sharply by their teachers in 1996 after they mocked and jeered at a passing funeral. Nobody had told them that death demanded respect. And in a world where blinds are not drawn down, and there are no hats to doff as the hearse goes by, how were they supposed to learn, and what does it matter anyway?

And yet, night after night, in the wards of a hundred hospitals, people die as they have always done, alone at the end and in many cases afraid of what is to come, more and more comforted by morphine, less and less by the Holy Ghost. We prefer not to notice. In the midst of death, we are in life and

John Lennon's wish in 'Imagine'—'no religion, no heaven and no hell, and all the people thinking for today'—has come true. How odd that the Church itself should have helped it to do so, by abandoning its cold and austere central truth, that we must all die and may be judged, the one piece of ground nobody, not even Hitler or Stalin, could ever have captured from it.

I find only anxiety and apprehension about the social effects of this pastime and especially about its effect upon small children.
—T. S. Eliot, *The Times,* 20 December 1950

SIX

The Telescreen Triumphs

FOR ONCE, WE *were* told exactly what to be afraid of. But it made no difference. Eliot's letter predicting the dangers of television must rank as one of the wisest and most prophetic ever published by *The Times,* and it was also in time to prevent the danger of which it warned. At Christmas 1950, most British households did not have a television set, and did not hope to obtain one. Britain had one television channel, which was transmitted for only a few hours each day. Radio, the cinema and a huge national variety of newspapers and magazines satisfied the wants of a literate, educated population for information and entertainment. Eliot himself was a highly influential cultural figure, publisher, playwright, poet and religious writer, who could claim to understand the USA better than most Englishmen, since he was American by birth. His letter was measured and cautious, and so important that even today, to read it is to experience a pang of loss, a feeling of a great opportunity missed.

> Sir, in your issue of 17 December you announce that the BBC proposes to spend over £4 million during the next three years on the development of television. I have just returned from a visit to the United States, where television (though

not, I believe, more developed technically) has become an habitual form of entertainment in many more households than here. I find only anxiety and apprehension about the social effects of this pastime and especially about its effect (mentally, morally and physically) upon small children.

Before we endeavour to popularize it still further in this country, might it not be as well if we investigated its consequences for American society and took counsel with informed American opinion about possible safeguards and limitations? The fears expressed by my American friends were not such as could be allayed by the provision of only superior and harmless programmes. They were concerned with the television habit, whatever the programme might be.

> Your obedient servant,
> T. S. Eliot,
> 24 Russell Square, London WC1

Eliot had already foreseen all the arguments about 'superb nature programmes' and 'dramas which lead children on to the classics' and the rest of the excuses which have been put forth by the broadcasting industry for the damage which they do to young minds. Eliot could see that television was something quite different from any previous medium. Probably instinctively rather than rationally, he sensed from the worried faces of his American friends that a revolution was in progress, a revolution that would damage and weaken millions of young minds.

Now we know what Eliot only foresaw through a glass darkly. It would be many years before British children were exposed to television on such a scale and at such an early stage in their lives that the damage would be too obvious to ignore. But by the mid-1990s, it was plain that something was going seriously wrong, with more and more reports of young children from affluent homes who could not behave or read or grasp simple concepts of behaviour and manners. In January

1996, I interviewed Dr Sally Ward, an expert on the speech development of young children. Dr Ward was perturbed by the number of children unable to speak normally at ages when they should have learned to do so without any trouble. At that time, she was certain that two things had greatly increased the problem—the launch of daytime television in Britain, and the increasing number of special videotapes aimed directly at young children.

These things arrived just as the number of women going out to work was rising sharply. (At Christmas 1997, the female workforce in Britain would outnumber the male workforce for the first time in recorded history, a development with such huge consequences that it has, of course, never been debated, directly legislated for in Parliament or discussed in a general election campaign). Thanks to these developments, the television screen had become, along with schools, a kind of national childminding service. Parents could use the television as they might once have used a nanny or a grandparent. They could no longer afford the nanny, and the grandparent probably lived hundreds of miles away, but the plastic box performed the same function, cheaply and apparently harmlessly. The extent of this use of television as third parent became clear on the morning after the death of Princess Diana, when millions of adults learned the news from children deprived of their Sunday morning cartoons by special news broadcasts. But it was not just older children who were dumped in front of the flickering tube. Infants as young as six months old were being abandoned to the output of broadcasters and commercial-makers.

What is the effect of this? Dr Ward says, 'I have seen children of two-and-a-half with virtually no ability to understand words'. Often they cannot even speak, and are capable only of animal, gulping noises, boundlessly horrible and depressing. In our early months, we *can* learn an enormous number of things: taking turns in conversation, telling when the other person has finished, reading facial expressions, the general rules which make civilized conversation possible. Planted in front of cartoons, or the TeleTubbies, we do not discover these things at all. This is because television's communication is all one way, encouraging people to be passive receptors rather than active partakers. The television carries on with what it is doing regardless of what they do, so they learn to do the same. And since they cannot understand what they are seeing and hearing, it does not matter if they are watching a high-level debate on *Newsnight* or violent rubbish such as *Power Rangers*. The effect is just as bad. Nor is the damage limited to conversation. Early exposure to television can mean a failure to understand how to behave as a social being, turning watchers into mere individuals unable to realize that they are connected by duty, affection or even fear to others.

Dr Ward describes a typical victim of this early exposure: 'He comes into the room and ploughs right past you. If you put a box of toys on the floor, he ploughs through that too, wandering rather aimlessly around and looking at nobody and nothing.'

'There's a lack of social awareness, a lack of knowledge of how to function in society. They aren't picking up vital clues about how others feel, or how to respond to them.'

Some form a sort of bond of love with the video player. 'They went berserk when it was turned off. They simply couldn't do without it, and when it was taken away they reacted as if their mother had disappeared.'

These, by the way, were not just the abandoned victims of single parenthood in collapsing tower blocks. The same problems afflicted the well-dressed products of wealthy, well-educated middle-class parents living in pleasant detached houses. At around the same time, researchers for the GMTV company discovered that children aged two and three were watching as much as eighteen hours of television a week, 80 per cent of it without an adult present in the room. These children, abandoned in a way only the late twentieth century could invent, are still climbing their way towards their teens, when they will be big and strong. It is frightening to think what kind of adolescents, what kind of adults they will become, and almost unbearable to imagine what kind of parents they will be. They are only the most developed cases of a disease which has been quietly spreading up the age range since Britain ignored T. S. Eliot in 1950.

Far from restricting television, the authorities encouraged it. Winston Churchill insisted that television cameras should record the Queen's coronation in 1953, giving the new medium its greatest fillip. A Tory government then went on to destroy the BBC monopoly, brushing aside traditional Conservatives who feared the moral effects and listening only to those for whom the free market was sacred above all. Lord Reith, the founding genius of the BBC, had warned that it was only the brute force of monopoly which allowed his corporation to take a conservative moral position. He was rapidly proved right, as competition for ratings became the unanswerable argument for laxer and laxer standards of taste and language, and bolder and bolder excursions into pornography and violence. The struggle for ratings also, quite predictably, forced religious programmes into a smaller and smaller corner, along with all unfashionable minority views.

An enormous power had been released into the land, and even if its controllers had wanted it to, it was not using its strength to keep things as they were, let alone to turn back the clock. It was also taking a stronger hold on the national mind with each generation, as children came to it younger and younger and were exposed to it for longer and longer.

But why is television so unique, and why is colour television so much more potent than black-and-white? Compare it first of all with the cinema, a medium which is at first sight so very similar. Cinema is a concentrated experience, available only for two or three hours at a special time and place. It is surrounded by ceremony—even now many theatres still use

curtains to signal the start of a programme, and there is a ritual to the order of trailers, advertisements, censor's certificate,
sale of food and so on. Until thirty years ago, performances
ended with the national anthem, incredible as this now seems
even to me. It is also usually done in company of around the
same age, with children still excluded by law from the most
violent or sexually blatant films. The cinema-goer usually
prefers to go with a companion, and is in any case watching
with all the other people in the audience. Films, even nowadays, are often applauded. There can also be genuine infectious laughter.

Television is available without ceremony, without a special journey and without companionship. Its pleasures are
increasingly solitary, especially in the millions of homes where
it is on most of the time and where there is a set in each child's
bedroom. It is also available in great quantity. If a viewer
chooses, he can watch the television almost without interrup-
tion from the moment he gets up, or comes home. There is
almost always something to watch, provided you are willing
to be passive. Anyone trained from his earliest years in the television habit is likely to be extremely passive, because his ability to imagine, to hold conversations, to think without prompt-
ing, has already been weakened and withered. He does not
need them.

In the 1950s, children simply could not do this in Britain.
There were long periods when nothing was shown except something called the 'test card', a series of geometric patterns
designed to allow engineers to tune the signal properly, sometimes accompanied by music, but now a fond memory. There
was also an event known as the 'closedown', usually well before
midnight, after which an announcer would remind viewers to
switch off their sets. The screen would then actually go blank,
emitting a high-pitched signal to wake those who might have
fallen asleep in front of it. In the 1960s, there were still size-
able gaps during which nothing was transmitted at all. Parental

authority also still existed in many homes, enforced by a mother who was there all the time. Perhaps most important of all, the programmes were in black and white, or, to be truthful, pale grey, medium grey and dark grey.

Colour came slowly, launched with Wimbledon tennis coverage in 1967, a tiny minority interest in 1968 with just over 20,000 licences, and not reaching a million homes until 1972. As late as 1974, there were still twice as many black-and-white sets as colour ones in British homes—11,766,424 to 5,558,146. But where colour came, even the bad programmes looked good, and by the late 1980s a new generation was growing up, to whom the bright, noisy plastic box in the corner was the most seductive, the cleverest, the most articulate, the most beguiling thing they had ever seen. Even the most brilliant storyteller, the most inspirational teacher, the most companionable parent or older brother, could not compete with colour television's virtuosity and variety. Sports, especially, were instantly transformed and far easier to follow. Even such things as snooker and darts suddenly became 'good television'. The pictures on the screen in the corner of the room were for the first time brighter, cleaner, sharper and more exciting than the room itself. It was harder and harder to take your eyes away from the screen. Even news bulletins became a sort of treat for the eyes, with the great capitals and landscapes of the world suddenly seen for the first time in their full, rich reality. There was no longer any need to imagine for ourselves, and the thing was so seductive that almost nobody could resist it for long. George Melly, that hopeless progressive, wrongly forecast in 1969 that there would be a 'small resistance movement of middle-class intellectuals, the children of those who in the early fifties wouldn't have the telly at all'. He thought they would equate black-and-white with high seriousness, but in fact such people either surrendered to the new and bought colour TVs, or continued to resist by refusing to have televisions in their houses at all. The only people who continued to watch in black-and-white were the elderly poor, who could not afford the new sets or the higher TV licence fee charged for colour.* Resistance to television was probably thanks to the miraculous survival of intelligent, national speech radio, kept alive by the BBC's continued accidental monopoly, and unknown almost anywhere else on earth.

The periodic battles over the two middle-class BBC radio channels—Radios Three and Four—are incomprehensible to most outsiders. They are defended, furiously and bitterly, by their small number of listeners precisely because they cater for the last serious section of the population who have not surrendered their imaginations to the television. They actually prefer to listen to the morning news on the radio than to watch it on the colour television. They are generally in young middle age, dating from the era when middle-class parents at least rationed the television. They are genuinely unhappy with television's short attention-span and its obsession with pictures above all things. Until recently, they had very little idea what the presenters of their favourite programmes looked like, a happy state brought to an end by the increasing use of radio figures on television. They are, while politically and socially liberal, puzzlingly conservative (from the BBC point of view) about the use of language, accent and grammar. Because of their backgrounds, they are present in large numbers among politicians, journalists, civil servants, churchmen and in university senior common rooms. They can write powerful letters to the editors of major newspapers. But they give a completely false impression of the state of public opinion or the broadcasting audience in Britain. They are, sadly, like the last people to escape the pods in *Invasion of the Bodysnatchers*, or like the refugees in the forest in *Fahrenheit 451*, each of whom has remembered one great book to preserve it from the televisual culture which burns all books on sight. Attempts to rejuvenate the Radio Four audience have all failed, and will continue to fail, because the rising generation, even at the very top end of the education and career range, mostly lack the concentration, curiosity, individuality and imagination required of a serious radio listener. It is unwise nowadays to assume that even intelligent young journalists have listened to Radio Four in the previous week.

This shows just how differently radio and television affect their audiences. Both become a kind of club, sharing a common knowledge of certain people, voices and serials with thousands or millions of others. But radio listeners do not pool their imaginations with anyone else, or lend their imaginative powers to others. At all times, they retain the ability to decide if a fictional character or even a real person is tall or short, dark or fair, sinister or engaging, good or bad. Television viewers have all this decided for them.

Come to television as an adult, literate and independent, and it may make you lazy and passive, but it cannot leech away the thoughts, memories and imagination you already possess. But what if you come to it as a tiny child, your memory undeveloped, your imagination a blank space, your social and conversational abilities as yet non-existent. Is it possible you will then be a different *kind* of person from your parents?

The American commentator Neil Postman certainly thinks so. In his book *The Disappearance of Childhood: How Television Is Changing Children's Lives,* Postman points out that 'even the idea of a children's game seems to be slipping from our grasp'. He noted, more than fifteen years ago, that games such as hide-and-seek had almost completely vanished. Television, he argues, requires 'perception, not conception'. How could it be otherwise when the average length of a single camera shot is now three to four seconds in programmes, two to three seconds in commercials? Its skills in delivering its message straight to the brain 'make the rigours of a literate education irrelevant'. He quotes Reginald Damerall's frightening observation that 'No child or adult becomes better at watching television by doing more of it. You have yet to hear of television-viewing disability.' This, of course, is the opposite of reading, where greater skills allow the growing child to read more deeply, more widely and with more taste, and a growing mind builds up the mental muscle needed to tackle the great works of literature and history.

Postman believes this matters enormously, because 'children are a group of people who do *not* know certain things which adults know'. At least, they used to be before they were seduced by television and its brothers, the video player and the virtual-reality computer game. By destroying this superior adult knowledge, and handing children the fruit of the tree of knowledge unmediated by adult wisdom, we have abandoned our young to powers and influences which we cannot control, and whose strength we do not know. To leave a child unsupervised in front of a television set is no less dangerous than giving it neat gin, or putting it within reach of narcotics.

One sign that this may be true is the way in which the old restraints on sexuality and aggressive violence are collapsing so quickly among the young, many of whom simply cannot understand what their parents are worrying about. Postman argues, 'Shame gives power and authority to adulthood. For adults know, whereas children do not, what words are shameful to use, what subjects are shameful to discuss, what acts are deemed necessary to privatize.' But 'shame cannot exert any influence as a means of social control or role differentiation in a society that cannot keep secrets'—i.e., a society which hands children over to the cathode-ray tube. This has great consequences for attitudes towards sex. Without shame and mystery, the system of taboos 'loses its dark and figurative character, as well as most of its moral force ... what was once shameful may become a "social problem" or a "political issue".

'In revealing the secrets of sex, television has come close to eliminating the concept of sexual aberration altogether'. This is vastly more important than the issue of sex alone. Postman quotes G. K. Chesterton's warning that 'All healthy men, ancient and modern, Eastern and Western, know that there is a certain fury in sex that we cannot afford to inflame, and that a certain mystery and awe must ever surround it if we are to remain sane.'

So the loss of parental control over the sex taboo is a far deeper danger than the mere destruction of the idea of right and wrong sexual conduct, catastrophic though this is. It has snapped some of the most important of the invisible chains which keep our society from satisfying its passions without restraint.

If that were all, it would be bad enough. But a generation brought up by Chris Evans* and the other skilled performers of youth television has not just been robbed of the moral subtleties of four hundred years of literate civilization. It has become easily manipulated because it has learned first to expect to be manipulated, second to enjoy being manipulated, and third not to care when it happens. Anyone who can control a major television channel can use it to pour out propaganda, but it is only this new generation which does not know how to resist it, provided it uses the right sort of codes, language and symbols. None of these codes, languages or symbols are conservative, or can be used by a conservative, because they are 'subversive' of the imagined 'authority' of a mythical 'establishment', which of course includes the Tories and poor old Mrs Whitehouse, along with the long-dead malcontent colonels who were the originals of 'Disgusted, Tunbridge Wells'.* A conservative message, in this medium, will always look as foolish as Mr William Hague in a baseball cap.*

Postman returned to the assault in *Amusing Ourselves to Death,* where he warned that we should not be complacent just because we had avoided George Orwell's nightmare totalitarian society, which he had predicted for 1984. What was actually coming true, he suggested, was Aldous Huxley's alternative nightmare in *Brave New World,* where nobody even realized that they were being oppressed.

What Orwell feared were those who would ban books. What Huxley feared was that there would be no reason to ban a book, for there would be no one who wanted to read one. Orwell feared those who would deprive us of information. Huxley feared those who would give us so much that we would be reduced to passivity and egoism. Orwell feared that the truth would be concealed from us. Huxley feared the truth would be drowned in a sea of irrelevance. Orwell feared we would become a captive culture. Huxley feared that we would become a trivial culture.

Huxley, in fact, warned directly of 'man's almost infinite capacity for distractions.' Postman believes that capacity has been fully engaged in the last twenty years.

His words could almost have been written to describe the cynical, puerile, bubblegum election campaigns fought by Bill Clinton in 1992 and 1996, and by Tony Blair in 1997, when he proclaimed himself a modern man. 'When serious public conversation becomes a form of baby-talk, when people become an audience ... a nation finds itself at risk. Culture-death is a clear possibility.' One thinks of 'Things can only get better', 'For the many, not the few' and, of course, 'Education, education, education', or of any of Mr Blair's much-praised but largely vacuous speeches.

This atmosphere of jaunty, funky emptiness is very hard to combat because, as Postman asks, 'Who is prepared to take arms against a sea of amusements? What is the antidote to a culture's being drowned by laughter?'

Echoing Eliot's dismissal of 'quality' television, he argues that 'we would be better off if television got worse, not better. ... *The A-Team* and *Cheers* are no threat to our public health. *Sixty Minutes*, *Eyewitness News* and *Sesame Street* are.' Spiritual devastation, he predicts 'is more likely to come from an enemy with a smiling face than from one whose countenance exudes suspicion and hate.'

But his central point in all these warnings remains that television robs adults of one of their most important tasks, as passers-on of culture to the young, mediating, explaining, sometimes hiding things until later when they will be less dangerous. Once, children became adults first by learning to speak and then by learning to read. Now we are travelling back to the primitive times before literacy, when adults could keep less from their young, when adulthood came far earlier, and the culture of the tribe was cruder and more immature as a result. If he is even half right, the implications for all settled cultures are large. For a culture such as Britain's, shaken and broken and bent and under reconstruction, the implications are immense.

Of course, other forces have marched alongside television, though it is hard to believe that they could have been half so successful without its aid. Modern popular music, with its strangely bisexual appeal and its carnal beat—part war-dance, part fertility ritual—would not have spread so fast unless pubescent boys and girls had been able to see the often androgynous faces of the stars, first on television and then on the videos which are now rock's most powerful marketing device. It is for others to explain why twelve-year-old girls screamed most wildly whenever the Beatles began to sing falsetto, or why the most enduring images of Mick Jagger are those of him cross-dressing and in full make-up in the rarely shown movie *Performance*. The appeal of rock musicians is a peculiar thing, though if Neil Postman is right it has much to do with the sexual awakening of children who until recently would have been thought too young for such things, and who are most easily seduced by ambiguous, half-and-half figures, partly themselves and partly the other, unknown sex. But all these things suggest that people brought up as Tony Blair says he was, are different. They do not just look different, but *are* different, in some deep way, from the twenty or so generations which went before them, and likely to respond in different ways to different stimuli.

One of those stimuli, and one Mr Blair has been keen to bring into every classroom and home in the country, is the computer. There may be a good political reason for this. Anyone who has spent any time with computers, even at their most crude and basic level, knows the way in which the screen can draw a person into it, making him forget normal time and place, even forget or ignore bodily desires such as hunger and thirst. Once again, a computer user with obligations, with an imagination, with other forms of literacy, may be able to fight off this influence. But someone who comes to the computer without these bonds and safeguards does not even *want* to fight them off. He can become more fully himself, more fully a self-indulgent individual and master of his own world, by plunging as deep as he can go into the electronic pool of wonders. When John Donne wrote that no man was an island, entire of himself, he could not have foreseen the way in which such devices make solitude not just bearable, but desirable above all things. Yet that solitude is not a proper loneliness. The computer-games player becomes even more of a receiver than his friends who are watching MTV in the next room. As he wrestles with his control pad, he is actually tuning his body and mind to patterns decided by the computer programmer, making himself even more of a robot than a normal couch potato.

His moral sense, and his ability to cope with the less-brightly-coloured reality of life, are also reduced. Many of these games are morally neutral, but others teach that destruction and violence come with no consequences. In the 1950s, teenage boys may have loved the sound of breaking glass, but they feared the approach of the policeman or the angry householder too. Now they can enjoy the same sound, together with the screech of tortured metal, the screams of their victims as they rip out their brainstems in Mortal Kombat or crush their cars to tinfoil in Carmageddon, and be sure that there can be no consequences, for there are no policemen or householders out there in cyberland. Who can wonder if, when they wander into real life, they drop bricks or breezeblocks through the windscreens of passing cars, or place small corpses on railway lines, or seek to speed up the dull cold world with fast-acting drugs which make the whole of life feel like a computer game?

But if they are the masters of their own tiny worlds, are they in control of anything else, or has their self-absorption left them at the mercy of those who make the programmes, create the rock bands, design the games and sell the narcotics? Plainly, we do not yet have a nation entirely made up of blank-eyed zombies dividing their time between violent computer games and the crack-house. But we do have a disturbing amount of violent crime in which the attackers are reported as being heavily drugged, and we do have a younger generation much of which seems closed to any non-conformist arguments. A survey of the so-called 'millennium generation' in November 1998 showed that Conservative support among the young has dropped to historically low levels, quite possibly a real change in consciousness which will affect them all their lives.

This does not record a mere change in political loyalty, which is not specially important in itself. It shows that, for the first time this century, the young are not inheriting prejudices, opinions, values, morals and habits from their parents. The continuity, which once ensured that most people followed their families in such things, has been broken. The post-revolutionary generation, whose families have often disintegrated and are usually weak, whose schools do not uphold authority or tradition, whose religious experience and understanding often do not exist, has also grown up with several immensely strong outside influences, all of them radical enemies of existing culture. The same generation has had little chance to develop its own critical, personal imagination through reading, and so has been a blank page on which the revolutionaries have been able to scrawl their own slogans.

They will grow up to be modern men and women, quite like Mr Blair, but even more so. For they will not have, as he did, any 'safeguards and limitations'. They did not have Durham chorister school, a devoted and strong family, Fettes College, Oxford University and the Inns of Court to keep them from being *too* modern.

CHAPTER SEVEN

Forty Years On

WE ALL KNOW HOW POTENT cheap music is, but the power of cheap jokes is greater still. Laughter, often guilty but usually irresistible, has brought down great fortresses that withstood Tom Paine and the Luftwaffe. The rotting doors of religious belief have been kicked in by the film *The Life of Brian,* which did more damage to faith among young Britons than every pamphlet and lecture which ever issued forth from the earnest spokesmen for rationalism and humanism. The coarse caricatures of *Spitting Image,* easier to understand than real-life politics, massacred the public image of Margaret Thatcher and did few favours to the Royal Family. One example of the power of this televised puppet show was the widespread belief in the 1980s that the Liberal David Steel was an insignificant figure in the pocket of a far more important Dr David Owen, leader of the rival Social Democrats. Only insiders knew that this was pretty much the reverse of the truth. The importance of a certain type of comedy in changing our national life is beyond calculation, since a well-turned, well-timed jibe can burrow into the national consciousness for decades after it is first made. The cartoonist Vicky turned Harold Macmillan into 'SuperMac', a name which outlived both the victim and the artist, who had meant the epithet to be damaging and gnashed his teeth when it became affectionate.

It is a tribute to its megaton force that *Beyond the Fringe,* the real starting point of the humorous cultural revolution, no longer seems funny or particularly clever. Yet for years after it first opened at the Fortune Theatre in London, on 10 May 1961, this little squib was so popular and controversial that it almost became a cause or movement. Its four stars, Peter Cook, Alan Bennett, Dudley Moore and Jonathan Miller, each went on to great worldly success, in the case of Bennett and Miller to become grand middle-aged men of British culture and the world of television, revered by people too young to have heard of *Beyond the Fringe,* or to recall the world in which it exploded like an enormous stink-bomb.

Look at the things it mocks: The national anthem, in 1961, was still played at the end of most cinema and theatre performances. *Fringe* opens with a group of Englishmen baffled that a Russian likes to play 'God Save the Queen'; the Royal Family is attacked indirectly by the sly device of making fun of an ultra-keen royalist; a vicar, a very silly one, is shown trying to suck up to 'youth'; Oxbridge dons are depicted as drivelling about linguistic philosophy; nuclear deterrence is repeatedly lampooned as an idea which is self-evidently absurd; Harold Macmillan and the Tories are assumed to be funny in themselves; Shakespeare is parodied as if meaningless; capital punishment is portrayed as cruel and insensitive without any reference to the condemned man's crime; the 'class system' is dismissed as nothing but petty snobbery; judges and, of course, the Lord Chamberlain, Lord Cobbold, then in charge of theatre censorship, are pilloried as 'out of touch' and 'élitist'. Only one sketch, jeering at an African dictator, could be described as anything but liberal, and that ends with him revealing that he has had his skin whitened and his hair straightened so that he can get lodgings in prejudiced England.

But amidst this is the section which probably seemed most daring of all at the time, 'Aftermyth of War'. It is nothing very special, except that it dares to giggle at what was then the nearest Britain had to a national religion, the idea that the Second World War had been a time of heroism, sacrifice, classlessness and national unity, all in the great cause of saving liberty. For some people this view may have been wearing a little thin by 1960, but for millions it was still unquestioned and unquestionable.

After a joke version of a portentous newsreel commentary ('Underneath the gaiety, stormclouds were gathering. Across Europe, German soldiers were dancing the hideous gavotte of war ...'), Alan Bennett plunged into a monologue which skilfully mixed propaganda and absurdity: 'I'll always remember that weekend war broke out. I was at a house party at Cliveden with the Astors, and we sat around listening to the moving broadcast by Mr Churchill, or Mr Chamberlain as he then was ...'

This quickly introduces the standard left-wing version of the pre-war era, created mainly by the communist propaganda agent and professional liar Claud Cockburn, and then seized upon and expanded by the Labour Left. According to this account, the Tories actively sought the appeasement of Germany because of alleged sympathy for the Nazis and a desire to destroy Soviet Russia. The only real foes of the Nazis, it suggests, were the Left and the Soviet Union (whose 1939–41 alliance with Hitler is explained away as resulting from disappointment at the failure of Tory Britain to seek an Anglo-Soviet alliance). There is some small truth at the heart of this, mainly based on a recorded remark of Stanley Baldwin that he hoped the Nazis and the 'Reds' would destroy each other. But it does violence to the far more complicated reality, especially the Left's dogged resistance to British rearmament, and the unquestioned patriotism of the vast majority of Tories. The idea of a closeness between the Tories and the Nazis is quickly rammed home again, as the headscarfed Bennett goes on: 'But I did not feel then that all was quite lost and immediately afterwards I got on the telephone to Berlin to try to speak to Herr Hitler, who had been so kind to us on our last visit to Germany that summer. Unfortunately the line was engaged. There was nothing I could do to avert the carnage of the next six years.'

Interleaved with mockery of upper-class pretension is the message that these braying fools were closer to Hitler than to their own fellow-countrymen. Not surprisingly, the next target is the idea that the British were a united people. A working-class couple are made to look fools and dupes as they listen to BBC bulletins and comfort themselves with endless cups of tea. The scenes are obviously meant to make fun of films such as *In Which We Serve* or *The Cruel Sea,* in which all classes suffer together for a cause that goes beyond class. Here are some samples:

> That was the night they got Pithy Street. I'll always remember it. I was out in the garden at the time planting out some deadly nightshade for the Boche. My wife came out to me in the garden and told me the abominable news: 'Thousands have died in Pithy Street.' 'Never you mind the thousands of dead,' I says to her. 'You put on the kettle, we'll have a nice hot cup of tea.'

And then:

> I never ever used to hear the nine o'clock news because I was always out in the garden round about nineish, planting out some carrots for the night fighters [this is a reference to a once-universally-believed urban myth that RAF night-fighter pilots were so successful because they were fed a special diet of carrots to improve their night sight, a cover story, designed to conceal their use of secret radars]. But I do remember that black, black day that rationing was imposed.

My wife came out to me in the garden, her face a mask of pain. 'Charlie,' she said, 'rationing has been imposed and all that that entails.' 'Never mind, my dear,' I says to her. 'You put on the kettle—we'll have a nice cup of boiling hot water.'

But by far the most daring of the war dialogues was this, performed by Peter Cook and Jonathan Miller. There is the sound of hearty singing; Cook steps onto the rostrum.

> *Cook:*   Perkins! Sorry to drag you away from the fun, old boy. War's not going very well, you know.
>
> *Miller:* Oh, my God!
>
> *Cook:*   We are two down, and the ball's in the enemy court. War is a psychological thing, Perkins, rather like a game of football. And you know how in a game of football, ten men often play better than eleven …?
>
> *Miller:* Yes, sir.
>
> *Cook:*   Perkins, we are asking you to be that one man. I want you to lay down your life, Perkins. We need a futile gesture at this stage. It will raise the whole tone of the war. Get up in a crate, over to Bremen, take a shufti, don't come back. Good-bye, Perkins. God, I wish I was going too.
>
> *Miller:* Good-bye, sir—or perhaps it's *au revoir?*
>
> *Cook:*   No, Perkins.

Of course it was funny; after years of cloying propaganda it was bound to be. The British war obsession had become almost as important as its Soviet equivalent in covering up and compensating for national decline and post-war failure. But for many people the laughter came with an aftertaste of shame that they should mock at such things. And once they had laughed at them, they could never again look back at the war in quite the same way. Every stiff upper lip, every brave widow,

every episode of courage, generosity and sacrifice would hence-
forth be seen through the cracked, yellow filter of 'satire'. What
the London audiences guffawed at in 1961, probably rather
shocked at themselves, would spread outwards and down-
wards and upwards until it made old-fashioned patriotism
seem pitifully innocent, humourless and unfashionable. The
'Establishment' itself sensibly realized that this sort of humour
could not be fought. But by joining in the laughter, it offered
a sort of surrender to the ideas behind the jokes. One unbe-
lievable evening, the Queen herself appeared, incognita, in the
Beyond the Fringe audience, accompanied by that future butt
of satire, the then Lord Home.*

The new humour, commercially successful and respected,
now took advantage of its secure bridgehead. It went further,
and spread its message far wider than the small audiences of
Beyond the Fringe. Bennett, by far the cleverest of the *Beyond
the Fringe* quartet, went on to write a much wittier work, *Forty
Years On*, which carried the attack way past the defences which
had been pounded and weakened by the earlier play. This
opened at the Apollo Theatre, London on 31 October 1968,
starring John Gielgud, Paul Eddington and Bennett himself. It
would later be made into a superb radio play by the BBC, a
recording which has rightly become a classic.

Forty Years On is more devastating because it is more
grown-up than the teenage balloon-pricking of *Beyond the
Fringe* and because it is more affectionate towards its target.
But it certainly has a target, and hits it very hard indeed. It is
set in Albion House, a decayed boys' public school about to
be handed over to a new 'progressive' headmaster. In the original production, the scenery was dominated by a war memorial 'with lists and lists of names, which run the whole height
of the set'. The directions also instruct that 'when the curtain
rises, the stage is dark. We hear the sounds of school, a chapel
bell, the sound of a cricket match and boys repeating by rote
in class. An organ plays softly.' These may have been 'the

sounds of school' in 1968 but it is a measure of our revolution that they would have seemed alien in most schools in 1998.

The retiring head has many speeches which could easily be truly moving evocations of loss and bravery, elegiac descriptions of the world and values swept away by the two great wars. But he is constantly subverted, by sexual double meanings, by the interruptions of the uncaring boys, by the grim practicality of the other staff trying to keep things going at a less exalted level, and by sudden stumbles into the ridiculous, direct from the sublime.

He is allowed some beautiful moments of reactionary, pessimistic truth, predicting the behaviour of his successor: 'The first thing he will do is abolish corporal punishment, the second thing he'll do is abolish compulsory games. And the third thing he'll do is abolish the cadet corps. Those are the three things liberal schoomasters always do, matron, the first opportunity they get. They think it makes the sensitive boys happy. In my experience sensitive boys are never happy anyway, so what is the point?'

And, confronted by references to naked breasts in the school play, he muses: 'I would merely say that if everyone who caught an unlooked-for glimpse of the female bosom chose to publish it in book form, civilization would very shortly grind to a halt.'

There is also this exchange between the head and his successor:

Headmaster: Would it be impossibly naive and old-fashioned of me to ask what it is you are trying to accomplish in this impudent charade?

Franklin: You could say that we are trying to shed the burden of the past.

Headmaster: Shed it? Why must we shed it? Why not shoulder it? Memories are not shackles, Franklin, they are garlands.

| Franklin: | We're too tied to the past. We want to be free to look to the future. The future comes before the past. |
| Headmaster: | Nonsense. The future comes after the past. |

And later:

| Franklin: | Have you ever thought, Headmaster, that your standards might perhaps be a little out of date? |
| Headmaster: | Of course they're out of date. Standards always are out of date. That is what makes them standards. |

Just as in *Beyond the Fringe*, the theme of Tory betrayal at Munich runs through the whole play, a bitter snarl amid the farce. A character called Hugh, a 'disillusioned Tory MP', speaks about Dunkirk: 'There was one boat-load landed right on the Commons steps. I only hope some of the Munichers were there to see that.'

And again as D-day begins: 'You'd never have guessed, listening to them cheering in the House today, that these were the same men who marched year by year, into the lobbies behind Baldwin and Chamberlain.'

A little later there is this sharp soliloquy:

I wish I thought we were all fighting for the same England. I thought when it started this war would see the end of the business-men, the property developers, the mulberry-faced gentlemen with carnations in their button-holes, the men who didn't want this war. As the end draws nearer you see they're still there. Ranged behind Churchill now are the very men who kept him out of office all through the thirties. And they will destroy him yet, because it is their England he is fighting for ... the England of Halifax who went hunting with Goering. the England of Kingsley Wood who wouldn't bomb Krupps because it was private property, the England of Geoffrey Dawson altering the despatches from Berlin. We shall win this war, but when it ends there will have to be a reckoning. Then they will go down, and they will drag Churchill with them.

As the play ends with the victory of 1945, the directions note: 'The stage is filled with flags, but they are rather worn and dingy flags, stained and brown, and full of holes, like the flags which have hung too long in the chancels of churches.'

For the final dialogue, we move forward to 1968, which was then the present day:

Headmaster:	In our crass-builded, glass-bloated, green-belted world, Sunday is for washing the car, tinned peaches and carnation milk.
Franklin:	A sergeant's world it is now, the world of the lay-by and the civic improvement scheme.
Headmaster:	Country is park and shore is marina, spare time is leisure and more, year by year. We have become a battery people, a people of underprivileged hearts fed on pap in darkness, bred out of all taste and season to savour the shoddy splendours of the new civility.
	The hedges come down from the silent fields. The lease is out on the corner site. A butterfly is an event.
Tempest:	Were we closer to the ground as children or is the grass emptier now?
Miss Nisbitt:	Tidy the old into the tall flats. Desolation at fourteen storeys becomes a view.
Matron:	Who now dies at home? Who sees death? We sicken and fade in a hospital ward, and dying is for doctors with a phone-call to the family.

Headmaster: Once we had a romantic and old-fashioned
conception of honour, of patriotism, chivalry
and duty. But it was a duty which didn't
have much to do with justice, with social
justice anyway. And in default of that justice and in pursuit of it, that was how the
great words came to be cancelled out. The
crowd has found the door into the secret
garden. Now they will tear up the flowers
by the roots, strip the borders and strew
them with paper and broken bottles.

Lectern: To let. A valuable site at the cross-roads of
the world. At present on offer to European
clients. Outlying portions of the estate
already disposed of to sitting tenants. Of
some historical and period interest. Some
alterations and improvements necessary.

If you had wanted a summary of the ideas which lay behind
the new humour of the 1960s, you could not have found a better one. Not only do we have the left-wing myth of Munich,
which is used to strip the old governing classes of their right
to carry on ruling; we also have a conviction that Britain is
finished, has lost its reason for existence and is an untenanted,
decaying estate in need of new masters and plenty of modernization and improvement. And why? Because of the absence
of 'social justice', which led to the cancelling out of the great
words—honour, patriotism, chivalry and duty, and which has
also led to the throwing open of the secret garden, a metaphor
for the golden life of the old landed classes before 1914. The
fact that it is done with some affection and style does not make
it any less of a manifesto, or any less harsh or misleading.

It was this same tradition of radical humour which gave
motive power to the BBC's extraordinary 'satire' programme,
That Was The Week That Was. Just thirty-seven editions of

this programme were shown, ending in December 1963, but there has been nothing like it since, and its effects continued long after it was taken off the air. It was unique mainly because it carried the hurtful and shocking attitudes of *Beyond the Fringe* into the suburbs, where such ideas were still unknown. To give one indication of how easy Britain was to shock at the time, and how *TW3* took full advantage of this, one of the most scandalous moments in its history came after a sketch when a woman informed a man that his flies were undone. Thousands of viewers were quite genuinely astounded to hear the word 'flies' on the BBC. Little did they know what else they were soon to hear. In the mysterious way of programmes whose time has come, *TW3* created an audience through word of mouth and by becoming a running story in the newspapers. Incredibly for a show beginning at 10.50 on Saturday night, it quickly gained an audience of twelve million. It was clever enough to get the British conservative classes to laugh, even sneer, at themselves, ashamed of not joining in the fun while knowing in their hearts that it was they and their beliefs which were being mocked.

Crucial to this success was the strange and novel character of David Frost, who would become a member of the new post-satire establishment. As Asa Briggs says in his *History of Broadcasting in the UK*, Frost's non-BBC voice was itself a break with the secure past. 'Some thought it "classless", others called it "cheeky". All called it "nasal". All, for or against, were aware that it carried with it no traditional BBC resonances.'

By 'traditional resonances', Briggs presumably means the Reithian idea of impartiality, rectitude and unquestioned patriotism.* Under its radical director general, Hugh Carleton Greene, the BBC saw itself at this time as a kind of vanguard party, with a duty to push the British people in directions most of them did not even know existed. It was not a party political stance, but a cultural one, formed partly in wartime, partly in literary and theatre circles, partly in the universities. But, while it was not pro-Labour in any specific way, it was certainly anti-Conservative as well as being pro-radical in everything from religion to fashion. Just as in the Thatcher years, the BBC excused the undeniably left-wing stance of the programme by saying that to be anti-establishment, it was necessary to be anti-government, which at the time meant anti-Tory.

One strange and rather embarrassing incident revealed a great deal about what *did* inspire the loyalty and enthusiasm of the *TW3* cast and production staff. President Kennedy was murdered on a Friday, paralysing both BBC and ITV transmissions and halting comedy programmes. The BBC radio flagship *Any Questions* was suspended, and the four panelists paid obituary tributes to the murdered President. Surely a satire programme with a rather smutty and irreverent reputation would have to be suspended in such circumstances? But rather than take the evening off, the *TW3* team hurried to the studio to improvise a special 'tribute' to the liberal hero JFK. If only they had known his true character, would these scourges of Macmillan and his handling of the Profumo sex scandal have been quite so keen to make this sickly eulogy? Or perhaps they would, just as many of Kennedy's supporters have never been able to abandon the progressive myth of Camelot. Tory scandal always seems so much more exciting than left-wing scandal.

Not long afterwards, the programme ended its run, plainly because an election was bound to take place in 1964, and the BBC wanted to avoid accusations of direct bias in the final months before the campaign. There does not seem to have been any Government pressure, though there were many protests about the programme's lack of balance from individual Tories. According to Briggs, Harold Macmillan refused to countenance any government complaint about *TW3*, partly because he enjoyed the way he himself was caricatured. But Macmillan must also have realized that government attacks on a comedy show would merely have made him look ridiculous, without gaining anything.

This is one of the reasons for the extraordinarily subversive power of comedy. No democrat dares to be seen as humourless, and only dictatorships are ready or able to punish jesters. As George Orwell pointed out, the goose-step is funny to watch, but the regimes whose soldiers march the goose-step are so frightening that nobody dares to giggle. Tyrants, recognizing that laughter is a serious business, are not afraid to punish those who mock them, and punish them in ways that hurt. They have also been known to try to control humour by licensing it, as happened in the East Berlin 'satirical cabaret' *Die Distel* (The Thistle) and the allegedly satirical Soviet magazine *Krokodil*. Democratic politicians do not want to ban or control subversive humour, and could not even if they did, although jokes can do more damage to a government than great piles of normal propaganda, slanted news or selective editorializing, and—because they are jokes—do not need to be measured against truth. If *Spitting Image* says that Mrs Thatcher was a bully and a dictator, slashing spending on health and welfare, there is no point in trying to correct this impression with facts.

What is interesting is that there has never yet been a powerful anti-establishment television comedy under a Labour government, nor is there likely to be. Of course the mimics and the caricaturists have learned how to lampoon Labour figures, but the feeling of righteousness, of mockery, as it were, from a position far above the Tory Party and all its works, just is not there. Humour and comedy have become a virtual monopoly of the cultural Left, because only they would ever seek to politicize humour in a free society. The only good conservative political jokes tend to come from countries under socialist oppression. Conservative humour, by its nature, is non-political and tends to deal with the wry acceptance of life, even in its mockery of other countries, the sexually odd and the other inhabitants of these islands. When Labour governments *are* mocked, on the BBC or elsewhere, it is from the Left that the mockery comes, pointing out the insincerity of their socialism, their ethical foreign policy or what have you. It has the feel of licensed satire, rather than the deadly danger of the real, subversive thing. The pendulum does not swing.

Beyond the Fringe, Forty Years On and *TW3* created a tradition of 'anti-establishment' comedy which continued long after its roots were forgotten. There may still have been an 'establishment' of snobbery, church, monarchy, clubland and old-school-tie links in 1961. There was no such thing ten years later, but it suited the comics and all reformers to pretend that there was and to continue to attack this mythical thing. After all, if there were no snobbery, no crusty old aristocrats and cobwebbed judges, what was the moral justification for all this change, change which benefited the reformers personally by making them rich, famous and influential?

The 'alternative' comedians who became prominent in the later Thatcher years were far cruder and more thoughtless than the founders of modern satire. They had no ideology and no history, only a simple-minded conviction that Margaret Thatcher was on the side of greed and wealth against decency, compassion and the poor, and their humour made no appeal to its victims. When Mrs Thatcher fell, they were reduced to attacking Michael Howard, the Home Secretary, who was subjected to an irrational torrent of personalized mockery. Just as much of the mockery of Margaret Thatcher was, if examined closely, old-fashioned snobbery against a lower-middle-class suburban person, the anti-Howard fury was probably more than a little anti-semitic, though in the post-Hitler age this could never be stated openly. Caricaturists would emphasize his lips rather than his nose. Mimics would massacre his strange pronunciation of ordinary words. But, of course, since these attacks came from the 'anti-racist' and 'egalitarian' left, most people failed to see the paradox. When the Tories eventually fell from power, 'alternative' comedy lost most of its bite, and at the 1997 Edinburgh Festival a group of Tory journalists from the *Daily Telegraph* actually interrupted one particularly feeble performance to point this out to the comics.

But it did not really matter. Millions of people in their twenties had formed their view of the Tories, and of businessmen as a whole, by tuning in to Channel Four comedy programmes in which they were mercilessly torn to pieces by Ben Elton and Harry Enfield. Worse still, the association of the Tories with something called 'greed' had gone deep into the minds of the young. What did this mean? During a debate on drugs in Manchester in September 1998, a young ex-addict demanded to know 'What is the difference between addiction and greed?' Baffled by the question, I asked what he meant by greed. He angrily spat out a list of costly consumer goods, BMW cars, mobile phones, expensive coats and suits. It was clear that he saw the ownership of these things as a wicked act in itself. Not since the Russian Bolsheviks, with their propaganda against wicked capitalists in silk top hats, has there been such resentment of wealth for its own sake. Jokes about 'loadsamoney' and caricatures of 'Fat Cats' have mobilized an ancient British envy of wealth and harnessed it to a political purpose. They may also have created an attitude which provides millions of people with a crude moral justification for crime, seen by many modern thieves as a form of taxation levied upon the greedy by the rest. What began as a thoughtful, if rather dishonest attack upon an élite class has gradually become more and more debased as its target has retreated and diminished.

The new, 'iconoclastic' humour changed the way that the British, especially the middle class, thought about themselves. But people who use the word 'iconoclastic' in a casual, almost approving fashion have little idea of the damage that image-smashers can do, not least because the vandalism, once started, is very hard to stop. It destroyed the national unity created by wartime, and made it impossible for people in serious public life to speak as they had always done, dress as they had always done, and take the sort of holiday they liked. Comedy killed the upper-class accent, the tweed jacket and the grouse moor. It made an entire class too ridiculous to rule. See and hear film or sound recordings of them now, after the laughter has done its work, and you cannot believe that such people took themselves seriously, let alone that they once peacefully governed much of the world and defeated the 'efficient' and 'modern' might of the German Reich.

It also made the middle class, especially the educated and well-off middle class, despise themselves and feel a sort of shame for their supposedly élitist prejudices, based upon injustice and undermined by their failure to defend the nation from its enemies in the era of appeasement. Thanks to this, in another paradox, they have often felt unable to defend things within Britain which they value and which help to keep them in existence, from the grammar schools to good manners. They are ashamed of being higher up the scale, though for most middle-class people this is more a matter of merit than birth, and nothing to be ashamed of at all.

But having once destroyed its immediate target, the anti-deference, anti-hierarchy, anti-privilege humour movement did not die away. On the contrary, it grew in strength. Why? When Bennett and the others began writing in the late 1950s, there were still aristocrats in the higher branches of the Tory Party, judges were still overwhelmingly privately educated in rigid hierarchical boarding schools, the armed services were rooted in traditions which sometimes went back to feudal times, the Lord Chamberlain still sought to keep four-letter words and sexual references off the London stage, bishops were more or less important figures and snobbery was a powerful force. Many of these things were probably doomed anyway, but the force of satire hastened their doom. The satirists and the alternative comedians sensibly preferred not to accept that they had shot their own fox. Neither they, nor the people who enjoyed and benefited from their work, wanted to acknowledge that the world they lampooned had faded away. They continued to pretend, long after it was true, that the old establishment still existed. Many people still believe, for instance, that the Bar is a closed profession full of public schoolboys and male-dominated, when this has not been so for years.

Meanwhile, look what has happened to the satirists: The magazine *Private Eye,* once almost a samizdat publication banned by headmasters and W. H. Smith, is now a lucrative corporation.* Jonathan Miller is at the heart of the new artistic establishment. Alan Bennett is now such an icon of television drama that his increasingly bizarre offerings are screened to near-universal praise and dignified with the best actors, producers and technicians available. Ned Sherrin, once scurrilous and camp, is now a mainstream presenter on BBC Radio Four.

Since the 1960s, when the Left began its conquest of the cultural battlements, it has always been surprised and annoyed by Tory election victories. The 1970 Tory triumph, though entirely predictable, took the cultural establishment by surprise. The 1979 Tory win, though even more predictable, infuriated them. They had won control of broadcasting, of the schools, of the universities, the church, the artistic, musical and architectural establishment; how was it possible that they could not also be the government? Their rage was enormous, and increased with each successive Labour defeat. It was an injustice. How could the people be so foolish? Now, instead of aristocratic snobs misgoverning the country, the establishment was portrayed as a sort of fascistic semi-dictatorship, hacking at the NHS and the welfare state, waging aggressive wars abroad and enriching itself while the poor lived in misery.

This series of falsehoods has now become a weapon ready and waiting for unscrupulous demagogues to harness, and perhaps use against the new 'establishment' which has benefited so much from the satire boom and the alternative comedians. Once you have begun to use dishonest mockery as a weapon, you can never be entirely sure that it will not eventually be turned against you, by others who have learned that abuse and jeering pay much easier and swifter dividends than hard fact or serious argument. It could be that the civilized mirth of the sixties leads in a direct line to the crude hyena cackling of the mob. In any case, there is no sign of the humour industry taking the side of traditional morality, patriotism or civility. The best it can do is dignify itself with noisy and public collections for sentimental and prominent charity. Once you step beyond the fringe, you sooner or later find yourself in very wild country indeed.

The age of social services had arrived.
—From the Workhouse to the Workplace,
National Council for One-Parent Families

EIGHT

A Real Bastard

I F YOU HAVE TO BE CRUEL to be kind, then you must accept the unpleasant results of your cruelty, including your own self-reproach, or the expression has no meaning. The unsettling and disturbing story of Britain's unmarried mothers is the story of a society which decided that it preferred to be kind to its own conscience, and so unleashed a new cruelty upon millions of children and their mothers. The older cruelty, which took the ugly form of workhouses, shame and stigma, was hard to bear because it required active harshness from the state and from individuals. The new cruelty, which leaves hundreds of thousands of children without a proper family, is imposed through many acts of generosity by the state and the taxpayers, and through the broad-minded tolerance of individuals and opinion-formers. It is therefore easier to bear in a society which has nationalized its conscience. The effects are absorbed passively, and cannot be blamed on any personal callousness by officials or politicians, though they condemn growing legions of women and their children to lives of noisy desperation.

As with so many aspects of our cultural revolution, it is futile simply to compare what exists now with what used to be. We are incomparably richer than our parents, and if we had held on to our moral standards we would not necessarily have held on to workhouses and similar cruelties. In fact, the history of this country's treatment of unmarried mothers until the early 1960s suggests that we could have reached a sensible compromise between stern duty and individual kindness. But in that strange decade, we abruptly changed direction from reform to revolution.

Despite the nasty moral chaos of the early nineteenth century, the people of the British Isles had for hundreds of years taken a sterner view of marriage than their continental neighbours. British people had long felt that the sexual morals of France, Italy and Spain were significantly looser than their own, and that the marriage bond was stronger in these islands than elsewhere. How else can we explain the central paradox of the Church of England, born out of a divorce, but more inflexible about lifelong marriage than Rome itself? There are probably ancient reasons for this, rooted in the plains of north Germany and Scandinavia and forgotten fears about inheritance and land tenure, but whatever they are, it is an undoubted truth. Or it was, for marriage has collapsed in Britain in the past thirty years, while illegitimacy—the very thing marriage is supposed to prevent—has become so common as to be the norm. Shame and stigma, which once both defended respectable marriage and heaped misery on the poor bastard and his wretched mother, have disappeared. Instead, there is the slower, vaguer, more indirect misery of a society where fewer and fewer children have two parents, and where more and more women are married to the State.

It has all been so quick. Two very different authors, writing in the early 1960s, described the attitudes of the time in a way that suggests they knew change was at hand, but not that they would ever have expected the world to be turned upside down in the way which actually took place. One of these authors was the socialist Margaret Drabble, in *The Millstone* (1965), in which the heroine—who has rich parents and much self-confidence—bears an illegitimate baby. The other was the conservative crime writer P. D. James, whose *Cover Her Face*

(1962) deals with the murder of an unmarried mother working for her keep as servant to a wealthy family. Both books are keenly observed and appear to be drawn from real knowledge. They make it clear that—at that time—an unmarried mother was a dangerous and awkward thing to be, not for economic reasons, but for moral and social ones.

Miss Drabble's heroine, Rosamund, becomes pregnant through a silly and unexpected lapse, half-heartedly attempts an abortion by the gin and hot-bath method which 'everyone knows about', but fails because she is too drunk to get her hot-water geyser to work. When she eventually accepts that she is going to have the baby, she visits an obscure NHS practice in the hope of not meeting anyone she knows. While it is still assumed that if she is pregnant, she must be married, there is no moral fury directed against her when she at length sees the doctor:

'He told me to sit down and asked me what he could do for me, and I said that I thought I was pregnant and he said how long had I been married, and I said that I was not married. It was quite simple. He shook his head, more in sorrow than in anger and said did my parents know.'

The doctor then urges her to see the 'Unmarried Mothers' people' in Kentish Town, and to begin thinking about adoption. When she pays her first visit to the maternity clinic, she discovers that all the women there are called 'Mrs' whether married or not. When Rosamund points out that she is a Miss, the Sister smiles coldly and sweetly and says, 'We call everyone Mrs here. As a courtesy title, don't you think?'

Her sister tells her that it is her duty to have the baby adopted 'by some couple who really want a child'. Keeping it 'would be bad enough for you but it would be far, far worse for the child. Through no fault of its own it would have to have the slur of illegitimacy all its life, and I can't tell you how odiously cruel and vicious children can be to each other, once they get hold of something like that.'

Like a true liberal, she adds: 'I know that ideally, in a decent

society, no child ought to suffer because of this kind of hand-
icap, but this isn't a decent society, and I can't bear the thought
of what your baby would have to go through, and what you
would have to go through on its account.'

As it happens, Rosamund, with her rich parents and her
independent spirit, has the baby (which survives a terrifying
operation) and goes on to have a book published too. Only at
the end do we discover that the experience has turned her hair
grey. Had she waited another few years, of course, there would
have been a 'decent society' in which her action would have
become positively fashionable.

In *Cover Her Face,* we see the problem from a more painful
angle. Miss Liddell, Warden of St Mary's Refuge for Girls, has
arranged for one of 'her' unwed mothers to work as a house-
parlourmaid. Miss Liddell is a guest at dinner, and her former
charge, Sally Jupp, is waiting at table. While Sally is absent,
Miss Liddell declares:

> I don't think that we should talk about the problem of these
> children too lightly. Naturally, we must show Christian char-
> ity, but I can't help feeling that society as a whole is getting
> too soft with these girls. The moral standards of the coun-
> try will continue to fall if these children are to receive more
> consideration than those born in wedlock. And it's hap-
> pening already! There's many a poor, respectable mother
> who doesn't get half the fussing and attention which is lav-
> ished on some of these girls.

There is then a fierce debate about unmarried motherhood,
adoption, and whether the state should pay any money to girls
like Sally Jupp. One guest snaps, 'This is a Christian country,
and the wages of sin are supposed to be death, not eight bob
of the taxpayers' money!'

Then comes a moment when it is clear that Sally Jupp herself is far from grateful for the charity she has been given, and
fiercely resents it:

Suddenly Miss Liddell was visited by an irrational spasm of affection. Sally was really doing very nicely, very nicely indeed! She looked up to catch the girl's eye and to give her a smile of approval and encouragement. Suddenly their eyes met. For a full two seconds they looked at each other. Then Miss Liddell flushed and dropped her eyes. Surely she must have been mistaken! Surely Sally would never dare to look at her like that! Confused and horrified she tried to analyse the extraordinary effect of that brief contact. Even before her own features had assumed their proprietorial mask of commendation, she had read in the girl's eyes not the submissive gratitude which had characterised the Sally Jupp of St Mary's Refuge, but amused contempt, a hint of conspiracy, and a dislike which was almost frightening in its intensity.

So might a French aristocrat in 1785 or so have seen in the sly look of a peasant or a servant the doom which was fast approaching. It is clear from both these stories that the old rules are losing their force, that people are no longer happy to abide by them and that those with most to lose, the respectable classes, are filled with doubts about what is right. As with so much of 1950s and early 1960s British life, the conventions are still being observed, but their moral foundations are no longer accepted.

These people are living in the afterglow of a moral code which has already sunk beneath the horizon.

Both books are still in print, but it is interesting to wonder what younger readers make of these conversations and remarks. Even the phrases 'unmarried mother' and 'illegitimate child' are hardly heard now, while the idea of 'Refuge for Girls' is more or less ridiculous, and prominent people are constantly having children out of wedlock. The word 'bastard' has become a mere term of abuse, whose actual specific meaning is probably unknown to most of the people who use it. They are as distant from today's attitudes as something out of a Charlotte Brontë novel. Yet they seemed perfectly normal to authors, publishers and readers, less than forty years ago.

But in both books there are strong hints of coming change. In *The Millstone*, the disapproval is qualified, weary and not at all frightening. In *Cover Her Face*, the prospect of state support for unmarried mothers is clearly growing, and some of the dinner guests are scornful of what they see as old-fashioned censorious attitudes. The defences, it is clear, are already crumbling and rusted. It will take only a small shove to knock them aside.

And so it was. The history of the National Council for the Unmarried Mother and her Child, *From the Workhouse to the Workplace*, shows that about this time, a charitable and moralistic movement changed its character completely, plainly sensing that the moment had come for an entirely different approach.

This organization was founded in 1918, because of a disturbing rise in illegitimate births during the First World War, and because of the misery which followed. Most unmarried mothers at this time were treated with considerable cruelty. If they could not find jobs in domestic service—and few could, because not many employers were prepared to allow them to keep their children—they were forced to go into workhouses where they were separated from their babies for much of the time. The death-rate among illegitimate babies was frighteningly high, double that for those born in wedlock, largely because many of these babies were not properly fed or cared for. The National Council campaigned on two levels, practical and moral. First, it urged the creation of homes where babies could be breastfed by their own mothers, instead of kept apart from them in workhouse wards; it also asked for stronger laws to force fathers to pay for their children. More controversially, 'an equally important principle became to try to alter public opinion to turn it away from the punitive and harsh attitudes of the past.'

To those who warned that this would undermine the marriage bond and condone immorality, the campaigners replied in 1918, 'The experience of countries in which such action has been taken as is here proposed, has been that it is followed by a decline in illegitimacy'.

Over the next twenty years, the campaign scored a number of successes, which made British society significantly more humane in its treatment of one-parent families (as they were then not known). However, they deliberately and consciously did not challenge the idea that unmarried motherhood was wrong. The stigma of bastardy, unfairly visited on illegitimate children, was one of their targets, and there was and is a strong case for saying that this cruel label did no good and a great deal of harm, while removing it would lighten the lives of innocent victims of their parents' selfishness, folly and defiance of the moral code. Queen Mary herself gave enormous respectability to the National Council, visiting their offices in 1924 and endorsing their work. The organization began to make small but important gains, including a long-delayed increase in affiliation payments to mothers. Adoption, then seen as by far the best fate for illegitimate children, was regulated and made easier. Charitable and church organizations set up a network of homes where mothers and children could stay together, and be trained for useful work. The Second World War made the problem more urgent, though evacuation to the country often improved the living conditions of both unmarried mothers and their offspring. Dislocation of normal life, uncertain wartime liaisons and the presence of foreign troops together managed to double the illegitimate birth rate between 1939 and 1945. But in the post-war years, as Britain struggled to recover its lost respectability and social peace, the number of births outside marriage actually dropped for thirteen years between 1945 and 1959.

The National Council's own official history regards this period rather caustically, recording in peevish tones that 'In the fifties, the priority of the Council seemed to be working with the mother to make her a responsible member of society, rather than on influencing society to be more tolerant of unmarried motherhood.'

However, a series of quiet but enormous shifts in the law and the power of the state were preparing the way for an astonishing amount of 'tolerance'. The NHS itself, with its free medical care, released unmarried mothers from the fear that they might not be able to afford medical treatment for their young. In 1947, a new abridged birth certificate allowed illegitimate children to conceal their parents' unmarried status. In 1959, the Legitimacy Act allowed post facto legitimacy to children whose parents had 'not been free' to marry at the time of their birth.

These were all humane changes, ensuring that the sins of the parents could not be visited on the children. But they also made it easier for the parents to commit those sins without so much fear of the consequences, and they assumed that the old forces of shame and disgrace were purely negative, nasty cobwebs in the corner of an unreformed society which could have no possible purpose in the modern world. Such changes seldom have an immediate effect, and their supporters must have felt entirely benevolent.

For the shadow of the old attitudes still fell across 1950s Britain, even if enlightened MPs, civil servants and churchmen were busy trying to remove it. The official history of the National Council is scathing again: 'Educating the public during this period seemed less a matter of trying to change attitudes to birth outside marriage than of trying to prevent it.' The Council's public statements became 'increasingly moral' during the Fifties, 'perhaps as a reflection of the mood of the times'.

'Proclamations were designed to rouse public interest in the evil consequences of illegitimacy, with the aim of preventing sexual liaisons outside marriage. Typical of the council's methods at this time was that it sought to meet increased need, not by campaigning for improved maternity benefits, but by appealing more widely to the public for prams and maternity equipment.'

The changing morality of the period was charted by quotations from its annual reports. In 1956–57, the report noted: 'Since our Council was founded in 1918 the whole social scene has changed, and with it the position of the unmarried mother. She is no longer 'ruined' as a matter of course, but can usually go back fairly easily, after her confinement, to whatever employment she had before.'

But the next year, 'Some correspondents felt that we were making light of sin ... alas there are some parents who entirely refuse to receive the erring daughter or her child.'

This period of cosiness and old-fashioned brutal certainty was to end abruptly: 'During the next two decades there was a complete transformation in society, which profoundly affected the work of the Council.'

In 1962 the 'energetic' Margaret Bramall took over the leadership from Isabelle Grainger, who had been general secretary since 1946. 'That same year, the Council spelled out its role as a "watchdog of the interests of the unmarried mother and her child". The implicit, sometimes explicit, criticism of the unmarried mother faded.'

It certainly did. In 1962, the Council sent Lady Prudence Loudon and Professor Leonard Schapiro to study conditions in Denmark, and they returned praising the advantages of providing services for fatherless families, irrespective of the mother's marital status.

By 1968, the organization was declaring that 'She [the unmarried mother] and her child should be accepted as integrated members of the community. Society should provide financial and practical services that will give the child the maximum chance of a stable and settled upbringing.'

In the end, it was the crumbling of marriage which ended the stigma. Suddenly, there were thousands of women, many of them previously married, bringing up children on their own. It was harder and harder for a society which accepted these women in its midst to be harsh towards those who had never married in the first place. The old problem was swallowed up in a new one.

Thus the swelling number of divorces after divorce law reform, which effectively turned many young women into *de-married* mothers, gave the council a new and wider purpose, and in 1963 the National Council took divorcées under its wing, with no objections from the divorced women who might once have objected to being bracketed with a very different type of lone parent.

The Council's report in 1959–60 had asked unhappily, 'Why are an increasing number of our young people caught in a web of irresponsibility and misunderstanding of so much of the true values of life?'

By 1964, its confidence in those true values was slipping away. It is a dangerous mistake to classify unmarried mothers as a homogeneous group, referred to as 'they'. 'However similar their ... needs may seem, unmarried mothers must be accepted as people who need social services flexible enough to help them as individuals.'

And one year later: 'Our society is more compassionate to the unmarried mother than it was a generation ago, but she and her illegitimate child are still seen as a threat to normal family life.'

Another twelve months went by, and the Council was saying, 'The unmarried mother's predicament may be the inevitable result of the more permissive code of sexual behaviour which the public in fact now accepts while still preserving a different standard of morality for men and women.'

The barriers were falling fast. The 1967–68 report demanded: 'She and her child should be accepted as integrated members of the community. Society should provide financial and practical services that will give the child the maximum chance of a stable and settled upbringing.'

In 1969, 'Hostility to unmarried mothers still exists ... but public feeling has moderated during the past five years and the decreasing number of children offered for adoption bears out the contention that more mothers are able to keep their children' (it might also have had something to do with the newly relaxed laws on abortion).

By 1973, the National Council sought to change the language to reflect altered morality, a small early example of the linguistic policing now so common. It pledged to 'Cease using language that is offensive and wounding to a group of people who have enough disadvantages without suffering the indignity of being referred to in pejorative terms'. This was the year when the campaign finally dropped the term 'unmarried mother' and replaced it with 'one-parent family'. This expression had first been urged by some members as long before as 1963.

Throughout this period of changing morality, the organization was quietly winning victories in Whitehall and Westminster. Some swept away stigma, others provided cash. In 1967 the special tax allowance for divorced or widowed parents was for the first time extended to unmarried mothers. In 1969, fathers were no longer required to be present at the registration of children's births. In 1974, the Finer Report, the result of long years' deliberation by a Royal Commission, urged a complete change in society's treatment of unwed mothers, though many of its more lavish recommendations were not implemented. In 1975 lone parents were granted the same tax allowances as married men. In 1976 family allowances were extended to the first child in any one-parent family. A year later, lone parents were given an extra payment because of their status. The introduction of child benefit, paid direct to the mother, ignored her marital status and so extended the payment to all her children. In 1975 illegitimate children were granted equal inheritance rights with their legitimate brothers and sisters. In 1979 the Law Commission urged that the law should stop taking any account of illegitimacy.

Two even more explosive changes took place around the same time, which finally removed any moral disapproval from the practical treatment given to unwed mothers. The 1968 Seebohm Report led to the creation, for the first time, of local authority social service departments to deal with single mothers. The National Council rightly says that this was hugely significant, 'for the first time providing a realistic source of assistance to those unmarried mothers who did not wish to approach religious bodies, bodies such as P. D. James's "St Mary's Refuge for Girls".' In 1962, out of 2,940 mothers who approached the National Council for help, 2,714 were referred to a religious social worker. By the mid-seventies, social services departments were taking over. 'The emphasis had at last shifted from charity to the state. The age of social services had arrived.' In 1976, the National Council stopped giving grants altogether. Its charitable activities had been completely taken over by the state.

The other great change also came thanks to local authorities, which in 1966 began to offer housing to unmarried mothers for the first time. This trend was enormously increased in 1977 when the Housing (Homeless Persons) Act placed responsibility for all but the intentionally homeless on the broad, tax-financed shoulders of local authority housing departments.

A campaign for more humane treatment, working within conventional morality, had now become a wholly different creature, calling for a change in the moral climate. At a special general meeting in 1971, the National Council for the Unmarried Mother and her Child was laid to rest. A new organization, the National Council for One-Parent Families, was brought forth. The change in name confirmed a change of direction which had taken place nearly a decade before, and symbolized modern Britain's rejection of supposedly outdated moral concepts. An organization which had begun by claiming that its ideas would actually lead to less illegitimacy was now openly calling for the acceptance of illegitimacy, with the implication that it would not be upset if it increased. It did.

So it can neither have been surprised nor particularly displeased at the 'success' which followed. In 1981, there were 91,300 births outside marriage in this country, 12.5% of the total. In 1991 they had risen to 236,100, 29.8%. In 1980 there were 940,000 one-parent families, one in eight of all families, with 1.5 million children. In 1992, there were 1.3 million one-parent families, one in five of the total, with 2.1 million children.

The number continues to rise, as the stigma continues to fade. Many prominent people, including the Prime Minister's own press secretary, Alastair Campbell, and Mrs Blair's press secretary, Fiona Millar, cheerfully live together without marrying, and would be astonished if they encountered disapproval from anyone in their own generation.

This one colossal change has been the single greatest blow to the ideal of marriage. Divorce is, in a curious way, an attempt to shore up marriage by making its bonds looser and by allowing people who fail the first time to try harder with the second spouse. The general loosening of sexual morals tends to affect the young and unattached, and minorities of what would once have been called deviants, more than it affects those who want to set a public legal seal on partnership and parenthood.

Pre-Sixties society could have, and did, live with the growing tolerance of illegitimate children. The cruel treatment of bastards could be, and was improved without damaging the fabric of marriage and the family. But the utter abolition of the taboo against women bearing bastards, so that the word is now only shocking if it is used in its precise sense, is a direct blow at the marriage bond. The state subsidies and the value-free intervention of social workers, who must help but cannot scold, are still more direct. But even more important is the way that the state has, piece by piece, granted all the privileges of the married to the unmarried. This looks like generosity, and the politicians who willed it certainly want it to be so.

But it is in fact a theft of privileges from the married. Generous treatment to those who have erred is offensive to those who have behaved well and get nothing, a story at least as old as the parable of the prodigal son, with the righteous brother's sulky resentment of the fuss made over his wastrel sibling. If marriage does not have exclusive privileges many people, and above all men, are less likely to bother with a public and enforceable legal contract which may well get them into a great deal of trouble and load them with inescapable obligations for the rest of their lives. By helping the unmarried, modern British society has de-privileged the married, so sending a flashing 5,000-watt signal to all young men and women that it no longer demands that they wed, or plans to support them if they do. Being married is no longer more respectable, more secure or more subsidized than being unmarried.

The stance of the National Council for One-Parent Families gives us some clue as to when this de-privileging began, and shows how its supporters explained themselves. But unlike many other of the combat units of the cultural revolution, these enthusiasts do not explain why. From the start, they have dressed their actions in the shining garments of kindness, tolerance and generosity.

There are crude materialistic explanations—that the new rules led to the creation of tens of thousands of permanent jobs in local authority social service departments, that the state and its mandarins were increasingly jealous of the independent power of the family, that employers had discovered in two world wars that women were cheaper and more pliable labour than men, and wanted to wean them away from marriage and motherhood. And all of these may have played their part. But perhaps the key to it lies in the rapid death in the early 1960s of religious and moral attitudes towards the treatment of the unwed mother and her child. British society no longer believed in God or eternity or the afterlife. It was therefore impossible for any decent human to justify to himself or herself the harshness of society's treatment of these unhappy people. What higher purpose did it serve, that could possibly excuse the cold hardness of the old rules? When there are no souls to be saved, only bodies—women and 'kids'—there is only one object: to make their living conditions better, even if they then grow up— as they often do—in grave moral poverty.

The misery which has followed has eventually forced governments and social workers to recognize that food, shelter and warmth by themselves are not enough, and even the Left is now groping towards the idea that moral poverty can be as wicked as physical poverty. But to this, authority has come up with no better answer than the old socialist panacea of work, urging single mothers to go out and become wageslaves for their own good, if not necessarily their children's good. If you do not believe in sin, then you can hardly be expected to use up much energy fighting against it. And if you do believe in sin, then you are 'judgemental', and automatically excluded from the debate.

*We must be free or die, who speak the tongue that Shakespeare
spake; the faith and morals hold which Milton held.*
—William Wordsworth, 'National Independence and Liberty'

*Breathes there the man with soul so dead, who never
to himself hath said, This is my own, my native land.*
—Sir Walter Scott, 'The Lay of the Last Minstrel'

NINE

The Queen's English

A PEOPLE WHO SPOKE the tongue, and held the faith, of Shakespeare and Milton could never have submitted to the hamburger and soap opera culture which now has the British working class in its greasy grip, nor to the anti-British 'Europeanism' which has so beguiled much of the educated élite. Before these things could happen, the British people had to be separated from their roots. One of those roots was their history, but their literature was even more powerful, since it was constantly present in daily speech, as history was not.

To anyone brought up when English literature, scripture, liturgy, poetry and hymns were still taught and learned, it is astonishing to find out how little they have in common with those who were raised and educated in the post-revolutionary culture. The pre-revolutionary survivor can finish other people's sentences, detect the rhythm in other people's speeches, recognize a score of allusions in a page of print. There is hardly a word or phrase which does not awake a richer thought, or an echo of something hauntingly similar. Where others see a bare plain, those with the gift of verse can remember when it was a great forest. The memory is of course profoundly conservative, being about such things as landscape, chivalry, fortunes lost and restored, families preserved, evil deeds revenged, invaders repelled, foreign tyrants defied and God glorified. No wonder that progressive schoolmasters found it all something of an embarrassment.

But until recently, however progressive they were, they had to put up with it. In 1950, the syllabus for the Cambridge Higher School Certificate, the equivalent of today's A level, covered these authors: Chaucer, Sidney, Spenser, Marlowe, Shakespeare, Bacon, Jonson, Milton, Bunyan, Pepys, Swift, Gibbon, Fielding, Defoe, Wordsworth, Byron, Shelley, Lamb, Hardy, Browning and Shaw. As John Marenbon said in the Centre for Policy Studies pamphlet *English, our English*: 'English specialists left *school* [my emphasis] with a knowledge of their literary heritage which would shame most graduates in English today.'

The end came swiftly, and it came hand in hand with a shocking decline in literacy itself, without which most of these works were completely inaccessible. By 1987, Marenbon complained, 'even among candidates for admission to the best universities, who have specialised in English, only a minority can spell with consistent correctness, use punctuation properly and construct complex sentences grammatically.'

What is more surprising is that many university dons were neither shocked nor angered by this. They shared the attitudes of their colleagues in the schools that the imposition of rules of spelling, grammar and syntax was wrong in itself. On 11 June 1993, no fewer than 576 university teachers of English wrote to the *Times Higher Education Supplement*, attacking the then government's 'doctrinaire preoccupation with grammar and spelling', as well as an alleged 'hostility to regional and working class forms of speech'.

Because of this attitude, their more conservative colleagues had to pick up the pieces when the results of language liberalism arrived at University, knowing almost nothing of the subject they had come to study. Marenbon reported that 'university teachers discover that many undergraduates, who have specialised in English at A level, arrive entirely ignorant of all literature written before the 20th century, except for two or three plays by Shakespeare and a few hundred lines of Chaucer.'

More than ten years later, that knowledge is probably smaller still, as both GCSE and A level require less and less direct knowledge even of Shakespeare plays. Fewer and fewer children actually have to read and study entire plays or works, or even have to pretend to have done so. Instead they are allowed to read summaries and excerpts. The effort of understanding, let alone speaking the richly woven English of the sixteenth century is assumed to be beyond them, though the similar language of Bible and Prayer Book were written to be understood by every poor ploughboy and became part of the common speech of the entire nation.

Until the 1930s, people with very modest schooling would at least have been familiar with the sweeter parts of English literature and poetry, with the patriotic speeches from Shakespeare, with some version of the Arthurian legends. Anyone educated up to fifteen or sixteen would have been expected to know a great deal more. This common knowledge was already breaking down before the Second World War, and by the late 1970s it was obvious that the young were almost entirely cut off from the culture of their parents and grandparents. Much of the older poetry and literature was about church and nation, both of which had been wounded in their hearts by the First World War.

The novelist Kingsley Amis, deeply depressed by the collapse of knowledge and good judgement in the literary and political worlds, wrote a withering satire on the decay of national culture at the end of the 1970s (*Russian Hide and Seek*, 1980). Just as Evelyn Waugh had once suggested that the Labour government of 1945 was similar to living under foreign occupation, Amis suggested that the trashing of our culture and literacy were so severe that only a ruthless foreign

invader could possibly make them worse. His book is a portrait of a nation without a memory, its ancient buildings demolished, its trees hacked down, its people barely educated and
bottomlessly ignorant of their origins and past, living on stewed
beets, pork bellies and windfall apples. A small and dwindling
group of 'pre-wars' maintain the memories of what has been
lost, but those memories are fading, and so all trace of them
will die with this elderly generation. Amis describes an attempt
to revive enthusiasm for Shakespeare after half a century of
Soviet occupation, during which British history, literature and
religion have been ruthlessly suppressed. A group of Soviet
'liberals' are trying to give the people their culture back, and
are staging a performance of *Romeo and Juliet* in a long-closed
provincial theatre.

The actress playing Juliet, an English girl brought up long
after the occupation, attempts to speak some lines from the
play. She does not understand the rhythm of the verse, the classical allusions to Phoebus and Phaeton mean nothing to her,
in fact she hasn't a clue what she is saying. But *nobody notices.*
The play's Armenian cultural commissar confesses:

> We've had a lot of trouble with it, you know. I suggested we
> might try another by the same author; it seems there's one
> about a Danish aristocrat who goes mad and thinks he sees
> a ghost which tells him to murder his uncle. More straight-
> forward than this, I'd have thought, but the director, that
> young fellow there, he assures me there's no time to make
> a fresh start now, it's this or nothing. Well ... it's so hard to
> understand the characters and to make out what one's meant
> to think of them. A young man meets a girl at a party and
> feels her up in public, in front of her parents in fact. We all
> know such things happen, but then instead of having an
> affair with her, he marries her, and after only one night with
> her he suicides when he thinks she's dead—very flimsy, that
> part—and she suicides when she finds him dead, and the

author makes no attempt at all to explain why; I mean, they're not insane or anything like that. I expect I'm trying to take it too literally, and that part's meant to be a symbol of a couple completely going off each other when they've been powerfully attracted only a few days before, but one can't tell the audience that. Still, there's a certain amount of violence which we can play up, and the costumes and the sets are going to be spectacular; I'm sure the thing will go down well enough.

It is clear from this that Amis was not really writing about a Soviet occupation, but about the degeneration of culture that was already well under way when he wrote his novel. A real occupation would almost certainly have produced a resistance, the circulation of banned texts and the holding of secret religious services. But a country which ploughs under its own culture, without violence or open suppression, has no such resistance. The objects of the attack are unaware that they are under attack, and there are no martyrs, no persecution to bring resistance into being.

Amis did for a while try to lead a resistance movement. He had been involved in the protests against the expansion of the universities, famously warning that 'more will mean worse', and had been a sharp and merciless observer of the decline in standards which followed in all areas of literary life. But, while his protests gained much publicity, the expansion of the universities and the watering down of cultural values went ahead untroubled by his protests or anyone else's.

In Amis's book, the actual performance of *Romeo and Juliet* is attended by a semi-literate audience in a bizarre caricature of formal dress run up for the occasion. They have been so effectively separated from the literature of their grandparents that they cannot understand what is going on. 'They had been looking forward to enjoying themselves and had been bewildered and bored. They had been told over and over again that this was a great play by a great Englishman and there was nothing in it. They had put on these ridiculous clothes and come all this way to be made fools of.' The evening ends in a near-riot, arson and death.

A similar attempt to hold a 'church service' fails more pathetically, but for the same reason. The ideas on which such an event was once founded have died. A young woman reciting the Creed wonders what it can be about:

> The whole catalogue was very odd—remote and fanciful. It made sense to believe in keeping oneself to oneself, in divorce for unhappy couples, in a hot-water-bottle on cold nights; to do so might be of use in each case; that could be argued about. But what difference could it make to think the Holy Ghost advisable, to be in favour of the life everlasting? How had they come to recommend things like that? And yet men and women had died for the right to say they thought well of them. Incomprehensible; though it should be said that these days no-one died for anything.

Most of the congregation, utterly flummoxed by the strange event and the alien language, leave quietly before the end. One Englishman (Dr Wright), who has been hoping against hope for some sort of genuine national revival, is broken by what takes place: 'Nothing had happened, so unequivocally and with such finality that the chance of any significant event, any change, was ruled out for ever. That was the day Wright finally despaired.'

The cultural revolutionaries have understood that a nation's literature is one of the ways, perhaps the most important way, in which values are transmitted unchanged from generation to generation. They understand that Shakespeare's Englishness is not an accident, and that Shakespeare and Englishness have helped to form each other. They know that poems and plays cannot be learned by heart unless there are authoritative teachers to insist on it, and a common agreement about what is worth learning. They have also grasped that much of the canon of English literature is about this country's separation from the European continent, about its Protestant, independent nature, about its good fortune in being set apart from the rest of the world. They would tend to classify these things as 'insularity', 'Little England-ism', 'chauvinism', 'xenophobia' and 'racism'. By its nature, this literature is also dominated by men. With the notable exception of Queen Elizabeth I, there are few great female figures in this historical landscape, and precious few female writers to record and celebrate it. In the different kind of country envisioned by the revolutionaries, women will play a far greater role, and therefore this past is generally classified as 'sexist'.

One of the most influential scholars in English literature, and one of the prophets of change, is the Marxist Terry Eagleton, now an Oxford professor, whose ideas have had a vast influence on students and other teachers of literature. In his *William Shakespeare,* he opens by declaring that Shakespeare's plays 'value social order and stability', which of course they do, having been written at a time when the dynastic Wars of the Roses were still a recent memory, when England's freedom was under almost permanent threat from abroad, and just after a period of terrifying religious turmoil and persecution. They were, to some extent, Tudor propaganda—there is a strong case for saying that *Richard III* deliberately blackens the last Yorkist king so as to please the Tudor dynasty which bloodily overthrew him in 1485, less than a century before Shakespeare was born. Eagleton then goes on to try to rebuild Shakespeare as some sort of Marxist critic of the social order.

Perhaps he was convinced by his own arguments, or perhaps he realized that it was never going to be easy to get the bard onto the barricades. His argument that 'The witches [in *Macbeth*] are the heroines of the piece, however little the play itself recognizes the fact, and however much the critics may have set out to defame them', is a tough one to sustain. Can anyone with a sense of humour possibly hold to the idea that

'It is they, who by releasing ambitious thoughts in Macbeth, expose a reverence for hierarchical social order for what it is, as the pious self-deception of a society based on routine oppression and incessant warfare.... The witches are exiles from that violent order, inhabiting their own sisterly community on its shadowy borderlands'? This sort of thing is enough to make you wonder if there really is such a thing as conservative satire, after all. For most radical teachers, less ingenious than Professor Eagleton, it has been far easier to liquidate, censor or exile Shakespeare than to get him to join the Revolutionary Party, where he makes a pretty unconvincing Comrade.

Which brings me to the National Association for the Teaching of English (NATE), a fount of radicalism in schools and teacher training colleges, and a prolific publisher of manifestoes calling for a new approach to the teaching of our language and literature.

One of its chief voices, is Gunther Kress, a Professor of Education at the influential Institute of Education, part of London University. In his 1995 book *Writing the Future*, Professor Kress declares: 'English is a carrier of definitions of culture.... English is a carrier of definitions of its society.... The subject English is the only site in the curriculum where all the modes and media of public communication can be debated, analysed and taught. There is nowhere else.'

And he adds, 'English is the site of the development of the individual in a moral, ethical, public, social sense.'

This is very perceptive of him, and explains the high importance given to the subject by the radicals who have clustered around NATE. In his proposals for a future curriculum he makes his purpose even clearer: 'Texts will have to be selected in such a way that the socially and culturally crucial values and principles can be adequately demonstrated and debated.'

So what are these culturally crucial values? The Professor gives a hint, asking, 'What kind of English curriculum can prepare children to be productively intercultural and polycultural in the society of tomorrow, rather than passively, anxiously or angrily monocultural? ... What kind of curriculum is needed to produce dispositions, a habitus which is at ease with cultural difference?'

He continues to worry at it, in a way that makes it quite clear he is concerned with far wider matters than a mere knowledge of existing literature or language: 'What contents of the new kind do we want children now in our schools to know; who do we want them to be; what values should they treat as natural, as normal, as human, in order to live full lives in the changed world of tomorrow?' And then, 'Literacy, like no other element in the culture of our society, is bound up with cultural and social possibilities. It represents a society's means of representing the world to itself; it is its means of representing itself to itself ... foundational in the shaping of the future.'

Brian Cox, one of the architects of the national curriculum, a former conservative turned 'progressive' explains the sort of contents the reformers would like to see. In *An English Curriculum for the 1990s* Cox says that many university teachers have written to him to complain about the new curriculum, saying it is too 'pluralist'. 'In France or Germany, they say, teachers would be amazed if their own great writers were not compulsory reading for all students.... We should be proud of the English qualities to be found in writers from Chaucer to Dickens, from Shakespeare to Jane Austen, from Milton to Pope.'

But Professor Cox is not impressed by this. He responds: 'This emphasis on an "English" tradition has come under continuous attack during the last 20 years or so; during their undergraduate training many young teachers of English will have discussed the assumptions that underlie that concern for our cultural heritage. The desire for a national culture is seen as damagingly conservative, often "racist" and almost inevitably unsympathetic to the rights of women. This may surprise many people who read English literature for pleasure.'

Indeed it may, but they should have been paying more attention to the background noise from the universities, and then they would have realized that their apparently harmless leisure activity was in fact a statement of racist, sexist complacency.

Cox asks: 'Should we insist that children spend all their time with a literature whose main non-white representatives are Othello, Man Friday in *Robinson Crusoe* and the savages in Conrad's *Heart of Darkness?*' He believes that the most dynamic English today is often found outside England, which is possibly true, but then lists, among others, Toni Morrison, Alice Walker, Anita Desai, Nadine Gordimer and Chinua Achebe as examples of this. It would be a bold person who suggested, now, that these fashionable writers will endure to become part of the great canon of English literature. Is it possible that they have been chosen not so much for their quality as for their sex, their colour, or their concern with modish causes?

There is perhaps a clue in Professor Cox's more recent *Cox on the Battle for the English Curriculum,* where he quotes at length and with apparent approval attacks on traditional poetry and literature taught to children, by the poet James Fenton and the broadcaster Michael Rosen. Fenton sniggers at much traditional verse, while Rosen homes in on an 'explicitly racist' and 'supremacist' story in Kipling's *Jungle Book* ('HM Servants'), while complaining that *Peter Pan* and *What Katy Did* are 'fanatic' in ascribing roles to girls and that there is snobbery about working-class people in *The Wind in the Willows, Just William* and in *The Railway Children.* As for *Little House on the Prairie,* its 'assumptions about "native Americans" apparently need "careful negotiation"'.

Cox also quotes from the famous letter to *The Times* (1/1/93) from Sally Feldman, editor of an important BBC radio children's literature series. Ms Feldman complains of 'a betrayal of children, their literature and of the experience of reading'.

She asks why our best contemporary writers have been ignored in favour of 'this outmoded spectre of childhood, frozen in a sentimental, ultra-traditional frame.' She asserts: 'The culture offered to our children is dominated by the values of the British Empire in its heyday. The books are mostly written from the point of view of the English upper middle classes for their children.' Feldman assails *Huckleberry Finn* as 'defiantly impenetrable', suggesting instead a book called *The Turbulent Term of Tyke Tyler*. She prefers the tediously anti-Tory *Secret Diary of Adrian Mole* to Richmal Crompton's allegedly snobbish William books. And of course her approved list features a book about apartheid, and another about that favourite topic of class warriors, wartime evacuation.

Feldman's mention of *The Turbulent Term of Tyke Tyler* makes an important connection with another part of the revolution, far lower down the literary ladder but—because it involves younger and more impressionable children—just as important.

Alice in Genderland was produced by NATE's Language and Gender Working Party in 1985. This waspish little volume denounces the 'gross gender bias and distortions of early reading schemes and many children's books'. One essay complains about the sexist representation, in a book called *The Little Chick*, of a cockerel, 'full of importance, as compared with the hens, who are shown as anxious and nervous about their chicks'. The fact that this is a true representation of chicken sexism is of course neither here nor there for these critics. They would have books full of docile bulls, and male eagles keeping nests warm, if they could. Their attitude rests on a denial that the different sexes have different characters, so it might as well be imposed upon the beasts of the field and the fowls of the air as well as upon humankind.

Something called 'the cult of the apron' is constantly attacked in the essays that make up *Alice in Genderland*. What is this cult? It is the idea that mothers are in the home, doing the sorts of things mothers used to do before they were all marched off into the factories and the office blocks to be wage-slaves, or perhaps teachers.

One of NATE's experts, Hilary Minns, purses her lips with disapproval as she describes a scene from a book called *Can I Keep Him?* The poor oppressed woman is seen 'sweeping, cleaning the lavatory, tidying the cupboards, vacuuming, washing up and scrubbing on her knees'. As for a series on famous writers, published by MacDonald Educational: 'In spite of the fact that the editor-in-chief was a woman, all 34 writers in the series are male.'

Ms Minns gives us a glimpse of her own stance, disclosing that she tried and failed to make the children in her class get changed in mixed-sex groups. But she successfully persuaded them to challenge the prejudices of our male-dominated society, by keeping a 'complaints about sexism' file and writing to the editor of the *Sun* about page-three girls.

A fellow campaigner, Linda Harland, complains about the Ladybird Key Words reading scheme in which 'Peter has to help Daddy with the car, Jane has to help Mummy in the house'. She also assails the sex bias in other early reading schemes, *Janet and John, Happy Ventures, Ready to Read* and *Nippers*. These criticisms have had a powerful effect, as most of these schemes have now been modified to suit the new prejudice, or abandoned, or replaced by others more willing to adapt to the spirit of the times.

Bridget Baines carries the struggle into the secondary school, pointing out that 'even in *Animal Farm* the animals are almost solely male'. She quotes a study of winners of the Caldecott medal for book illustration, showing that these winners contained 261 pictures of male humans to 23 pictures of female humans. When animals were included the imbalance was even more severe—95 to 1. She calls for 'the addition of book titles and short stories providing more varied images', and recommends 'a spate of letters to exam boards' pointing out the effects of these omissions and 'suggesting suitable titles for inclusion in syllabi, possibly with sample questions as well'.

A fellow comprehensive teacher, Elaine Millard, alleges that the literature taught in the past effectively stifled the sense of a female self. And she also recommends *The Turbulent Term of Tyke Tyler*, a book I have never seen in a bookshop or library but which she seems to admire because the sex of its tough main character is hidden until the end. Guess what Tyke turns out to be.

When *Alice in Genderland* was written, it was critical and revolutionary, even subversive. Now, not much more than a decade later, its ideas are more or less orthodox. It is, as so often, amazing that change has come so swiftly. But on almost all fronts there has been no coherent, organized resistance to the cultural revolution. The other side has lost its nerve, and no longer really believes in itself.

Those teachers of English who have rejected or weakened the teaching of traditional grammar, given up correcting spelling mistakes and encouraged children to believe that their dialect or accent was just as valid as standard English did not, then, just do this because they were lazy and did not choose to exercise their authority. Some of them at least must have felt that they were undermining one of Britain's most powerful bastions, the domination of spoken and written language by people who have been brought up in a certain way, to follow certain traditions. They must also have felt that they had a strong ethical reason for doing so, to comfort and encourage the poor and disadvantaged, and to make newly arrived immigrants feel welcome. These are not despicable motives, even if their results have been wretched, and their power is a tribute to the genuine idealism of many who supported these ideas, as well as yet another warning that idealists are the most dangerous people in the world.

Do we, then, want to break marriage? If we do break it, it means
we all fall to a far greater extent under the direct sway of the State.
—D. H. Lawrence, *Apropos Lady Chatterley's Lover*

TEN

Difficulties with Girls

THE GREATEST FORTRESS of human liberty, proof against all earthly powers, is the family. In its small private space, it can defy the will of authority and the might of wealth. It is without doubt the most effective means of passing lore, culture, manners and traditions down through the generations. Its loyalties are stronger than those of the state, more powerful even than patriotism. All serious tyrannies have sought to undermine or infiltrate it, socialist tyrannies most of all. Perhaps the most powerful symbol of this offensive was to be found in a mosquito-haunted Moscow Park where, until 1991, there stood a statue of a child, Pavlik Morozov. Morozov was a peasant boy who was murdered by his grandfather during Stalin's destruction of private farming, after he denounced his own parents to the secret police for 'hoarding' grain—that is, keeping what was their own. Many of us might sympathize with the grandfather, but the children of Moscow—and of all other Soviet cities—used to be taught to pay homage to young Morozov, one of the chief martyrs of the Soviet State and the Communist Party.

This was only one of many invasions of the citadel of family life by the USSR authorities, though perhaps the most shameful and outrageous. Much of the attack took the form

of apparent generosity. The Soviet system offered comprehensive 'care' for children in often squalid nurseries, but
demanded in return that both parents went out to work. One
strictly limited salary was not enough to pay the normal bills
of a Soviet household. Nor did the state-supplied apartments,
many communal, offer enough space for even a Western-size
family. Millions of couples limited themselves to one child,
and those with two or more were often the results of serial
marriage and divorce, so that the second child was a step-sister
or a half-brother. Marriage was a civil ceremony sanctified by
a trip to the nearest war memorial, but lightly regarded. The
huge, wedge-shaped Palace of Weddings in Kiev was known
locally as 'The Bermuda Triangle' because so many of the marriages solemnized there later disappeared without trace. Divorce
was deliberately made as easy as possible, while abortion was
an out-patient treatment, so trivial and cheap that many women
had seven or more abortions in a lifetime.

There are many explanations for authority's mistrust of
the family. The main one must be that it cannot control what
goes on there, what ideas are taught, what wealth stored up,
what loyalties fostered. Perhaps more galling for those who
believe that government action solves all problems, a fully
functioning family does not *owe* the state anything much. If
it feeds itself, clothes and schools its children and cares for its
old and ill, it does not need to show the almost feudal fealty
to government demanded of the rest of us in an age where the
authorities, rather than God or the Squire, seem to be in charge
of everything and to require most of our money to pay for
their services. In his *History of England 1914–45*, A. J. P. Taylor
points out that the only agents of the state a Victorian Briton
was likely to meet were the postman and the local policeman.

Full family independence would undermine the government's supposed right to demand heavy taxation. It would also
leave people free to cling to individual ideas of conscience,
rather than the nationalized 'social' conscience which measures

a citizen's value by how much tax he is willing to pay. The freer a society is, the more it leaves the family alone. D. H. Lawrence, that apostle of liberated sexuality, may seem a surprising advocate of married life, but his fierce defence of the free human spirit compelled him to take this view. In *Apropos Lady Chatterley's Lover* he wrote,

> It is marriage, perhaps, which has given man the best of his freedom, given him his little kingdom of his own within the big kingdom of the State, given him his foothold of independence on which to stand and resist an unjust State. Man and wife, a king and queen with one or two subjects, and a few square yards of territory of their own: This, really, is marriage. It is a true freedom because it is a true fulfilment for man, woman, and children.

And he warned inter-war Britain, and especially the Church, of the dangers it faced if it took a hacksaw to the marriage bond:

> Make marriage in any serious degree unstable, dissoluble, destroy the permanency of marriage, and the church falls. Witness the enormous decline of the Church of England. The reason being that the Church is established upon the element of union in mankind. . . . The marriage-tie, the marriage-bond, take it which way you like, is the fundamental link in Christian society. Break it, and you will have to go back to the overwhelming dominance of the State, which existed before the Christian era. The Roman state was all-powerful.

So the family, for all its faults, was one of the main pillars of the older British culture, including the idea that an Englishman's home was his castle. Its defeat during the last five decades has helped to produce the most conformist and least individualist generation in known history. Without a strong family, the growing child is much more easily influenced by his own age group, themselves under pressure from TV pro-grammes, advertisers, teachers and fashion.

There is no single cause for the family's decay. Like much of our revolution, it has its roots in the rationalist, secular ideas of the eighteenth and nineteenth century, and it was encour-aged by the double shock of two devastating wars. Families also fare better in the countryside, where their strengths are more obvious, and where divorce and confusion can lead to the breakup of farms and other disasters. When the Irish Repub-lic held a referendum on divorce in 1995, the division was as much country versus city as it was Catholic versus secular.

English marriage law was one of the oldest and most inflex-ible in the Christian world. At the time of the Reformation, the Bishops were prepared to annul marriages after lengthy hearings, but not to allow remarriage except with special per-mission. They tended to grant separations instead, but by the middle of the nineteenth century, a more secular urban and pluralist people were not content to be told what to do by Anglican divines. The introduction of civil marriage in 1836 was the first early warning of revolution. It was followed in 1854 by church legislation to allow divorce on the grounds of adultery, when the Bishop of St David's warned (quite rightly, as it turned out) that this would eventually lead to cheap divorce in the county courts, available to all and sundry.

By 1857, when the power of divorce was taken from the Church and given to the secular courts, Parliament was pass-ing an average of three private Acts each year, licensing remar-riage of a divorced spouse.

From then on, most of the more radical changes have been made not in Parliament, but in the courts. The courts have tended to stretch the grounds of divorce, keeping a keen eye on moral fashion but mainly motivated by the greatest con-venience of the greatest number. By their nature, the law and legal profession seek a secular balance, not a moral outcome. It is not and never has been their job to defend moral absolutes.

The history of divorce law reform has been the history of lawyers doing what was most expedient for the clients who could afford their services. That is what they might be expected to do. The interesting thing has been the response of those who are supposed to be the guardians of unchanging moral authority.

It is worth giving a short history of this turbulent period in English matrimonial law, and of the law's changing view of the conditions under which divorced partners should then live. Custody of children, maintenance and property division, are now the crucial rules of engagement in what has become a fearsome sex war. The changes have all been in one direction. The original principle was that divorce was possible if one party had repudiated the marriage by his or her behaviour—provable acts such as desertion, cruelty or adultery. Until very recently, fault or guilt were vital parts of the law. A husband who was the guilty party had to maintain his wife, even if she had divorced him. If the husband were innocent, and his wife guilty, he did *not* have to maintain her, though he was obliged to make sure she was not completely destitute. The guilty party, whether husband or wife, would *not* get custody of the children.

In 1948, in the case of Allen vs. Allen, the old custody doctrine was blown to pieces. A prisoner of war returned to find his wife and eight-year-old daughter living with another man in the house. The Court of Appeal refused him custody of his child. From that moment, guilt ceased to be decisive in custody cases. The 'biological' right of women to their children was upheld over the Christian moral right of a blameless parent. In the following years, the courts took broader and broader definitions of 'cruelty', increasingly making their own subjective judgements on the state of the marriage and dissolving it if they did not think it was viable.

In 1965, the Law Commission was set up under a liberal judge, the future Lord Scarman, and the development of divorce reform effectively handed over to the lawyers. The Commission would quickly come up with fault-free 'irretrievable breakdown' as the main ground for divorce, and no right for either spouse to keep the marriage in existence beyond five years. In effect, the judges had produced not just 'divorce on demand' but *unilateral* divorce on demand. This was such a radical revision of the idea of marriage that it would have taken away the breath of bishops, MPs and lawyers alike, even thirty years before. But the old certainties had crumbled so fast in the hearts of the British people that it took place with hardly any fuss at all. Parliament from then on would tend to confirm what was already legal practice. It also worked hard at shifting the balance of power away from the husband and towards the wife. A case in 1973 led to a ruling that 'conduct is not relevant to maintenance'.

The courts more and more relied on 'unreasonable behaviour' in granting divorces, a subjective judgement not easily disproved, instead of the harder definition of cruelty. Then, in the early 1980s, a husband was ordered from his own home *without* any suggestion that he had behaved violently towards his wife. A growing mountain of case law during the same period gave women rights over the joint property of husband and wife. The courts also increasingly failed to enforce husbands' rights to visit their children. The 1994 creation of the Child Support Agency, with its powers to order husbands to provide maintenance, followed by the still more liberal divorce reforms rammed through in the dying months of the Major government, sent a clear signal to anyone who was still in doubt: The state was on the side of the wife, whether she was in the right or in the wrong. It was hardly surprising that not only did the number of divorces rise steeply, but that the sex balance changed. Once, petitions from husbands and wives had been roughly equal. Now, the overwhelming majority were from wives, who also tended to benefit more than their husbands from legal aid.

All this had followed a Royal Commission which had actually urged a completely different course. The legal and political establishment virtually ignored the 1956 Morton Report on Divorce Reform, which wanted to keep the idea of fault and blame at the core of the laws. The debate launched by this Commission was probably the last time that absolute morality was brought into the argument at a high level. It had followed the withdrawal of a 1951 Private Member's Bill, introduced to the Commons by Mrs Eirene White, which would have allowed marriages to be dissolved after both parties had been separated for seven years. The Second World War had destroyed a huge number of marriages; many men had returned to find their wives living with other men, and—worse still—bringing up other men's children. Existing divorce law, dating from 1937, allowed the dissolution of a marriage only if an offence had been committed, for which one spouse or the other took the blame. The offences were limited to adultery or cruelty, and the process was painful, embarrassing and difficult.

The late 1940s were a period of what would now be called 'moral panic', with teenage violence, the appearance of firearms on the streets, a rising curve of illegitimacy and marriage breakdown. It was this feeling that things were coming apart which led to the hanging of Derek Bentley after his under-age accomplice murdered a policeman. The then Home Secretary, David Maxwell-Fyfe, could easily have reprieved Bentley, who had not actually fired a shot, but felt he needed to make an example and erred on the side of harshness in a case which is still not forgotten or forgiven. These were confusing times. Princess Margaret, faced with a choice between marrying a divorced man and doing her Royal duty as upholder of traditional morality, bravely chose duty. The afterglow of 'old-fashioned' Christian belief was still strong. Britain was faced with a choice between giving in to the new tide of looser, humanist morality or girding its loins and standing firm.

To begin with, the old order seemed to be holding fast. In the debate which followed Mrs White's Bill, the Church of England sternly defended the old truths. In its document *The*

Church and Marriage it spoke with Biblical austerity: 'It is of the first importance for the nation that this divine law (of life-long marriage) should be upheld', declared the then Archbishop of Canterbury. 'Nothing but lifelong monogamous marriage can adequately establish home life; provide for the birth and nurture and training of a family of children over a period of years.'

It listed the likely effects of easy divorce, saying it would distort ideals, foster lawlessness, encourage self-will, weaken the sense of obligation, offer a cloak of respectability to sin, encourage extra-marital affairs, encourage evasion of parenthood, contribute to family instability and offer children a precedent for divorce when they came to maturity.

'In spiritual matters,' it argued, 'men have powers of choice and can be educated. Weak laws and unsound public opinion can spread an attitude to marriage dangerous to the national well-being, and so encourage the spread of divorce.'

Answering critics who said its attitude would cause hardship to many, the Church retorted with this scornful question: 'Whoever succeeded in raising the moral tone of any society without causing the frustration of some natural desires, and the hardship of having to forego them?'

Only six years before, the Lambeth conference of Anglican bishops, deeply disturbed by the post-war increase in marriage breakdown, had said: 'We earnestly implore those whose marriages are unhappy to remain steadfastly faithful to their marriage vows, relying on the unfailing resources of God's grace.' It is a measure of our turmoil and change that such words and attitudes now seem almost impossibly remote.

Already, within the Church, there was a strong movement for compromise with the twentieth century. By 1966, when the Church was again asked to consider divorce law reform, the language and the philosophy had changed so completely that it is hard to believe they issued from the same organization. In *Putting Asunder: A Divorce Law for Contemporary*

Society, the Church had switched from defiance to appeasement, though it was not ready to accept the likely outcome of
its retreat. It acknowledged that the divorce courts were quietly and deliberately weakening the law already, so that the
idea of fault was dying. It believed that this meant the law was
'moving in company with the mind of society.'

Far from hoping to change the mind of society on this issue,
the Church wanted to join in the revolution itself. Viewed from
this distance, *Putting Asunder* seems to be a flabby, inconsistent document which tries to have it all ways, and deceives
itself about the likely outcome. The fact that its title is a reference to the unequivocal declaration of Jesus Christ himself
that 'those whom God hath joined together, let no man put
asunder' makes its evasions even more repellent. Yet in the
strange spirit of those times, serious, educated religious men
were happy to produce such a document. Perhaps the Bishops
were unaware of D. H. Lawrence's prophetic warning, perhaps they could not see for themselves the link between their
own authority and the strength of the marriage bond, perhaps
they merely thought that the best way to refill their emptying
churches was to swim with the tide.

At the time, opponents of weakening the law warned that
the abolition of blame would lead to what they called 'divorce
by consent'. Instead of being a public promise to family, friends
and society, wedding vows would become a private contract
that could be broken at will. Strangely, they were less concerned
about what would actually happen—that no-fault divorce would
make it weaker still, a mere one-sided contract, which either
partner could tear up after enough time had elapsed.

Putting Asunder declared: 'We find no reason to suppose
that the doctrine of breakdown of marriage would favour
"divorce by consent" in the objectionable sense of these
words.... The conception of marriage underlying the doctrine
of breakdown seemed to us to be neither unworthy nor incompatible with a covenant of lifelong intention.' The authors

believed that the change 'would not only accord better with social realities than the present law does, but would have the merit of showing up divorce for what, in essence, it is—not a reward for marital virtue on one side and a penalty for marital delinquency on the other; not a victory for one spouse and a reverse for the other. But a defeat for both.'

This was, of course, humbug. Divorce was permission to remarry, usually pursued by one spouse at whatever cost, and it made a nonsense of the promises of lifelong fidelity clearly stated in the Church's own marriage service. Who cared if, in the course of the break up, divorce was 'shown up for what it was'? What they were recommending was do-it-yourself morality, the bending of the rules to suit current fashion, and the abandonment of four hundred years of doctrine. The Church had not been happy with civil divorce since it was introduced in 1857, and had never given its blessing to the older, narrower law. Now, entirely forgetting its past, it joined the most radical, utilitarian reformers, pretending as it did so that its views would have no important effects.

'We arrived at our primary and fundamental recommendation that the doctrine of the breakdown of marriage should be comprehensively substituted for the doctrine of matrimonial offence as the basis of all divorce.'

Then they asked what would or should happen if an innocent spouse were divorced against his or her will. Their answer was useless and empty: 'The sense that it *is* harsh persists and we cannot claim to have found how to dispel that sense entirely. The fact of the matter is, we believe, that when a marriage comes to grief, wounding cannot be avoided.'

What an astonishing reverse this is, compared with the 1954 declaration that it was always painful to *uphold* moral absolutes. Now they were saying that pain was inevitable when those absolutes were tossed aside.

The main arguments against the old morality were made day after day in the law courts as couple after couple came

before the bench to ask for release. The fading afterglow of
Victorian religious morality grew dimmer in this area of life
more quickly than in any other. Perhaps the exposure to North
American divorce morals, developed in a vast country where
it was always possible to start a new life hundreds of miles
from your old one, had something to do with it. Hollywood
had introduced America to Britain before the war, as had Wallis Simpson when she stole King Edward VIII from his subjects ('Hark the herald angels sing, Mrs Simpson stole our
King', sang the schoolchildren in the playgrounds of the 1930s),
and the occupation of the British Isles by American troops during the war had shown many people that there was a different way of doing things. Normally, utterly different cultures
are kept apart by the barrier of language, but here as in so
many other ways, America's combination of English speech
and continental customs overcame the outer defences of British
reserve, self-control and tradition, allowing the spread of ideas
and manners developed for an alien and much bigger nation
in which great space allowed for less restraint, and allowed
people to use geography to escape the consequences of their
own actions.

But there were, of course, other homegrown influences.
The 'advanced' views of Bloomsbury intellectuals, confined to
a tiny clique before the war, were now much more widespread,
in such places as the universities and the rapidly expanding
BBC.

Two sets of Reith lectures, chosen and promoted by the
BBC, gave currency and respectability to new ideas about the
family. Professor Edmund Leach, an anthropologist, shocked
a still-conventional audience with several passages in his broadcasts *A Runaway World?* in 1967. His opening was aggressively post-Christian: 'Men have become like gods; isn't it about
time that we understood our divinity?' It was also openly rel-
ativist. Leach simply did not accept that there were any absolute
rules outside time and space. Everything was up for negotia-

tion, like a salary or the price of a house: 'Morality is specified by culture; what you ought to do depends on who you are
and where you are.'

And where were we? Professor Leach thought we were
imprisoned by outdated ideas of family life: 'Perhaps it is the
family itself that needs to be changed.'

It was a persuasive, if shocking, position. Leach believed
that modern society had wiped out the old and healthy extended
family, and replaced it with the tiny nuclear family, too small
to bear the burdens placed upon it. On this narrow foundation he based a much broader attack:

> In the past, kinsfolk and neighbours gave the individual con-
> tinuous moral support throughout his life. Today, the domes-
> tic household is isolated. The family looks inward upon
> itself; there is an intensification of emotional stress between
> husband and wife, and parents and children. The strain is
> greater than most of us can bear. Far from being the basis
> of the good society, the family, with its narrow privacy and
> tawdry secrets, is the source of all our discontents.

Leach, rather incredibly, protested later that he was 'astonished by the public animosity provoked by this very ordinary
remark'. Perhaps he really was, but only because in academic
circles such ideas were by then very common.

He went on:

> We need a change of values here, but it is not at all obvious
> what the change should be....
>
> I do not pretend to know the answer. All I am saying is
> that it seems very likely that 100 years from now the gen-
> eral pattern of domestic life in Britain will be altogether dif-
> ferent from what it is now, and we should not get too upset
> if symptoms of this change are already appearing....
>
> Our present society is emotionally very uncomfortable.
> The parents and children huddled together in their loneliness

take too much out of each other. The parents fight. The children rebel. Children need to grow up in larger, more relaxed domestic groups centred on the community, rather than on mother's kitchen: something like an Israeli kibbutz perhaps, or a Chinese commune.

The Professor was later to claim that this did not mean the kibbutz or the commune had been proved to be a viable alternative to the nuclear family. He certainly cannot have envisaged the sort of arrangements discovered in October 1998 on a Glasgow council estate, where an eleven-year-old child was equally welcome, and equally neglected, in the tower-block flat occupied by his mother or the flats occupied by his father or his uncle in the same building. It took police twenty-four hours to work out which was his permanent address. His plight (or otherwise) was revealed when he was found at his primary school with a large supply of heroin, which he believed to be sherbert.

Professor Leach (who died in 1997) would surely not have approved of this new kind of extended family, but could it have been a consequence of the ideas he helped to make respectable? He chided society because 'We worry about privacy rather than loneliness' and noted that visitors to Eastern Europe, then communist, often reacted badly to the lack of privacy there. He urged, 'It is we who need to change, not the others. Privacy is the source of fear and violence. The violence in the world comes about because we human beings are forever creating artificial boundaries between men who are like us and men who are not like us.'

And, well before the triumph of youth culture, he felt that adults were wrong to fear the new attitude towards sexual morality then spreading among the young. 'The young have seen through our absurdities. . . . they deserve encouragement, not reproach.'

Much of this argument has now become a sort of liberal common sense. The idea that family rows are more damaging than divorce, the allegation (supported by dubious statistics) that marriage is a trap in which men violently mistreat women, the suspicion of child abuse behind the veil of married respectability, are now common ground among many liberal commentators and social workers, who treat marriage as, at the very least, a suspect institution.

In the world of the law, the almost resigned acceptance of the new realities was exemplified by Brenda Hoggett, later Mrs Justice Hale, a law professor turned judge who did much to remove the idea of blame from divorce law. In a 1982 article, 'Ends and Means: The Utility of Marriage as a Legal Institution', Professor Hoggett pointed out, 'Whether it would have been possible to remove the inequality between the sexes, improve the protection given to the weak, and at the same time promote lasting marriage, we shall never know. Instead, the efforts of English law to remove the defects of the marital package deal have succeeded not only in virtually destroying whatever value it has as a stabilizing or restraining force but also in an ever-closer approximation of the legal consequences of marriage and extra-marital cohabitation.' In other words, by trying to reform marriage, English law made it less and less worth bothering to get married at all. She concluded:

> The legal system has clearly abandoned one set of moral principles in favour of a pair of social goals which have proved incompatible. Family law no longer makes any attempt to buttress the stability of marriage or any other union. It has adopted principles for the protection of children and dependent spouses which could be made equally applicable to the unmarried.
>
> In such circumstances, the piecemeal erosion of the distinction between marriage and non-marital cohabitation may be expected to continue.
>
> Logically, we have already reached a point at which, rather than discussing which remedies should now be

extended to the unmarried, we should be considering whether
the legal institution of marriage continues to serve any useful purposes.

The Professor's logic is undeniable, if the issue is a purely practical one. A post-Christian, practical attitude to the marriage
bond was not really shocking by the time she wrote those
words. A revolution in views of chastity and constancy had
already taken place.

One of the important precursors of that revolution was
the 1962 series of Reith lectures delivered by the psychologist
Morris Carstairs (*This Island Now*). These include a fascinating statistic, almost incomprehensible in our post-marriage
society, that in 1961, 31% of girls who married in their teens
were pregnant at the time of their weddings. (Local newspaper reporters, who used to write up weddings from standard
forms filled in by the happy couple, always sniggered when a
young bride was wearing an Empire Line dress, a shape
designed to conceal the growing bulge of pregnancy.) To
Carstairs, the significant thing was that they were pregnant.
To us, it is that they then felt it wise and necessary to marry.

Carstairs upset his 1960s listeners by taking a very 1990s
position. Blaming the 'authoritarian' St Paul and the 'reformed
libertine St Augustine' for Christian sexual morality, he set out
a number of thoughts which would soon become liberal orthodoxy: 'It has always been those whose own sexual impulses
have been precariously repressed who have raised the loudest
cries of alarm over other people's immorality.'

And: 'I believe we may be quite mistaken in our alarm—
at times amounting almost to panic—over young people's sexual experimentation'. (What, by the way, are these 'experiments' and the other 'experiments' in drugtaking seeking to
prove or disprove, which is not already known? It is interesting that this word is so frequently used for wrong actions taken
by the young.)

And: 'Contraception is still regarded as something wicked, threatening to chastity, opening the way to unbridled licence. But *is* chastity the supreme moral virtue?'

Obviously not for Professor Carstairs: 'Many societies get on quite well without pre-marital chastity. It seems to me that our young people are rapidly turning our own society into one in which sexual experience, with precautions against conception, is becoming accepted as a sensible preliminary to marriage; a preliminary which makes it more likely that marriage, when it comes, will be a mutually considerate and mutually satisfying partnership.'

Mournfully, he declared that popular morality was now 'a wasteland, littered with the debris of broken convictions. . . . Concepts such as honour, or even honesty, have an old-fashioned sound; but nothing has taken their place.'

As for sexual morality, Carstairs talked of a new concept, which now sounds very familiar indeed. It was of sex as 'a source of pleasure, but also as a mutual encountering of personalities in which each explores the other and at the same time discovers new depths in himself or herself. This concept of sex as a rewarding relationship is after all not so remote from the experience of our maligned teenagers as it is from that of many of their parents.'

Carstairs was also a prophet of modern feminism. Describing marriage as an 'unromantic compromise between sensuality and drudgery', he looked forward to a society where women would enjoy social and economic equality with men. 'We have not known such a society, but during this century we have moved a long way towards it,' he said, approvingly.

The effect of these pronouncements, delivered through the majesty of the BBC, was enormous. Those who had privately held such ideas must have felt greatly encouraged. Those who disagreed with them had the first nasty taste of an experience which would become common. Their moral opinions, which they had never questioned and which had been reinforced throughout their lives by home, school and church, were now being attacked by the voice of authority. As time passed, the private beliefs of the majority would hardly ever be reflected on the broadcast media, so convincing them that they were in fact a minority and had somehow been left behind. As time went by, they lost confidence in a morality they had once been proud to support, and became ashamed of it. Enfeebled, isolated and pushed to the margins, the majority were not merely silent, but dumbstruck and powerless, afraid to defend themselves.

The relaxation of divorce laws had another effect, impossible to measure but hugely influential on late-twentieth-century opinion and morals. When the law had been inflexible and divorce rare and costly, few people knew more than one or two divorced couples. Children whose parents broke up were regarded as exceptions, to be pitied and treated with tact.

As the reforms took effect and the sheer number of divorces grew, the balance swung the other way. Suddenly it seemed as if we all had divorced classmates, colleagues, neighbours, friends, relatives. They were still treated with tact, but it was a different kind of tact. Instead of not wanting to upset them by mentioning their sad state, the British *stopped disapproving of divorce in public*. Whatever they thought in private, they knew that they risked giving serious offence if they openly voiced their views. The subject became a taboo. Everywhere from newspaper editorial conferences to gatherings of clergymen or groups of parents at the school gate, it was bad manners to insist on what had—until a few years before—been a cultural consensus in favour of lifelong marriage.

And from there it was but a step towards the new morality in which any assembly of adults and children was reclassified as a family unit. For one of the most startling and alarming features of cultural revolution is the speed with which it overwhelms the past, along with its savage intolerance of the opinions and customs which it has replaced.

ELEVEN

Last Exit to Decency

THE TOP SHELVES OF NORMAL newsagents now sag with explicit pornography that would once have been hidden in dingy rubber-goods shops in the wrong part of town. A daily 'newspaper' has made its owner a millionaire with its open, blithe exploitation of female nakedness. Mainstream papers cheerfully display half-clothed women on prominent pages, and bare breasts are now so common on television that nobody is willing to admit to being shocked—though many certainly are in secret. Magazines produced for well-off, educated, professional women are packed with blatant articles about subjects which were once judged so intimate that few would have dared mention them even to a doctor, and then only in low voices and the strictest privacy.

Yet, while millions of people probably shudder inwardly when they catch sight of all this gynaecology and orgasmic prose, they know that it is *not respectable* to make a fuss. The only acceptable reason for opposing or criticizing any of this sort of thing is militant feminism. If a radical MP such as Clare Short condemns the *Sun*'s casual display of the female bosom on its Page Three, the fashionable world is impressed if a little embarrassed, while the equally forceful protests of the un-radical Mrs Mary Whitehouse are ignored as embarrassing, suburban and repressed. Why the embarrassment, when very recently it would have been Page Three that was embarrassing, rather than the objections to it?

The cleverer leftists, such as the barrister and playwright Sir John Mortimer, always understood that there was a connection between the liberal cause and the pornographic revolution. One of his most notable defences of the new culture took place during the trial of the once-notorious Schoolkids Issue of *Oz* magazine in 1971. I shall return to this, the least serious of Britain's legal debates on how openly sex could be discussed in a society based upon restraint. But to understand this sector of the cultural revolution, it is compulsory to begin with the Lady Chatterley affair, identified by that should-have-been Poet Laureate Philip Larkin as the moment when 'sexual intercourse began', along with the Beatles' first LP. Larkin's poem dates it wrongly, in 1963. The trial actually took place in October 1960, when history still happened in black and white, before Myra Hindley,* before Harold Wilson, before *That Was The Week That Was*.

We are inclined to giggle now about the Chatterley affair, now that the once-banned novel has been serialized in full and fleshly colour on prime-time, mainstream television, and we are all sophisticates about adultery, impotence and nakedness. But we were more innocent then. The House of Lords debated the verdict, and one peer mourned: 'Purity is sacrificed on the altar of promiscuity as woolly-headed intellectuals pour their vociferous sewage into the ears of the public', while another snapped: 'What are we coming to? It is all very well for one noble Lord to laugh. This is not a laughing matter; it is a very serious issue that we are facing today.' The old booby was right. It *was* a serious issue they were facing, and one which we still face.

By the end of the 1950s, the country was seriously divided on the issue of obscenity. It was not a party division—few of the great clashes of the past fifty years have been. It was between generations and between the 'respectable' and the 'advanced'.

Before the Second World War, books deemed pornographic had been regularly condemned, and barred from the country—not very effectively, as we shall see. Among the books which ran into trouble was the turgid lesbian romance *The Well of Loneliness,* by the eccentric Sapphist Radclyffe Hall, whose most shocking passage ran 'that night they were not divided'. This prosecution was a sort of prototype for the Chatterley affair, except that the times were very different, and so was the law—which allowed a book to be condemned for individual passages rather than as a whole. It also did not allow publishers to plead literary merit as a defence. So while *The Well of Loneliness* attracted a great crowd of 'witnesses' prepared to swear to its cleanliness and virtue, they were ignored by the magistrates who ruled that such evidence was inadmissible.

Censorship at that time was very much a matter of social class. Wealthy, well-connected people were able to get hold of banned titles without much risk by travelling to France, but the wider population were cut off from such things almost completely. When *Lady Chatterley's Lover* came to court, it was noticeable that almost all the expert witnesses, respectable and established members of the academic élite, had been able to get hold of unexpurgated copies in their pre-war youth. But this sort of furtive availability was not enough for the reformers. The liberal thinking classes were annoyed that these sweets were not generally available, and they felt provoked and embarrassed by the censorious behaviour of the Conservative Home Secretary, Maxwell-Fyfe (who had refused to reprieve Derek Bentley), who saw it as his duty to rebuild the barriers broken down by six years of war. In 1954, he oversaw *five* prosecutions of novels for obscenity. Radicals, among them the future Lord St John of Fawsley, a Tory, became alarmed and pressed for a new law in which 'literary merit' would, in effect, excuse obscenity. They did not want the courts to be able to ignore the sort of witnesses who had queued up so fruitlessly to help Radclyffe Hall before the war.

A Bill first drafted by Lord St John was eventually steered through the Commons in 1959 by none other than Roy Jenkins, who appears at the barricades in so many skirmishes of the culture wars that one feels he should have some kind of medal to show for it. The new law's central clause insisted that works accused of obscenity had to be taken as a whole, not in part. It also said that the courts had to take account of 'all relevant circumstances'.

Encouraged by this, and by the acquittal of Lawrence's banned book in a U.S. federal court, Penguin decided that the ideal moment for a test case had arrived. The classic account of the trial by H. Montgomery Hyde nowhere openly states this, but the whole affair has the air of a legal system going through the motions of prosecution, without any great hope of success, or any desire for it. It *was* a test case, but one in which both sides seem to have been hoping for the same result. Hyde says that nine of the jury were for acquittal from the start. The accused were not required to sit in the dock, and freely admitted that they had already printed 200,000 copies of *Lady Chatterley*, hardly the action of a company seriously afraid of conviction. The Prosecutor, Mervyn Griffith-Jones, leaned over backwards to be fair, at one point saying to the jurors, 'Your task is really this—to determine what in a free country should be tolerated and what should not be tolerated.... You may or may not disapprove of the book. However much you disapprove of the book, you will not convict the company [Penguin Books] unless you find that this book is obscene in the sense that it tends to deprave and corrupt.' They had, he stressed, to judge the book as a whole: 'You are not to look at it as censors; your verdict is not to be based upon the fact that you may disapprove of the book. It must be obscene. Allow, as far as you can, the right of writers and publishers to express their talents, and approach the book from the widest and most liberal point of mind.'

These remarks are far more important than Griffith-Jones's often-quoted and ludicrous question: 'Is it a book you would

even wish your wife or your servants to read?' Even his lists
of rude words (30 f-words, 14 c-words, b***s 13 times, s***
six times, a*** six times, 'cock' four times, p*** three times)
have a half-hearted feel to them. He produced one witness, a
police officer who described how co-operative Penguin Books
had been in providing copies of the work. And that was it.

By contrast, the defence barrister, the future Lord Chancellor Gerald Gardiner, had thirty-five witnesses ready to testify to the book's merits, and another fifty in reserve if needed.
The cast list of these witnesses is a wonderful catalogue of cultural liberalism in our society. Some of them were extremely
silly, and Mr Griffith-Jones made sport of them. Others were
halted in mid-flow, for baffling legal reasons. Roy Jenkins himself made an appearance in the witness-box which was much
briefer than he must have expected it to be. But the general
effect was to spread the idea that respectable, educated, Christian people, headmasters and suchlike, could happily accept
the publication of this not-very-good book, with its lewd conversations, its wearisome descriptions of the sex act and the
home life of the penis, its coarse language and its scorn for the
marriage of the Chatterleys.

Many of the witnesses would later admit that *Lady Chatterley* was not one of Lawrence's best works, and contained
some positively atrocious passages, but the Bishop who said
this was a book which all Christians should read and the distinguished professor who opined that it was a puritan work
were not likely to be prosecuted for perjury whatever they said.
And on Wednesday 2 November 1960, after retiring for less
than three hours, the jury supplied the expected and, one has
to say, required verdict of 'not guilty'. It would never again be
possible to ban a book in England unless it could be proved
to have no literary merit whatsoever. And there would usually
be someone on hand to say that it had at least *some*.

Turn the clocks forward to 23 June 1971 and the wigs and
gowns were once again assembled to pass judgement upon a

very different work: the twenty-eighth issue of *Oz* magazine, more often known as the Schoolkids Issue. To a 1990s mind, *Oz* would seem to be an amateurish, ordinary and messy production. Its thoughts on sex and drugs now find their way into glossy women's monthlies or respectable Sunday newspapers, and its cover in this case, a tableau of black women in vaguely lesbian positions, seems tame compared with modern fashion photography. Even its centrepiece, a perversion of the well-loved children's cartoon character Rupert in which the homely little bear is endowed with a giant penis and grotesquely rapes a fat slut with few details spared, no longer has any real power to upset. We have seen all this. Even the gardens of childhood have been invaded by the sexualizers and pornographers. But in 1971, despite the Sixties, many of the moral defences of an older Britain were still—just—standing.

At the same time as the *Oz* editors stood in the dock for obscenity, a manual of sexual licence for the young, *The Little Red Schoolbook,* was also being prosecuted (and also being defended by John Mortimer). When its publishers were fined £50, the moral campaigner Mary Whitehouse was jeered in the street outside by a liberal mob of 'youths'. The publisher declared, 'What is at stake here is not sex education for young people, but the ability of any people to question authority.' Much of the advice he had offered would be issued at government expense to schoolchildren less than twenty years afterwards. In its defence, Caspar Brook, director of the Family Planning Association, described the book's amoral section on contraception as wholly admirable. A comprehensive school headmaster, Charles Stewart-Jervis, said the little manual was 'healthy and wholesome'.

Similar people had assembled to defend *Oz*. George Melly, jazz musician and *bien-pensant,* admitted the magazine was full of dirty jokes but claimed that it fulfilled an important function: 'Anything that can be done to alleviate the guilt complex about sex is good. . . . The more open sexuality is, the less

the feeling of guilt and the less the misery.' Asked by the prosecution if smutty jokes were told in front of his children at
home, Melly retorted, 'You are trying to make me out to be
an NW1 monster'—a reference to the North London postal
district then thought to be the haunt of militant liberals (much
as Islington is now) and satirized in Marc Boxer's cartoons
Life and Times in NW1.

The editor himself, Richard Neville, explained that his
magazine worked on the assumption that many people took
drugs, but it was quick to point out the dangers of doing so.
One of his chief aims was to abolish something he called 'under-
cover puritanism'. The more relaxed people were in sex, the
healthier the community would be. Miss Caroline Coon, on
behalf of the charity 'Release', said that *Oz* was a 'responsible publication which did not advocate the taking of drugs,
adding: 'Unless you give children the facts, they are prepared
to take anything to find out what the experience is'. This view
would be orthodoxy in the 1990s, when the policy of 'harm
reduction' elbowed aside the idea that young people should
be told quite simply not to take drugs because it was always
wrong.

The long queue of the great-ish and the good-ish continued to shuffle up to the witness-box. Dr Lionel Haward, a con-
sultant psychologist, testified that *Oz* was a good magazine.
'It has a number of beneficial features which I would like to
see incorporated in many school magazines.' His hopes were
to be fulfilled. Dr Haward said the message of the Rupert Bear
cartoons was 'to criticize the lack of dissemination of sexual
education'.

Another psychologist, Dr Josephine Klein, said the magazine 'would not debauch or corrupt the morals of young children'. Dr Michael Schofield of the Health Education Council
pronounced the magazine 'a giggle'.

A Dr Michael Segal, former head of TV programmes for
the Rediffusion TV company which had held the franchise for

the London area, said he had allowed his four children to read *Oz*. This permission included his twin boys, aged eleven. Professor Ronald Dworkin, now a lion of the political correctness movement, was then so little known that *The Times* at first thought his name was 'Ronald Walker'. He pronounced that 'this prosecution is in a sense the corruption of public morals'.

Mr Michael Duane, a former headmaster then lecturing in a teacher training college, said 'mentally deranged' people had brought the process of law to bear. The comedian Marty Feldman, in his testimony, audibly called the Judge (Mr Justice Michael Argyle) a 'boring old fart', asked him 'Am I waking you up?' and suggested that there was more obscenity in the Bible than in *Oz*.

If it had not been a conflict between generations before, it certainly was now. The prosecutor, Brian Leary, asked the jury to set a standard: 'Ask yourselves what alternatives are before you; the dropping out of society; expecting the state to provide for you, and by that I mean you and me and the rest of us who don't mind working?'

Despite John Mortimer's comment that Shakespeare would have had a thin time at Mr Leary's hands, the jury convicted Neville and his colleagues on four obscenity charges on 29 July, and Judge Argyle, quoting from St Matthew's gospel and the prophet Malachi about the duties of adults towards children, sent them off to prison.

It was then that it became clear that the only long-term effect of this trial would be on prison haircuts. As Neville, Felix Dennis and James Anderson arrived at Wandsworth, their fashionably long hair was lopped off by a prison barber, causing such outrage that the Home Office rules on prisoners' hair were there and then amended.

Recognizing that a whole way of life was under attack, the new orthodoxy hit back. On 6 August, four hundred 'young people' demonstrated for two hours outside the Old Bailey. A round-the-clock guard was placed on Judge Argyle's house. If there was an establishment, it rapidly concluded that the case had had the 'wrong' result. On 6 November, the Appeal Court quashed convictions and sentences on the grounds that Judge Argyle had misdirected the jury.

There was a fascinating account of the trial in the *New Statesman* magazine by Jonathan Dimbleby, who, if not part of the establishment in 1971, is certainly one of its members now. He said the judge, in his flowing robes and tight white wig, was just as bizarre as the defendants in their shoulder-length hair, flowing robes and dungarees. 'Here is the confrontation that matters,' he presciently wrote. 'One morality set resolutely against another, an "alternative" challenging the Establishment.' He concluded: 'After constant exposure ... to "****ing in the streets," "masturbation", "deviation", "lesbianism", "corruption" and "cannabis", this middle-aged group of British householders—the jury—was asked quite simply to set the standard. What an invitation.'

Look at the offending magazine now, and it is clear who won the confrontation. The cover's lesbianism is understated. The adverts for vibrators and homosexual contact magazines would shock nobody under forty. Nothing in it would be specially out of place in a London listings magazine or a colour supplement, except perhaps for the Rupert cartoon, which is deliberately tacky and disgusting, and that would easily find a home in a New Lad's monthly.* The puerile anti-teacher cartoons—in which tweeded, middle-aged men masturbate or cane each other's bare bottoms—summon up nostalgia for an age when most teachers were indeed male, did wear tweeds and used canes. The c-word, then a tremendous taboo, is now used in plays on BBC radio. The children quoted 'hate their parents' and 'turn on regularly'. A 'schoolkids' manifesto' has mostly been implemented: 'More freedom was everybody's cry. Get rid of the primitive examination system, get rid of teachers who can't see beyond their own prejudices, give us the freedom to smoke, to dress, to have sex, to run school affairs.'

The *Oz* and *Little Red Schoolbook* trials were a last futile skirmish in a lost war, significant because it extended the issue of pornography into the related battles over drugs, education, homosexuality, swear-words, fashions in clothes and hair, and authority in general. A much more significant battle had been fought four years before over the limits of censorship. It concerned the book *Last Exit to Brooklyn* by the American Hubert Selby. Nobody seriously argued that Selby was another Lawrence, even if his writing had a certain raw style and power. The book was a revolting and not specially moral tour of the lower depths of New York City. When it came to trial, in November 1967, this is what the *defence* lawyer said: 'This book will shock and nauseate. You may think it is unbearable and horrifying, but it is not a crime to write a book that shocks or disgusts, or even nauseates.'

The Judge, Graham Rogers, ruled that no women should serve on the jury, saying that they 'might be embarrassed at having to read a book which dealt with homosexuality, prostitution, sadism, drug-taking and sexual perversion'. At the time, nobody considered this ruling to be strange.

Once again, the avant-garde lined up to be counted among the legions of the blessed, by defending Mr Selby's right to be published. Professor Frank Kermode declared himself 'much moved', and suggested that 'It is a book which George Eliot would have recognised as having to do with the urgent issue of morality, which puts it in what one might describe as the great tradition of fiction-writing.' It was also 'very much in the tradition of Dickens', and in an argument now exhausted by constant use in the defence of modern screen bloodshed, he compared Selby's violent scenes to the blinding of Gloucester in *King Lear*.

When John Matthew, the prosecutor, suggested that 'a normal, well-educated, average, intelligent person who picks up this book might come to a different conclusion about its moral aspect', Professor Kermode replied that he didn't think so.

The book's British publisher, John Calder, said he had been

shocked and repelled by the book when he first read it. 'But the power of the writing and the integrity of the author made it one that a serious publisher could not ignore.' He predicted that in fifty years' time it would be read by 'senior teenagers' in school, a prophecy that now seems rather modest.

Another literary critic of note, Al Alvarez, declared that it was a masterpiece of quite outstanding merit. He echoed the Chatterley trial by saying, 'In many ways it is a work of very considerable purity.'

Among other arguments for the book was the suggestion that, in the aftermath of Hitler's concentration camps, anything at all was allowable in literature.

However, this time the old guard put up something of a fight. Professor George Catlin, a political scientist from Canada's leading university, McGill, told the jury, 'I cannot imagine anything being obscene if this book isn't', which was more or less the issue at stake in the trial. Professor Catlin suggested a cynical motive rather than a high-minded one for the publishers' enthusiasm: 'These books are giant moneymakers. I think over a quarter of a million copies of this book have been sold in America.' He said Selby's much-praised dialogue could have been obtained by tape-recording the conversations in a hippie centre in San Francisco, and pointed out that several major arbiters of literary merit—the *Times Literary Supplement, Sunday Times* and *Observer*—had not reviewed it.

The publisher, Sir Basil Blackwell—the only witness whose age, seventy-eight, was recorded by *The Times* in its report— said the book had 'slight' literary merit. In brave and candid testimony, Sir Basil revealed he had only read the book so that he could appear as a witness against it. He said, 'Dickens was a great artist. He certainly portrayed wicked and evil men but he made them live. He did not produce them as mere lay figures in an endless stream of filthy language and foul behaviour. It is all one thing, abominable thoughts, abominable words and abominable conduct.'

Did it deprave or corrupt? Sir Basil replied frankly: 'I felt it depraved because I felt that my memory and my mind was impaired, vitiated and defiled by the language that I read. . . . I felt I was seriously hurt by the book and wanted to go away and cleanse my mind.'

Sir Basil said he had stopped the sale of the book at his Oxford shops when he discovered its true character, and confessed, 'I would rather do anything than read it again.'

The Church, too, was divided. The Reverend Kenneth Leech, curate of St Anne's in Soho, said he would be prepared to recommend it to his parishioners, which was perhaps a reflection on his unusual parish. The future Bishop of Liverpool, David Sheppard, confessed that he was 'not unscathed' by reading *Last Exit*. He felt it was 'pandering to all that was worst in me' and said, 'I would not like to say that I could read a book like this and suffer no damage from it.'

Prosecuting counsel asked the jury, 'Do you think these nauseating details make it a work of such outstanding literary merit that the public must have it at all costs—because that is what it comes down to in the end?'

The jury took nearly six hours to rule the book obscene. But as usual the case did not end there. The following July, John Mortimer told the Court of Appeal that this was 'the type and status of work that the [Obscene Publications] Act was passed to protect'. He also pronounced that 'what is on trial here is literature'.

If so, literature got off lightly again, for the court quashed the conviction because of 'fatal flaws' in the judge's summing up. He had, said Lord Justice Salmon, 'failed to put to the jury the defence case on the question of obscenity, and failed to give proper directions on whether publication was for the public good.'

A clear pattern can be seen in each of these trials, that of an establishment anxious to relax the rules, sometimes obstructed by the old-fashioned views of Sir Basil Blackwell, of David Sheppard and of middle-class jurors, or of judges brought up in a different tradition. There is also a struggle evident between common sense, which is almost always conservative, and the desire of the élite to spread its own ideas to the masses.

The battle may have been fought over a few books and over the censorship of stage plays (where official control was abolished in November 1968), but of course the effects were hugely increased when television, radio and the cinema realized that the restraints were off. Nakedness, explicit portrayals of the sex act, liberal use of swear-words, 'frank' and 'non-judgemental' depictions of drug-taking, homosexuality and prostitution were at first tentative, but quickly became so commonplace that they ceased to count as news. Only a few years before, wondering foreigners such as George Mikes had recounted the repression and restraint of the British, laughing that while other men had mistresses, the British had hot-water bottles, while their wives sheltered from the cold in nightgowns made of tweed. Now the entire country seemed to be obsessed with staring at naked female chests, swearing and making dirty jokes. Like the pagans of old, unaffected by climate, the British were now dancing round a giant phallus. Unlike the pagans theirs was a sterile phallus, disarmed by condoms and pills—the first heathen sexual cult to be based around sterility rather than fertility.

This outcome had been achieved by the route of arguing 'literary merit' to justify the breaking of old taboos. It is a curious country which abandons an entire moral code on the grounds that immoral works might be an uplifting read, but that is roughly what we have done. Literary merit is so utterly subjective that there will always be some professor or parson willing to bestow a good reputation on the vilest garbage. Other, perhaps better, arguments have been advanced—that pornography is a safety valve rather than a stimulant to perversion; that censorship is in itself bad and should be abandoned. The question of whether total licence imposes any obligations on free men has seldom been discussed, because sexual liberation of all kinds is such an important part of the new post-Christian Britain. The arbiters of the new morality believed that one's sexual life did not need to be regulated either by law or by conscience. An interesting insight into these rather Edwardian views comes in C. P. Snow's 1968 novel *The Sleep of Reason,* a lightly disguised account of the Hindley child murder case, in which the author wonders if his youthful ideas about sexual freedom may have led unintentionally to horror. Few other liberals have ever bothered to consider the connection between their campaigns and the worrying increase in perverted and violent sexual activity.

This has led to the collapse of an agreed idea about what virtue is, combined with a belief that human freedom is the highest law. Even the Christian churches have suggested that sexual puritanism was an aberration, the work of St Paul and St Augustine, rather than a central part of the faith. These ideas, yet again, date back to the Victorian and Edwardian eras, when they became common among the educated and wealthy élite, who believed that religion was for the servants and the workers, and who went to church—if at all—for the sake of appearances. This was the period when hypocrisy truly was the tribute which vice paid to virtue, but because of its deep dishonesty, such an arrangement could not last for ever. Sooner or later the educated classes either had to remoralize themselves, or extend their liberation to the rest of the population. Given that men often seek companionship as they slither down the slippery slopes of immorality, it is no surprise that they chose to extend it. Nor is it any surprise that the fiercest resistance to pornography came from the lower middle class and the respectable working class, the people who have always believed most passionately in order, hierarchy and morality, because they live closer than anyone else to the edge of chaos. They have, once again, been proved right in their fears—not that it has done them much good.

It is clear to anyone with eyes in their head that
Deirdre Rachid is innocent and should be free.
—Spokesman for the Prime Minister and First Lord
of Her Majesty's Treasury, 31 March 1998

The whole nation is deeply concerned about Deirdre Rachid.
—The Rt Hon William Hague MP, Leader of Her Majesty's Opposition, 31 March 1998

TWELVE

Suburbs of the Mind

DEIRDRE RACHID DID NOT EXIST. She was a fictional character in the television soap *Coronation Street*, who had been sent to a fictional prison by a fictional court for a fictional crime. Everybody, including the Prime Minister and the Leader of the Opposition, knew this. And yet they also knew that millions of people cared rather more fiercely about this figment than they did about much of the real world. Both of them would have felt it unwise to boycott the strange national festival of protest against Deirdre's 'harsh' sentence.

They were only following the example of most popular newspapers, which had for years treated the major soap opera series as if they were real, sometimes confusing their stars' television identities with their actual ones. Among the middle classes where it was still slightly shameful to confess to watching TV soap operas, it was respectable to own up to an addiction to the radio soap opera, *The Archers*. There was a genuine confusion in people's minds about which was real and which was not.

The Prime Minister's own stepmother-in-law (if there can be such a thing) was the actress Pat Phoenix, far better known by her *Coronation Street* name, Elsie Tanner. She provided her services as a campaigner in his first hopeless by-election campaign in Beaconsfield, where she drew far bigger crowds than he did. When a *Coronation Street* character was written out of the series, and said to have retired to the remote village of Cartmel, thousands of 'Street' watchers made weekend pilgrimages to this beauty spot in search of their lost friend. The actor, of course, had not retired or gone anywhere near Cartmel. A group of satirists calling themselves the Archers Anarchists produce a quarterly bulletin whose theme is that 'there is no cast' and that all the characters are real. They are only half-joking.

It is tempting to wonder if there is an alternative Britain somewhere, where all the soap operas meet up. Is there a soap railway on which Soap Virgin Trains can carry people from Coronation Street in Wetherfield to visit friends in Albert Square, in the London Borough of Walford? Is there a soap motorway which can take you to Brookside or Hollyoaks, and a soap telephone network through which all these people can ring each other up? There ought to be, because for tens of millions of people these places, along with Ambridge and Emmerdale and Grange Hill, have become at least as real as life, if not more so. And for some, especially schoolchildren returning to empty homes, mythical suburbs in Australia are more important than real ones in Britain.

For English rural, urban and suburban life has been strangely denatured. People live in places, but are not of them. Communal activities, or even activities which bring people into contact with each other, have died away. Front gardens, once a source of neighbourly competition, are now increasingly concreted over and turned into car parks.

The ebbing of wartime solidarity, the increasing mobility of people so that neighbours changed more often, the way in which almost everyone became car-borne and never left home or arrived there on foot—all these things reduced the opportunity for contact. Then the growth of female full-time work depopulated the suburbs during the day, so that the once-familiar sight of women walking down the road with children became a startling rarity. Incidentally, it also greatly increased the opportunities for burglars, who could count on large areas being completely deserted during the working day. While this was going on, telephone ownership and the spread of hi-fi equipment allowed the millions to have electronic relationships and private electronic entertainment. It was no longer necessary to leave the house and go to the pub or the cinema to get away from each other.

In the affluent 1980s, as millions of children acquired their own televisions and computer games, the house became a self-contained unit with almost no outside needs. Parents, scared either of dangerous traffic or of sexual predators, were afraid to let their children wander physically, so they allowed them to wander mentally instead. They swapped the old dispensation—moral authority, power over ideas and the development of the imagination—for the merely physical power to limit movement. The liberation of children's minds was, in part at least, the price for their loss of physical freedom.

For the television companies, the Soap Opera formula was cheap, predictable and popular with advertisers. With the right sort of publicity and clever storylines, it delivered a large audience of habitual viewers, at the point in the evening where people were deciding which channel to watch.

For the viewers, the formula provided a network of imaginary friends and neighbours who were both more interesting and less demanding than they would have been in real life. For the schoolchildren, there was *Grange Hill,* for the northerner or the traditionalist, *Coronation Street,* for the more modern-minded southerner, *EastEnders,* for the middle-class person dreaming of village life while stuck in a pebble-dashed semi, there was *The Archers,* and so on.

And that might have been that, except for the way in which these suburbs of the mind took on a life of their own, and a social agenda. The BBC pioneers who troubled the nation with avant-garde Wednesday Plays, with *Cathy Come Home* and *Up the Junction* and *Poor Cow* and *Edna the Inebriate Woman* back in the 1960s and 1970s must be incredibly jealous of the vast popular audiences reached by these banal, ill-written and cliché-infested little dramas with their mass-produced acting and dreary sets.

Everyone now knows that *The Archers* was originally designed to spread government advice and propaganda among farmers, which may make it the longest-running agitprop series in the world. But radio has a much more limited power than television, since it works in the individual mind, rather than pushing the imagination aside and replacing it with a collective one produced in a studio. Perhaps the first example of social engineering by television was a BBC early-evening series, *The Newcomers,* which dealt with the tensions between long-standing residents of a town and the 'newcomers', then rather insultingly known as London overspill, who had started to move into new housing estates nearby. In the mid-1960s, this reflected a huge migration out of the big cities to the semi-rural suburbs (dealt with in Chapter Four) and perhaps allowed some people to see their difficulties as part of a larger problem.

But this was nothing compared to the new wave of social realist soap operas pioneered by the genius of the genre, Liverpudlian Phil Redmond. His first successful invention was *Grange Hill,* the unending saga of life at a suburban secondary school. Redmond, a 1970s sociology graduate, was one of the first children to go through a comprehensive education. This is something he has since complained about, saying, 'I was a social experiment, which I wasn't pleased to be. I came out at 17, factory fodder assigned to the scrapheap, and fought my way back.'

Grange Hill began in 1978, and must have formed the early world-view of millions of schoolchildren. The setting is London outskirts, more east than west, multicultural, multiracial and with inmates described as 'streetwise', the modern word for 'sly and knowing'. From the moment it began it was attacked by the sort of people TV programmers *want* to be attacked by. Mary Whitehouse quickly condemned it for undermining teachers' authority, which of course it did. In 1980, an official of the National Association of Schoolmasters—then a far more conservative organization than its current incarnation—said: 'The teachers come out as buffoons and all we see are strikes and sit-ins, larceny and violence.' The *Daily Telegraph* said the programme encouraged bad manners and discouraged scholarship. It was also disliked for making Estuary English—the universal classless patois of southern England—widely fashionable. None of these criticisms, of course, had the slightest effect. The ratings were good. Television's regulators are powerless against the mere spreading of attitudes, even though those attitudes ultimately make it possible for programme-makers to go on to break important barriers against bad language, violence and sexual display.

There were also plenty of people ready to praise the programme, and to make use of it. To them, it 'tackled' social issues, mainly those dear to the hearts of the cultural revolutionaries: racism, drug abuse, teenage pregnancy, disability and AIDS. *Grange Hill* regularly benefited from bouts of Fleet Street outrage, such as the 'sexy chat in the girls' toilets' in January 1990. One girl talked lewdly about her relationship with a boy, another confessed to sleeping with an older man, whereupon her friend advised her to take 'precautions'. Criticisms from Mrs Whitehouse simply bounced off, and one of the actors, Rene Zagger, then sixteen, told her and others, 'Lay off us. We are serving a purpose. We are dealing with realistic situations which youngsters face. It's wrong that we've come under fire for covering realistic issues just because we have young viewers.' And they are young. *Grange Hill* at its peak was watched by three-quarters of children between eight and eleven years old. Its supposedly realistic style was copied by others hoping for the same sort of ratings.

The Home Office openly used the series, suggesting a sto-ryline about a stabbing in the playground—following the national knife panic and new laws which illogically resulted from the stabbing of a London comprehensive school head-master, Philip Lawrence. This was by no means the only exam-ple of blatant social engineering by soap opera. One *Grange Hill* character, Zammo, was turned by the scriptwriters into a heroin addict and a criminal over two years. The mother of one *Grange Hill* child was infected with AIDS through a blood transfusion, so that the child could then be subjected to per-secution and made to have an HIV test. The BBC said: 'We hope the story will help shatter some of the prejudice and igno-rance surrounding AIDS', a task which might have been harder if the victim had contracted the disease through the more usual and more morally tricky routes such as sharing dirty syringes. No wonder Phil Redmond has said, 'Every lobby group in the country wants to be in *Grange Hill*.'

Every lobby, that is, except for those who would like Britain to return to the older order. It is hard to imagine the produc-tion team including a storyline which attacked abortion, sug-gested homosexuality was wrong, or urged teenage girls to 'just say no' to sex, let alone one which focused on the prob-lems of a clever child from a poor family who has been forced to go to Grange Hill because the government has abolished grammar schools and Assisted Places scholarships.

As to the effect of this on the young mind, Jeremy Etting-hausen made a frightening point in a fascinating retrospective on twenty years of *Grange Hill* in the *Daily Telegraph*:

> For many of those who have grown up with the show, mem-ories of their own schooldays are distorted by school life as depicted in *Grange Hill*—a testament to the realism of the show. The whack of a classmate's ruler on the back of the hand while teacher's back is turned, self-conscious paranoia in the changing rooms, a rashly uttered phrase that leads to a nickname that sticks—did these things actually happen to

us, or are we suffering from *Grange Hill*-induced false memory syndrome? The programme shadowed and guided us through childhood and adolescence, and its influence lingers.

Or as Keats might have put it, 'Do I wake or sleep?' There can be few better descriptions of the way in which television invades the private portion of the human mind, substituting its own ideas and even memories for genuine ones, so subtly that we can no longer be sure which is which. Both Huxley, who warned of sleep-teaching in *Brave New World,* and Orwell, whose two-way telescreens observed us as we watched them, failed to predict the far more insidious form of mind control which we have inflicted upon ourselves without any need for Fordism or Big Brother. We welcome into our homes the machines that vacuum the thoughts out of our heads and pump in someone else's. John Berger in *Ways of Seeing* said that television advertisers succeeded by persuading viewers to envy themselves as they would be if they bought the product. These programmes do something similar, by persuading the viewer to envy himself as he would be if his life were that little bit more exciting and melodramatic than it actually is. They can make things seem normal that are not.

But, oddly enough, they often fail to make the positive moral points that their defenders cite in their defence. The Broadcasting Standards Council in November 1990 found that children, in particular, just viewed the scenes in front of them as a neutral reality. They could not identify the 'goodies' and the 'baddies' and were confused when a policeman turned out to be a criminal and when a school caretaker took to thieving. The same survey found that children as young as three were watching programmes such as the Australian serial *Neighbours,** and that six- and seven-year-olds did not realize the characters were being played by actors.

Each of the successful soap operas takes place somewhere reasonably accessible to the rest of us, a comfortable village, a small close, a street or square with a pub and a shop. For many of us these things are nostalgic images of life as it used to be. There are very few Coronation Streets left in our northern cities, and most of the sort of people pictured in Albert Square would long ago have headed off to the Essex suburbs. The soap opera suburbs of the mind are more settled, more interesting, more sociable than anything we find in real life—not least because the scriptwriters cannot very well show people doing what they do most of the time: watching the *television* or exposing themselves to deafening noise of one kind or another. The Queen Vic and the Rovers' Return would be useless settings if the clientele were listening to rock music or watching Sky Sports with blank expressions on their faces.

Having created this idealized network of imaginary friends and places, the producers and writers can move things in many different directions, provided they do not go too far. *Brookside* upset many viewers in its early days because the characters used too much bad language. Phil Redmond immediately toned it down. Yet the same programme has featured a mercy-killing by suffocation, lesbian kissing and incest between a brother and sister. As Anna Pukas wrote in the *Express* in 1997, 'In *EastEnders* and *Brookside,* the taboos fell thick and fast. Drug addiction, male and female homosexuality, incest, child abuse—sometimes it seemed as though the writers had been told to churn out scripts on Perversion of the Month.' The actress in the incest scenes found herself receiving strange looks from passers-by, and was once shouted at by a man on the London Underground, who reproached her: 'Hey, you're the one who's bonking her brother, aren't you?' Did he think she had really committed incest with her brother? At least part of him probably did, enough for him to think differently about a subject which had probably never crossed his mind before.

The incest storyline—which ended, predictably, with an abortion—also attracted two million extra viewers to *Brookside,* and provoked forty complaints. It is hard to imagine what

variety of perversion could work the same trick for the programme. For the problem with taboos is that once broken,
they are well and truly destroyed. They do not linger for long,
and what seemed abnormal and even horrifying a few years
ago rapidly becomes usual, even dull. The British 1960s film
Victim, about the blackmail problems faced by respectable
homosexuals, must seem incomprehensible to anyone under
forty-five, who has no memory of times when homosexuality
was openly and unashamedly viewed with the sort of contempt
and disgust now reserved for paedophilia.

How deliberate is all this? The actress Sophie Langham
was recruited to *EastEnders* to take part in its lesbian kiss
scene in 1994. She was spotted by a casting agent when she
appeared in a stage play called *The Year of the Family.* Sophie
described this play as being 'about incest and weird family
antics. In the play I had to put my hand up my skirt and fon-
dle my breasts.' It is telling that this is the kind of production
which mainstream soap operas trawl for their cast and, perhaps, their ideas.

And what ideas they are: A plane crashed onto fictional
Emmerdale, shamelessly cashing in on the Lockerbie disaster.
Brookside's six houses suffered nineteen deaths in the course
of twelve years. When *EastEnders* had its first AIDS victim
she was a heterosexual who didn't use drugs and who managed to pass the infection on to her husband, an event as
unlikely as a hurricane in Hackney. When the programme
decided it needed a rape case, the victim was subjected to an
offensive police interrogation, long after such behaviour was
abandoned by the real police. In *Coronation Street,* residents
were made to undergo the arrival in their midst of a male-to-
female transsexual, who was denied access to the ladies' loo
at work by cruel prejudice. By a strange and thought-provok-
ing paradox, this person was played by a female actor, subtly
suggesting that a switch from one sex to the other really is possible. The storyline was immediately praised by a Labour MP,

who suggested it would help to win full civil rights for trans-sexuals, full civil rights meaning the ability to alter the facts on their birth certificates.

The pattern in all these events is the same: Behaviour which was once deviant is made to seem mainstream, or at least acceptable, and those who are unhappy about it are portrayed as narrow-minded, old-fashioned, prejudiced and wrong. The effect of this implicit propaganda upon public opinion has been enormous, causing many people to be ashamed of views they had held since their childhood and had thought until recently were normal.

The Archers' village of Ambridge seems to have fallen under some sort of Biblical curse, with spouse-beating, racial harass-ment, outed homosexuals (who of course emerge as heroes, as their persecutors are shamed) and the appointment of a female parson, all in the course of a matter of months. Middle-aged Tory farmers are also made to speak in metric measurements which they would never normally use. Critics have rightly pointed out that the village of Ambridge is no longer really rural, and has become a suburb—a suburb which just happens to be in the middle of some of the last unspoiled countryside in England.

The editor of the programme, Vanessa Whitburn, is just as much a creature of the new culture as Phil Redmond. She has said, 'I have sought to capitalise on increased realism, and sharpen the focus of the drama.' And she criticized her far-less-political predecessor, Jack Smethurst, for seeing the pro-gramme 'primarily as social comedy' with a lighter anecdotal side. Defending herself, she said: 'Just think of the debates sparked off by the strong storylines of the past few years; the imprisonment of Susan Carter, Elizabeth's decision to have an abortion ... the racist attack on Usha Gupta.'

Jack Smethurst derided the new programme as having been taken over by feminists. He, and many listeners, were confused to find their familiar landscape suddenly peopled with tractor-driving wimmin and softy new men, as well as an unlikely Asian female lawyer, who seems to have moved into the BBC's best-loved midlands village solely so that she could be the victim of a racial attack. Conservative characters have as usual been portrayed as either old or stupid or vicious or insensitive.

Ms Whitburn believes, tellingly, that 'single women are much more interesting dramatically than dull married ones', and admits to having killed off one male character to 'liberate' his wife. She once declared her colours thus: 'To be PC (politically correct) is really to be moral. It is having a correct moral stance. PC is, in fact, my moral plank. I don't think that wishy-washy liberal ideology works any more.'

She has also said, 'Drama always has to move you to make you think, and distress you for a purpose.' It is a phrase which sums up well the attitude of many of her rivals in Britain's huge and ever-spreading soap opera industry, whose task seems to be to provide the millions with a substitute for real life, one which helps to accustom them to a new social order, which will seem less distressing because they have already been so thoroughly distressed in the imagination of their hearts.

Ms Whitburn is unique in having provoked real resistance and resentment among existing listeners. When *Coronation Street* was seriously revamped, there was nothing like the wave of objections which followed the changes in Ambridge. Perhaps this is because, uniquely, *The Archers* is a radio series and each listener has his or her own strong personal vision of what the fictional Ambridge is like. Perhaps it is because the BBC Radio Four audience has been among the slowest to adapt to the new culture. But whatever the reason, their objections failed to make any impact upon the programme, which went on to provide Ambridge with a homosexual pub landlord, the better to expose the outdated prejudices of country folk. Who cares if it is unlikely, or that it destroys an innocent entertainment for a few hundred thousand people?

THIRTEEN

The Pill That Cured Morality

H E SHOULD BE NEXT TO Lenin, Mao Zedong, Gandhi and Freud, in the dubious pantheon of men who changed the world for better or worse this century. But most people have never even heard of Gregory 'Goody' Pincus, inventor of the female contraceptive pill, nor of his two patrons, Margaret Sanger and Katharine Dexter McCormick. This bizarre trio did more to alter the post-war world for ever than anyone else. Because Britain had been such a sexually puritanical society, the effects of their discovery may well have been greater in this country than anywhere else on earth.

In fact, it is reasonable to suggest that the strange mood which swept through the richer countries in 1968 is mainly the result of their discovery. In so many fields, people now say 'It was never the same after 1968', which just happens to have been the year by which use of the female contraceptive pill had become accepted and universal enough to affect individual behaviour. Older ideas could not survive side by side with the new ones. In 1966, Paul Jones of Manfred Mann could sing 'I'm hers, she's mine, wedding bells are going to chime' in the top twenty hit *Dooh wah Diddy*, for along with almost all the other bands of the age, they still treated marriage as the end of courtship. Thirty years later, The Beautiful South sang a rather different tune, *Don't Marry Her,* **** *Me,* a highly popular hymn of hate against the married state. Pincus and his invention made this change possible. He may even have desired it himself, and his allies certainly did.

Margaret Sanger, like her British equivalent Marie Stopes, was a highly scandalous figure in her early life, as she campaigned for the cause of contraception, against what she saw as Protestant puritanical prudery and Catholic dogma. One of her friends, Mabel Dodge, explained that Mrs Sanger's beliefs went much further than a mere desire for limiting families.

> It was she who introduced us all to the idea of Birth Control and it, along with other related ideas about sex, became her passion. It was as if she had been more or less arbitrarily chosen by the powers that be to voice a new gospel of not only sex-knowledge in regard to contraception, but sex-knowledge about copulation and its intrinsic importance. She was the first person I ever knew who was openly an ardent propagandist for the joys of the flesh. This, in those days, was radical indeed. . . . Margaret Sanger personally set out to rehabilitate sex.

She was also a genetic fascist, urging the gradual elimination of weaker and handicapped people, favouring sterilization of the unfit and advocating the exile of unwanted people to special supervised farms. She spoke of creating a 'race of thoroughbreds', language which in the post-Hitler era seems shocking but which was quite common among the socialist rationalists of the time, who believed that man could perfect himself. The enthusiastic, indeed passionate adoption of such ideas by the Nazis caused Mrs Sanger and her allies to soften their tone. (The term 'Birth Control', for instance, was dropped in favour of 'Family Planning'.) But there is no doubt that they were social revolutionaries, just as certain of their rightness as any Marxist–Leninist Commissar or National Socialist storm-trooper.

Like many such world reformers, she was a libertine bundle of trouble in her personal life, perhaps hoping to bring other people to her level so as to feel less alone. When, in 1913, her marriage began to break up, she acted accordingly. David Halberstam, in his study of the American 1950s, gives an extraordinary account of this driven and outrageous woman and her role in the sexual revolution. He says:

> She wanted to put theory into practice regarding greater sexual freedom, but Bill Sanger did not. She increasingly began to regard him as a bore and even suggested that he take a mistress. He was appalled. 'I am an anarchist, true, but I am also a monogamist. And if that makes me a conservative, then I am a conservative', he protested.

At one point she fled the country and went to Europe to have an affair with sexologist Havelock Ellis. Facing prosecution for illegally distributing contraceptives, she went to the journalist John Reed for help. Reed, who would become famous for his wide-eyed admiration of the Bolshevik revolution in his book *Ten Days That Shook the World,* became Margaret Sanger's spin-doctor. He advised her to have her picture taken in a Quaker collar, with her two sons at her side. This misleading portrait, of an apparently pure and lovely woman with her young, won the public's heart and forced the prosecution to abandon the case.

Mrs Sanger would never quite become respectable, but from then on she met increasing success, helped by the heavy-handed response of America's Catholic hierarchy to her activities. When New York's Catholic Archbishop persuaded the police to shut down one of her meetings, outraging American feelings about free speech, Mrs Sanger said, 'It was no longer my lone fight. It was now a battle of a republic against the machinations of the hierarchy of the Roman Catholic Church.'

In 1948, Mrs Sanger got into touch with an old friend, Katharine McCormick, a woman so rich that her lawyers said she 'couldn't spend the interest on her interest'. She provided large sums to Mrs Sanger to support her campaign, but was very specific about the sort of projects she wanted to help. They had to put women thoroughly in control, freeing them from what she viewed as the tyranny of motherhood. When, in 1958, a scientist mentioned the possibility of a *male* contraceptive to her, McCormick told Sanger: 'He was rather shocked when I told him I didn't give a hoot about a male contraception, that only female research interested me.' Much later, when the pill was close to public launch, Mrs McCormick confided to a female colleague that her deep desire was to separate the sex urge from reproduction, and hinted rather strongly at lesbian feelings, which would be a logical extension of this view. She may have been influenced by the fact that her immensely wealthy husband was schizophrenic, and she feared she would pass the disease on to her children.

The two women, Sanger with her passion and McCormick with her millions, made contact with Gregory Pincus in 1950, when he was already famous for his test-tube fertilization of rabbit eggs. (The *New York Times* ran an alarmist headline about his work that now seems rather prophetic: RABBITS BORN IN GLASS; HALDANE–HUXLEY FANTASY MADE REAL BY HARVARD BIOLOGISTS.)

From this work, he began to suspect that hormones could be used to control fertility. But big business was at first not specially interested in Pincus's Worcester Foundation, where the key research was carried out, so money was short. According to David Halberstam, Pincus was cautious when the two women first approached him with offers of assistance. However, he quickly warmed to this work. His task was made far easier by the recent discovery that the hormone progesterone, once rare and costly, was easily extracted from wild yams which grew in the Mexican desert. Through the early 1950s, work progressed on methods of fooling the body into thinking it was pregnant, Pincus's chosen course. He even enlisted a prominent Catholic doctor, John Rock, to the project, believing that this would give it respectability and make it acceptable to conservative medics and scientists. As Mrs Sanger said, 'Being a good R.C., and as handsome as a God, he can get away with anything.'

In 1954, the first three women guinea-pigs were given Pincus's pill but not as a contraceptive. Rock, whose Catholic views weakened in these years, wanted to use progesterone to *help* couples have babies, rather than stop them, and quickly found that the hormone did this rather successfully. Then, in April 1956, contraceptive tests were carried out on a hundred women in San Juan, Puerto Rico. From then on, progress was astonishingly rapid. The U.S. Food and Drug Administration licensed the pill Enovid to treat miscarriages in 1957. In May 1960, the FDA approved Enovid as a contraceptive. Within three years, 2.3 million American women were taking it, and it was a worldwide force, surging through the lives of every family in the Western world. One prominent American woman campaigner for sexual equality, Clare Booth Luce, declared triumphantly: 'Modern woman is at last free as a man is free, to dispose of her own body, to earn her living, to pursue the improvement of her mind, to try a successful career.'

She might also have said that the balance of power between the sexes had been destabilized, and relations between mothers and their children transformed from a natural and accepted one to a mere option. The enormous implications of Dr Pincus's pill were still unclear. It would take thirty years more before they would fully reveal themselves in this country.

Before the pill, women had a powerful argument against sex before marriage. Virginity was not just a fanciful ideal, but a wise precaution. In Kingsley Amis's 1960 pre-pill novel *Take a Girl Like You*, Jenny Bunn uses all her wit and wiles to fight off the insistent Patrick Standish and his incessant demands for sex. The conversation will have a ring of truth for anyone who came to adolescence before the pill was readily available. It will be archaic for anyone brought up in the post-pill Pincus era:

'You are a sweet little thing. You've got a lovely face and a lovely figure. And beautiful colouring. You're an absolute little smasher.'

'Thank you,' Jenny said in the voice of a bus-conductor going round for the fares. . . .

He took hold of her again, and in less than a minute was back at the stage where she had taken his wrist. He seemed to think that by saying what he had just said, or even by going on talking as long as that, he had altered everything, he had shown that what he was trying to do was much more harmless, much more important in one way and much less in another, than what he had been trying to do before. She took his wrist again. 'I think we came round this way about an hour ago,' she said.

'Oh, please.'

'No please,' she shifted her position to a more upright one.

'Oh but please ... honestly, I won't do anything ...'

'I know all about you and your won't do anything. I've read about you in books.'

Later on, things get more philosophical:

'I can't see it, Jenny, honestly. Why wouldn't you go on? I wouldn't have shocked you or anything, would I? And I'd have—you know, taken care of ... You'd have had a lovely time.'

'Yes, I know I would. It's not that I wasn't tempted.'

'Then what the hell is it? You religious or something?'

'Patrick, please don't say it in that sneering way. No, I'm not particularly religious, if you want to know. I haven't been near a church for months. It's just that I don't believe in this—whatever you call it—this free-and-easy way of going on.'

Then Patrick gets to the point:

'Right, now shall I tell you why you feel like that? I'm not being sneering now, I promise you. It's because you've had the kind of upbringing—very excellent in its way, I'm not saying anything against it—but it's the kind with the old idea of girls being virgins when they get married behind it. Well, that was perfectly sensible in the days when there wasn't any birth control and they thought they could tell when a girl wasn't a virgin. Nowadays they know they can't so every-thing's changed. You're not running any risk at all. But you've had that kind of upbringing, and that's why you feel like this. Do you see? It's just your training.'

'Maybe it is, but that doesn't make any odds to me. I just don't care why I think what I do, it doesn't change any-thing. What about why you think what you do? There must be reasons for that too.'

'The difference is that I haven't got my ideas from any-one else, I've thought them out for myself.'

Patrick's view, that his ideas are freethinking and uncon-ventional, is wonderfully typical of the sexual left, who have always acted as if they were dissident free spirits making their own minds up, rather than succumbing to the most basic prim-itive hedonism, crude desire rationalized, the conformism which existed everywhere before religion and civilized ethics rose up and fought against it. Jenny, on the other hand, has no rational argument against Patrick. She is 'not particularly religious', because by the late 1950s that has become rather a shameful, ridiculous thing to be.

If anyone doubts the hatred that the sexual liberals and cultural radicals felt for Christianity, they should read the words of Virginia Woolf, Queen of Bloomsbury, describing in a letter to Vanessa Woolf, 11 February 1928, a meeting with T. S. Eliot soon after he became an Anglican:

I have had a most shameful and distressing interview with dear Tom Eliot who may be called dead to us all from this day forward. He has become an Anglo-Catholic believer in God and immortality and goes to church. I was shocked. A corpse would seem to me more credible than he is. I mean there's something obscene in a living person sitting by the fire and believing in God.

That hatred was watered down among people such as Kingsley Amis and the educated, literary characters he wrote about, but was still strong enough to make Jenny, a north-country primary school teacher, unsure and embarrassed about her childhood faith.

Patrick, in a way, is right. Jenny is continuing to act as if she lived in a Christian world, when it has in fact been dismantled some time before. Sooner or later, thanks to contraception, girls of her sort will come round and give in. But the contraceptive sheath, relying on male good behaviour and competence, is not quite convincing enough. Had there been an effective pill which Jenny could have taken, this scene would have ended quite differently. She would then have had at least the impression that she was in control, though it would have been Patrick who really benefited from her supposed freedom. But we are still in the pre-Pincus fifties, and the episode finishes with a chaste kiss and 'I really think I'd better be getting back, sweet'.

Patrick wouldn't have needed to 'get back' if he had been born a few years later. The whole power of morality, and indeed of parents, was about to be shattered.

Valerie Riches, one of the most persistent critics of the new morality, says:

> In the 1960s, arguments were put forward by the Family Planning Association that making contraception available to the unmarried would reduce illegitimate pregnancies, an argument subsequently taken up by the abortion law reformers. On the contrary, rising figures of illegitimate pregnancies and abortions followed the easy availability of

contraception and abortion. So the propaganda line became that a *free* contraceptive service would reduce the number of abortions. Pressure on Parliament culminated in the passing of the National Health (Reorganization) Act 1973. This made birth control services available to *all,* including children.

Soon afterwards, the Health Department issued a memorandum saying that the parents of a child of whatever age should not be contacted without the child's permission. Victoria Gillick, in a famous legal action, briefly persuaded the courts to overrule this for girls under the age of sixteen, the legal age of consent. Despite false claims of suicides among young girls and predictions of an epidemic of unwanted babies, the brief months when doctors were obliged to consult parents were statistically little different from the rest of the year. In December 1984 the Law Lords voted by three to two to over-rule parents' rights, and since then doctors have been permitted to prescribe the pill to under-age girls without asking their parents, if they thought it justified (they almost always did). In Scotland, there are even fewer conditions, and in December 1998, Boots the Chemists in Glasgow began a pilot scheme to give morning-after pills to under-age girls. It seemed likely that something similar would soon exist in England and Wales. The attitude of the birth controllers was well demonstrated in an FPA publication *Learning to Live with Sex,* published as long ago as 1972: 'All these places (birth control clinics etc.) will treat your problems sympathetically and not tell your parents unless you want them to know.'

In an account of a Brook Advisory Centre for unmarried girls, published in *Just Seventeen* magazine on 15 April 1987, an official is quoted as saying: 'We are not here to say "tut, tut", we are here to help, so if we think a girl is at risk of getting pregnant and she seems responsible enough to make decisions for herself, we will always be able to assist her. Whatever happens, her parents would not be told.'

The family planning enthusiasts do not seem to have any real minimum age for their advice to begin. Sex education programmes are often designed for children in primary schools, and many others start at the age of eleven. One Family Planning Association leaflet *You Can Be Any Age to Ask for Advice* carries little pictures of teddy bears on it. In answer to the question 'When is the right age to have sex?' the leaflet replies cautiously, but interestingly:

> There's no 'right age'. If you believed everything you read or heard, you'd think that everybody is 'doing it'. It's not true. The average age when people first have sex is 17, but you're not unusual if you wait until you're older—many people do.
>
> Don't feel you should have sex just because all your friends say they are. You may want to be one of the gang but what's right for *you* is what's important here. Sex before you're ready or with the wrong person can leave you feeling bad. If you have any doubts or you think you'll regret it, why not wait?

The advice to wait is admirable, but is entirely *ad hoc* and subjective. The only basis of choice is how you 'feel', or 'expect to feel'. And of course, peer pressure, drink, drugs or mere mood can influence feelings enormously. Without a clear moral rule about when sexual intimacy is right, and when it is wrong, the poor inexperienced teenager, or even twelve-year-old, is left with nothing to guide her but an unreliable and inconsistent 'feeling' which could well be misleading.

And even this carefully written let-out is contradicted by everything else in the leaflet, which is entirely devoted to methods of contraception, including the morning-after pill, and to details of venereal diseases. The only imaginable bad consequences of promiscuous sex, it implies, are unwanted pregnancy or an infection. The potential emotional and moral damage cannot of course be dealt with through a pill, or contained in a condom, or aborted.

One of the most startling things about the liberal policy is that it continues to fail, yet is never seriously questioned. Despite frequent claims by the FPA that it aims to reduce the numbers of abortions, these continue to hover round the 150,000-a-year mark. Some experts believe that contraception actually increases the demand for abortion, because it raises the expectation that sex will not result in birth, and so persuades disappointed users of failed contraceptives to choose abortion without much further thought. They have already accepted that sexual intercourse does not and should not lead to a baby. The idea that they are going to have one therefore seems unjust, even outrageous. The numbers of under-age pregnancies continue to rise, though the increasing use of the morning-after pill—an abortion in all but name—is likely to bring them down or level them off in time.

The Netherlands is often cited as following a policy of enlightened sex education, but the story is more complicated than that. Denmark, with similar policies on education, has a far higher level of illegitimate births. Two different forces operate to reduce the illegitimate birth-rate in the Netherlands. In urban areas, where church and family are weaker, there is widespread use of the morning-after pill, and of a form of abortion known as 'menstrual extraction', which does not show up in abortion totals because it can be carried out in unlicensed clinics which are not obliged to report their activities. But the Netherlands also has other important special features: a larger number of stay-at-home mothers than most Continental countries, and a church-going, village-based rural culture which still disapproves strongly of unmarried motherhood.

Meanwhile in Britain, the failure of the sex education lobby does not seem to have upset it, or persuaded it to change its tune. It continues to expand and grow in respectability, wealth and power. And occasionally it gives a glimpse of its deeper beliefs.

Lady Helen Brook is the founder of the Brook Advisory Centres which dispense contraceptive advice to the unmarried, now that the state has taken over the job of giving contraception to the married. She wrote to *The Times* on 16 February 1980: 'From birth till death it is now the privilege of the parental state to take major decisions—objective, unemotional, the state weighs up what is best for the child.'

And what the state seems to have decided is that the child is best guided into a world where sex is treated as a recreation, its link with parenthood and responsibility forgotten. This also means that the state must also be neutral between competing forms of sex-play. The anus and the vagina, equally sterile thanks to powerful drugs, equally 'safe' thanks to heavy-duty condoms, are now just alternative orifices in which we seek or receive pleasure.

An FPA Primary School Workbook of 1993 maintains:

> Many children know their parents are not married, and may have parents who are single, divorced, lesbian or gay. Rather than discussing relationships within the context of marriage, talk about commitment and the specialness of a sexual relationship. However, you should point out that in some cultures and religions, marriage is required before two people have a sexual relationship. This approach offers them a balanced view.

Of course, it is not balanced. It is neutral between marriage and non-marriage. Its authors would no doubt say that it was 'preaching' to suggest that marriage was better than cohabiting. But they do not accept that stripping marriage of its privileged position is also preaching—immoral preaching if you like, but purposeful and effective preaching for all that.

In a survey of local authority sex education policies Paul Atkin recorded:

> All sex education guides studied were implicitly hostile to the view that the two-parent family based on marriage was the best possible place for children to grow and develop.

Writers of many Local Education Authority syllabuses go to imaginative and often ridiculous lengths to avoid references to traditional family life.

Although 72% of children live with their two married parents and only 1% live with neither, some sex educators appear to be writing for a generation of orphans and go to great lengths to avoid the word parent.

Guidelines from the National Curriculum, drawn up by an ostensibly Conservative government, described children as living with 'important adults'. Atkin added:

Most guidelines relegate the nuclear family to one option among many 'different types of family', giving the impression that it does not matter if you have one parent or two. This defies both common sense and all the evidence which shows that the real family has no equivalent. Despite this, many LEAs begin relationship reductionism early, between the ages of five and seven, when it is difficult for children to cope with any implied criticism of their home arrangements.

Some authorities refer to marriage as 'a ritual', and it is often only mentioned in connection with divorce. In another example of immoral preaching, Atkin notes that 'While bisexuality, homosexuality, fetishism, lesbianism, masturbation and pornography all feature in Oxfordshire's "ABC of sex education", chastity, fidelity, right and wrong do not.'

There is also propaganda against 'sexual stereotyping'. Atkin says, 'What is normal is ignored or portrayed as negative, whilst the odd, unusual or unlikely are held up as something to aspire to.' Some programmes also suggest that men and women are attracted to each other only because of social pressure, an implicit endorsement of homosexuality as an equal lifestyle choice.

These are all predictable and rational results of separating sex from procreation, procreation from marriage, and pleasure

from duty—separations achieved by contraception so universal it is practically obligatory, and by freely available, destig-
matized abortion. Parents, quite possibly brought up when
different rules applied, are therefore an obstacle to the preaching of the new gospel, and must be brusquely pushed aside at
the earliest opportunity. Instead, the State will thrust itself ever
more deeply and intimately into areas of life once seen as utterly
private.

For instance, many parents will be disturbed to discover
what the FPA considers to be appropriate for children between
seven and eleven years old: '1. Work with a small group of five
or six children. Begin the session by saying the word "masturbation". Ask the children to call out all the words that they
have heard for masturbation. Look at the words and discuss
them.' The teacher is also supposed to explain what masturbation is and to ask pupils to call out all the 'myths and stories'
they have heard about it, presumably in case any of them have
been told that masturbation is not necessarily a good idea.
There is even a sexual activity word puzzle, in which the words
'masturbate', 'gay', 'lick', 'sex', 'intercourse' and 'lesbian' are
mingled with the words 'hug', 'kiss', 'talk' and 'laugh'.

Psychologists are divided about the effect of exposing children of this age to sexual secrets and taboos. But, like so many
of the other influences upon their young lives, this sort of material is bound—if not consciously designed—to break the existing link between parent and child, and to make it impossible
for the older generation to pass on its morals and beliefs.

This is strikingly similar to the modern form of anti-drug
campaigning, increasingly accepted by British authorities as
the only way of combating the astonishing level of narcotic
abuse among school-age children. The alternative amoral
method, warning of the physical dangers, has largely failed.
The 'Heroin Screws You Up' poster campaign, showing sickly
heroin users, became a cult fashion item because of the unintended glamour it gave to heroin abuse. The miserable death

of Leah Betts and some others, after taking Ecstasy, failed to persuade most teenagers that there was any serious risk. So 'harm reduction' became a more and more favoured option.

This approach assumes that the young will take drugs, dignifying the act with terms such as 'experimenting', though few are thought to take notes of these experiments. It then suggests ways in which this may be done 'safely', an approach taken to its limits in the output of the Manchester-based organization 'Lifeline'—but also endorsed by the government itself. In licensing legislation approved for Scotland in 1997, ministers inserted a requirement that certain types of clubs provide supplies of water and 'chill-out' areas, facilities which could only be of use to people who had been taking the dance drug Ecstasy. This was the first open acceptance of officially illegal narcotics in any UK law, but it was reflected in the unofficial policies of many UK police forces, to prosecute only when drug users were also selling narcotics. Drug use was not itself wrong, but damaging your body was, and selling an illegal substance was. In most cases, the offence of possession was met with no more than a 'caution', police jargon for 'doing nothing at all'.

The parallel with the approach to sex is not accidental. The only serious arguments against drug-taking, especially among the well-off middle class who can often (but not always) cope with a certain amount of drug use without too many harmful effects, are moral ones. But there is no universally accepted moral code, so people take drugs and nobody—including the law—disapproves. Therefore the authorities, adopting a joshing and matey tone, seek to mingle with the young, trying to speak their language, with purely practical advice. They may take it or not, as they choose. If they do not, then medical treatment, water, chill-out zones and counsellors will be available for drug abusers, just as pills and abortions and counsellors will be provided for the promiscuous.

By doing this, in both cases, the state defies the will of most parents, who generally take a much harder line on these issues.

Worse than that, it makes itself responsible for their children's welfare *whether the parents wish this to happen or not.* It does not offer a choice when it preaches its gospel of practical containment, for this gospel is not tolerant of rival views. Those who want to use other arguments, especially moral ones, soon find that their messages are incompatible with the official line.

If the new system worked, this argument would be simpler—a choice between an old-fashioned morality, which had cruelly restricted human pleasure and had been rendered obsolete by science, and a new system of ethics which increased the sum of human happiness. But it does not work. Unwanted pregnancies, sexual disease, and the sad consequences of drug abuse continued to grow throughout the last three decades of the century. Yet neither government, nor family planners, nor educators, retreated one inch from their positions. On the contrary, they insisted that they had not been given enough freedom, and sought to expose children to their propaganda at ever younger ages, and in more and more shocking forms. When these fail, it may well be too late to re-establish what went before. But that is what the cultural revolution wanted all along, the complete, irrevocable destruction of the inconvenient, embarrassing restraints which reached out of the past, whatever the cost might be. We are all free now.

FOURTEEN

Health Warning

S MOKING AND BUGGERY can both kill you, by exposing you
to diseases you would not otherwise get. If homosexual
acts were as common as smoking we would have to bury the
victims in mass graves, because AIDS slays so much faster than
cancer, heart disease or emphysema, and carries away the young
as well as the old and middle-aged. Smoking and homosexuality are also actions of choice, except in rare cases of rape.
There is no scientific evidence supporting the dangers of second-
hand smoking, though they are widely believed in by anti-
tobacco fanatics. Both activities are considered to be pleasures
by those who do them, though their delights are a mystery to
those who do not do them. Yet, despite these parallels, modern Britain treats them almost as opposites.

Cigarette smokers are blamed for their illnesses, and doctors occasionally threaten to withhold treatment from persistent offenders who have carried on with their unpleasant
habit despite having to suffer amputations and other hideous
consequences. Homosexuals and drug addicts are not, however, blamed for becoming HIV-positive. On the contrary, the
authorities will go to almost any lengths to avoid saying that
intravenous drug use and anal intercourse are the actions most
likely to lead to this devastating illness. A doctor who refused

to treat a promiscuous homosexual, on the grounds that he had brought his problems on himself and was continuing to do so, would be ostracized by his profession and probably hounded from his job. None has dared do so.

Far from concentrating their warnings on homosexuals, the government foster propaganda suggesting that the whole population is at risk, and make much of exceptional victims, such as haemophiliacs, who have been infected through no action or fault of their own. As for drug addicts, once despised and treated as wrongdoers, they too 'benefit' from the hedonism of the new ruling élite, which has no moral objection to drug-taking among its own members, and must therefore indulge it among the masses as well. Such people are increasingly treated not as offenders against the moral and legal code, but as victims of evil 'pushers', suffering from a disabling disease and therefore not to be condemned. In visitors' waiting rooms at Her Majesty's prisons, menacing signs warning of drug searches sit side by side with leaflets containing advice on how to obtain clean needles with which to inject illegal drugs. Television soap operas, as I point out elsewhere, have also been used to suggest that non-drug-using heterosexuals can and do contract AIDS. Of course they can, but it would be unlikely and atypical. Frequently, there are other factors which explain this, but which often do not emerge.

The disease AIDS is treated as a public enemy, in some way to be blamed for existing at all, and its foes wear red ribbons on their lapels to demonstrate their sympathy with its victims and their desire for a cure to be the first and most urgent target of medical science. In contrast, the very idea of ribbons to show 'awareness' of lung cancer, heart disease and emphysema is absurd. It is universally accepted that smokers have brought these plagues upon themselves and must change their behaviour if they want our sympathy. Increasingly, in offices, public places and restaurants, smokers are treated as pariahs. People are even denied jobs because they are smokers, and couples who smoke have found difficulty in adopting children. In a famous incident, a (heterosexual) couple who had sexual intercourse in front of fellow passengers on a train were not upbraided or rebuked until they lit up post-coital cigarettes, an act of which everyone could disapprove. Smokers are never encouraged by the health authorities to indulge in 'safer smoking'; in fact tobacco companies have specifically avoided the promotion of 'safe' or 'safer' cigarettes. All their products carry blood-freezing health warnings, however low the tar. It is true that few now smoke Capstan Full Strength untipped, perhaps the strongest cigarettes still marketed, and only available as a 'ghost brand' in a few specialist outlets. But no health spokesman would ever actually advise smokers to use the low-tar brands. Their unequivocal advice is to give up, as soon as possible. Anything else might well open them up to lawsuits, in an atmosphere where the tobacco industry is assumed to be an evil pedlar of addictive substances. It is interesting that the motor car, another product which will, if used according to manufacturers' instructions, damage the health of its users (mainly by depriving them of necessary exercise), is not targeted in this fashion—yet.

There is not even a hint of disapproval of anal sex or illegal drugs in official or semi-official propaganda about AIDS. Officialdom plainly fears that if it offends, it will lose its audience. Active homosexuals are urged to enjoy 'safe' or 'safer' sex ('safer' is actually less safe than 'safe'—the word was introduced to avoid giving the impression that homosexual acts could ever be totally safe). And drug addicts are advised, through jokey pamphlets such as 'Grandpa Smackhead Jones', published by the Lifeline organization, to ensure that they behave hygienically.

The truly odd thing about this is not that the government and its health quangos have adopted two opposite approaches to two similar public health problems. It is that, despite the fact that these are two of the most outstanding public health campaigns waged by the new establishment, nobody even seems to have noticed that the approaches are contradictory.

The reason why the inconsistency goes unchallenged is that both campaigns are a key part of the cultural revolution, the propagation of a new morality. To examine the contradictions would be to reveal that something disturbing was taking place.

Smoking was the great pleasure of the wartime generation. During a time when death was never far away, when couples were separated, when most pleasures were rationed or simply unavailable, when strain, loneliness, tiredness and danger were ever-present, cigarettes became one of the few solaces available to all. And, as anyone who has been to a war zone will know, they are also a breaker of barriers, something that can be shared even among people who face the same danger but have no common language.

None of this should be taken as a defence of smoking, an ugly, malodorous and expensive habit which undoubtedly hurts many of those who do it, often in deeply unpleasant ways. But it helps to explain why it was so popular, almost universal in fact, among the parents of the 'bulge' generation which was born once the war was over. Incredible as it may now seem, mothers smoked over cradles and in the kitchen, teachers smoked in classrooms, shopkeepers smoked behind the counter, and no-smoking compartments were rarer than smoking compartments on trains. Look at any film made in the 1950s: most of the people in it are smoking, some of them almost the whole time. In novels written at the time, from those of Nevil Shute to those of Margaret Drabble, smoking features as unremarkably as crossing the road or having a cup of coffee. These scenes are true. This is what it was like, even as the evidence grew that the tobacco habit was desperately bad for most people.

By the 1960s, the rising generation were learning to smoke themselves. But, while most working-class and poor children would carry on doing so, the educated and ambitious middle classes would later give up in huge numbers. In some cases, their rejection of smoking was purely to improve their health, while others liked to mock their parents' addiction to one weed as a way of justifying their own taste for a different one.

But it seems likely to me that the decision not to smoke, or to abandon cigarettes, was a declaration of independence similar to, but more lasting than, the growing of hair or the wearing of deliberately unrespectable clothes. It went deeper than these because it involved a refusal to share in the companionship of the cigarette, a social custom of an older generation dating from the war era. And, in a rather nasty way, it was an assertion of superiority over fathers and mothers. Younger generations do this all the time to their parents, but seldom *en masse*. What they were also rejecting was fatalism, the belief that death will come anyway, and that it is worth taking some pleasures even if they are risky—people had *always* known that cigarettes were in some way bad for them, long before scientific research conclusively showed just how bad they were.

Brought up without any serious religious faith or belief in an afterlife, in a world where progress once more appeared to be unstoppable, they felt they owed it to society and themselves to be as healthy as possible. Quite possibly they also sought to remain young as long as possible. Most of the baby-boom generation's pleasures demand either a healthy, youthful body or the appearance of one, and the onset of age is particularly dreadful to them. They are also influenced by the way in which the National Health Service has become a kind of religion substitute. Thus, it is irresponsible to behave in a fashion that might cost the NHS money. In the same way, it is irresponsible to ride a motorbike without wearing a helmet, or to travel in a car without buckling up one's seat belt. The freedom to take risks with one's own life has been undermined by the new belief that others should be responsible for paying for your care if you were injured. In that case, you are obliged to avoid injury or illness as a civic duty. We no longer own our own health. The state owns it and holds it in trust for us, and we have to respond by taking care.

This is a perfectly rational view, though if taken to extremes it becomes dangerously totalitarian. It is possible to see the huge number of abortions, and the increasing pressure for some sort of euthanasia of the old and ill, as part of the same logic: if you are unproductive and a drain on the national resources, you have no absolute right to life. Yet when AIDS first emerged as an identifiable disease, the rule that it was a social duty to preserve and guard your own health—even at the expense of pleasure—suddenly ceased to apply. The authorities did try to be consistent, but simply found it impossible to be honest and open about the real dangers of this highly specific ailment. To begin with, we were warned that we would all die of 'ignorance' in a menacing advertising campaign full of dark images. But even if it had been true that heterosexual promiscuity was just as dangerous as homosexuality or filthy syringes, the government's campaign did not urge us to change the way we were behaving. It just told us to use a condom while we were doing it. Had AIDS been as easy to catch as these advertisements suggested, the country would have been swept by a terrible epidemic despite all the warnings. Condoms would have been poor protection. As almost all the world knows, condoms are unreliable things in the prevention of pregnancy, and there is no reason to think they would have been any better at saving the world from AIDS.

This publicity, then, flew in the face of scientific knowledge. We can only assume that this deliberate avoidance of the truth was meant to avoid offending or 'scapegoating' homosexuals. It also went directly against the experience and practice of the well-established anti-smoking campaign, which had long ago brushed aside such sops to guilt as filter-tips and low-tar brands, demanding nothing less than full and total abstinence.

Why was this? The answer is surprisingly simple. Homosexuality, as an activity, could not be attacked in a society which had accepted heterosexual liberation. Drug-taking could not be attacked in a society whose hedonist new élite had almost all taken drugs for pleasure and still saw nothing wrong in having done so.

The pill had turned heterosexual intercourse into recreation rather than procreation. It had therefore destroyed the practical foundations of all the old moral rules. Once, if girls lost their virginity outside marriage, they could either be 'ruined' or forced into unwanted marriage. If women betrayed their marriage vows, they could find themselves with a baby who was clearly not their husband's. Now, sex was most unlikely to lead to pregnancy, unless the woman deliberately chose that it should do so. Abortion and the older, more cumbersome contraceptive methods had not had this effect. Before, because people expected intercourse to result in pregnancy, they didn't automatically resort to abortion when contraception failed, a failure they didn't find surprising. They were more willing to accept its consequences, less ready to stop something which had already started. The pill removed all these *practical* punishments for promiscuity, and made women much more willing than before to contemplate abortion if for any reason they found themselves expecting an unplanned child.

All that was left to regulate sexual behaviour was a Christian morality that even the Church of England no longer appeared to support.

And now came the awkward part. Logically, there was now no difference between sterile heterosexual sex and sterile homosexual sex. In fact, in some ways, homosexuality was the purest expression of the new doctrine that sex was fun and that we should explore our bodies and experience pleasure as self-fulfilment. Nobody who believed in pre-marital or extramarital sex could object to homosexuality without serious hypocrisy.

This is why the relaxation of laws on homosexuality, first proposed in the 1950s Wolfenden Report, was delayed until the 1960s. Before the pill, the liberalization could not happen because of the distaste most people felt for homosexual acts. After the pill, the governing class *had* to relax the laws, because they were no longer consistent with the national mood or with their own pleasures.

Nothing else, after all, had changed. The majority of people in Britain, as they are now, were uncomfortable about homosexual acts and feared that legalization would lead to popularization. But the liberal élite, whose moral standards had for years been laxer than those of the masses, were nervous and unhappy about enforcing a law which was often pointlessly cruel to people who were gentle and harmless, ruining careers and lives, and leading to much private misery. The moment for change came in February 1966, in Year Two of the Roy Jenkins Era.

The Sexual Offences Act was passed on a wave of tolerance and compassion, intended to lift an awful burden from individuals who were seen as sad victims of a needlessly harsh morality. Most MPs could not see any reason for a law which led frequently to blackmail, a threat vividly portrayed in the successful film *Victim,* in which Dirk Bogarde played a highly respectable, middle-class homosexual whose life was blighted by fear of exposure. Nor were they happy with the cruel effects on the lives of men who were prosecuted, their careers and lives ruined amid shame and embarrassment. It had happened quite recently to a Tory minister, Ian Harvey. The prominent Labour MP and journalist Tom Driberg incessantly risked his reputation with half-crazed excursions into homosexual low-life. Many others, less well-known, took lesser risks. Few in the Commons, as Roy Jenkins had pointed out in *The Labour Case* (1959), disapproved of homosexuality when they met such people in their private lives.

But it was the bill's opponents who saw quite clearly what was really at issue: legalization would lead to social acceptance.

Some of the speeches by opponents and supporters are extraordinarily prophetic. The liberal Tory Humphrey Berkeley promised that the bill's age of consent, twenty-one, would not be lowered, saying: 'It is something to which we attach a great deal of importance.... (Commons Hansard 11.2.1966) ... Adolescence is a period of emotional instability and there protection should be given.... Whatever we might think of the unpleasant nature of the physical acts involved, looking at the problems of homosexuality as a whole, we see that it is the appalling emotional loneliness and frustration which leads to so many mental breakdowns. That is something for which we should offer the protection of society for adolescents.'

It is interesting that even the liberal Berkeley accepted that homosexual acts might be seen as unpleasant, and expected a fair hearing for this view. Any MP making such a statement in today's Commons would be treated with contempt by the majority.

The same conformist majority would simply howl down Sir Cyril Black, who warned that the bill would 'result in a great increase in unnatural vice'.

Sir Cyril inquired, 'Does anyone doubt that if the Bill passes into law, the ink will not long have been dry on the Royal Assent before efforts are made to reduce the age to eighteen or even to sixteen?

'If we pass the Bill, we are in the eyes of adolescent boys and young men putting the offence on much the same level as other offences which are subject to an age limit, such as smoking or drinking.' Little could he have known that thirty years later there would be proposals to make the minimum age for smoking higher than the minimum age for homosexual acts.

Sir Cyril undoubtedly spoke for a large number of people then and now when he added: 'Nor do we help the solution of what is admitted to be a difficult problem by the state withdrawing its existing disapprobation from acts which most people regard as loathsome and debasing'.

Other MPs sensibly warned that the House might be relying too heavily on the Kinsey research which claimed that about one man in ten was homosexual, then widely accepted but now known to have been seriously flawed by the use of ex-convicts and male prostitutes in its sample.

Sir Cyril Osorne (Parliament had a surprising number of Cyrils in those days) said, 'If we were to legalise homosexual practice in private between consenting males, we would in some way be putting a hallmark on it, and taking away some of the disagreeableness that has hitherto been attached to it. And we would tend to increase the number of homosexuals.' He compared the bill to the recent laws to liberalize gambling, which had also had the opposite effect to the one intended, by making it more common and harder to control.

One of the bill's supporters, Richard Wood, contended, 'A strong aversion will continue towards homosexual practices. It is unlikely that the relaxation of the law will lead to the orgy of homosexuality which some seem to fear.'

If Sir Cyril Osborne and Mr Wood could now walk together down Old Compton Street in London, with its open display of homosexuality, its homosexual pornography shops and video parlours, or study the Gay Listings section of the London *Evening Standard,* or attend Gay Pride marches in Manchester, Sir Cyril might be the more repelled, but Mr Wood would be the more surprised. Others who might feel vindicated would be Labour MP Frank Tomney, who predicted, 'Once we start by legislation to debase our moral standards in a period of lush rich civilization, of material greed ... we are really heading for trouble', and Tory Sir Spencer Summers, who said, 'The public will interpret this step as condoning these offences. It will be seen as another relaxation of the conventional code and a further step along the road of moral laxity.'

William Deedes, now Lord Deedes, also made a telling contribution. He argued that in a time when religious and

ethical sanctions were weak, the criminal law had special significance—a warning which might well have applied to the
whole Jenkins programme. He predicted, 'The effect of these
changes will be larger than some people suppose.'

In 1998 Lord Deedes revealed privately that the Tory
reformer Rab Butler had recruited him to try to persuade Tory
MPs to support the bill, but he had advised Butler that, human
nature being what it was, the homosexual lobby would not
stop at decriminalization. Soon after the act was passed, to
prove his point, he sent Butler a copy of a homosexual magazine calling for greater social acceptance. 'Rab Butler normally gave *me* advice,' said Lord Deedes. 'I remember it because
it was the only time I gave *him* advice.' Ever the gentleman,
he declines to gloat over the accuracy of his prediction.

The curmudgeons, once more, have been proved right by
events, but are reluctant to say so because they recognize the
battle is comprehensively lost. The liberals, who were wrong,
do not care, because they were always prepared to pay a high
price for their new society. Once again, as in the case of hanging, the reactionaries lost because they did not really believe
in their case. The utilitarian argument failed because a wealthy,
stable, peaceful society, in which sex of all kinds was a recreation thanks to the pill, no longer cared where people put their
penises. The deeper argument, about where they were putting
their souls, was one that nobody had the conviction to make
any more.

Lord Deedes was quite right. In a society where there were
no serious religious and ethical forces, the Sexual Offences Act
rapidly had far greater effects than anyone could have dreamed
of. People who are used to the ready acceptance of homosexuality now would, once again, be surprised if they slipped
into the recent past. Take this scene in the successful 1950s
political novel *No Love for Johnnie,* in which a homosexual
young man is scathingly described by a Labour MP, Johnnie
Byrne. Byrne, an ambitious left-winger whose career has been

thwarted and whose wife has just left him, is at a party in north London, hoping to find a girlfriend.

> The first one to make a move though was one of the sweater and jeans young men. He wore jeans of exaggerated narrowness and a yellow sweater, bright yellow, that matched the corn yellow of his hair, which was crew-cut and stunted close to the skull. Round his wrist was a wire-thin gold bracelet, which sought to excuse itself by the identity disc which hung from it.
>
> 'Hullo, Susie,' he said to the girl in a high-pitched whinny, but his eyes were on Byrne. 'Simply *ages*, dear, since I saw you. Been on tour?' Byrne gazed in astonishment. This was a type new to him.
>
> 'My name's Ronald—Ronnie, they call me,' the effeminate young man gurgled. 'You're the MP, aren't you? I had an MP once as a very special friend.' He mentioned the name, and Byrne was not surprised. Tea-room gossip had rumoured that there was something odd about this particular member, and tea-room gossip was usually founded on hard fact and cynical observation.
>
> I've got to get away from this creature, he thought. This is my first night out and one of these tries to pick me up. He nodded vaguely and pushed rudely past the youth.

The author of the book, the Islington Labour MP Wilfred Fienburgh, can hardly be described as a backwoods reactionary. Until his early death in a car crash in 1958, he had been one of the most talented men on the party's Left. But in 1958, enlightenment and progressive views did not necessarily mean a kindly view of homosexuality. The general view of it, among educated people, was similar to the hostility most people now feel towards child molesters. It was an embarrassing, even disgusting, perversion, not spoken of if possible.

Now, thirty-three years after the bill, many of the arguments against its passage have become quite simply unspeakable, because legal acceptance has led first to tolerance and then to respectability. The suffering of AIDS victims, as portrayed, for instance, by Tom Hanks in the propaganda movie *Philadelphia*, has also been used to sentimentalize homosexuals as modern heroes—not because of actual bravery, but for endurance of suffering. Princess Diana's visits to homosexual AIDS victims were said to be useful in dispelling the idea that AIDS was contagious. In fact, this idea was fostered by the ludicrous pretence that it would spread to heterosexuals, a pretence which depended on the implication that it was easy to catch, and which obscured the distasteful truth that some fairly abrasive and bloody contact has to be made.

The real effect of Diana's visits was to make homosexuality acceptable as it had never been before, blessed by both royalty and glamour. The effects of this change in attitude are cumulative. As with divorce and remarriage, the existence of a significant number of openly homosexual people—colleagues and friends as well as actors and artists—makes it seem bad manners to criticize the homosexual lifestyle. Social disapproval has shifted, in many places, from the homosexuals themselves to those who openly disapprove of their actions. A word has been invented, 'homophobia', to describe the feelings of those who do not accept homosexuality as the equal of heterosexuality. Like its twin, 'sexism', it is intended to produce guilt by association with the utterly unrelated sin of racialism. It is also intended to impute personal failings, even some sort of mental disorder, to those who are against further relaxation of the rules. This is one of the most unpleasant techniques of the new conformism, which finds it very hard to accept that any normal honest person could disagree with its ideas.

A significant moment in this process came when the allegedly Conservative Prime Minister, John Major, invited the homosexual campaigner and actor, Sir Ian McKellen, to Downing Street to discuss the issue. Soon afterwards, a Labour government came to power in which one Cabinet Minister, Culture

Secretary Chris Smith, was openly homosexual. Mr Smith drew attention to this fact, and allowed newspapers to write profiles of his live-in lover. That lover was also invited to a Buckingham Palace dinner as his official consort. The Leader of the Opposition, Mr William Hague, was *not* allowed to take his then fiancée Ffion Jenkins, to the same occasion, because they were not married. Mr Hague, a supporter of an equal age of consent for homosexuals and heterosexuals, chose not to make a fuss about this bizarre piece of royal *in*equality. Several Labour MPs elected in the 1997 landslide were also openly homosexual, and one, Ben Bradshaw, had won a West Country seat despite clear references to his 'sexuality' by his Tory opponent.

And yet several months afterwards, the Cabinet Minister Peter Mandelson was unfeignedly furious when his homosexuality was publicized on a BBC television programme. Mr Mandelson's tastes had been well-known for years among the London political classes, and had even been publicized in the mass-circulation *News of the World,* though at the time he was far more obscure, and many readers may not even have noticed. Mr Mandelson was said to believe that an openly homosexual politician could not become Prime Minister, a post he was thought to covet. He may have been wrong or, as it turned out, worrying about the wrong thing. Two of his colleagues, Welsh Secretary Ron Davies and Agriculture Minister Ron Brown, were also revealed to be homosexual, in embarrassing circumstances. But Mr Davies lost his job only because it appeared he had been attacked and robbed while seeking companionship on Clapham Common. It was his indiscretion and recklessness, not his homosexuality, that did for him. Many even said that the same would have applied to a minister caught kerb-crawling for female prostitutes. A few months later, former Conservative Defence Secretary Michael Portillo revealed in a national newspaper that he had had homosexual experiences in his younger days, and had only ceased to have them when he entered public life. Mr Portillo's past had long been widely rumoured, and remarkably few people were surprised or hostile. Shortly afterwards he was selected without any serious difficulties as Conservative candidate for Kensington and Chelsea.[†]

At about the same time, the government began preparing to remove the rule preventing schools from teaching that homosexuality was a lifestyle choice equal to and comparable with heterosexual marriage. A series of legal judgements awarded homosexual couples rights in areas such as continuing tenancies, where married or co-habiting heterosexual couples had previously had a privileged position. These moves were widely seen by fashionable opinion as sensible extensions of the law, rather than what they really were: the final demolition of the remaining privileges of marriage. However, it was difficult for pro-marriage campaigners to attack them, since many such rights had already been given to unmarried heterosexual 'partners', and it would have been entirely inconsistent not to give them to homosexuals as well. There were, in any case, serious proposals for the introduction of some sort of homosexual 'marriage', which no longer seemed to many people to be a contradiction in terms. The unspoken idea behind the 1966 reform, that homosexuals and heterosexuals were now equal—denied by its own supporters at the time—seemed to have become an accepted fact. Perhaps Mr Mandelson need not have worried.

[†]Declaration of interest: The author opposed Mr Portillo's nomination and sought it himself, but on the grounds of the former Cabinet Minister's politics, not his past sexual preferences.

*There is the need, independently of the State, to create a climate of
opinion which is favourable to gaiety, tolerance and beauty, and
unfavourable to puritanical restriction, to petty-minded disapproval, to
hypocrisy and to a dreary, ugly pattern of life.*
—Roy Jenkins, *The Labour Case*, 1959

FIFTEEN

Is Britain Civilized?

CHINA'S CULTURAL REVOLUTION was led by Mao Zedong. Britain's cultural revolution was led by the very different figure of Lord Jenkins of Hillhead. Jenkins might seem to be a natural aristocrat and an instinctive supporter of tradition and privilege. His rich voice and elegant Oxford oratory, his comfortable waistline, his ease with the nobility and his obvious erudition and breadth of mind suggest to many that he was born to the élite. Yet buried beneath the outer layers of polish and *gravitas* is the sharp-witted son of a Welsh coalminer, Arthur Jenkins. Arthur Jenkins was one of the many distinguished men who never quite climbed to the top of the British Labour movement, in his youth one of the few routes out of crushing manual work. He was by turns union official, MP and militant socialist, and was unjustly imprisoned after a picket-line clash during the bitter miners' lock-out which followed the General Strike in 1926.

Roy Jenkins, even though he entitled his autobiography *A Life at the Centre*, is also an outsider, from a class of outsiders and a country of outsiders. Knowing this, it is less surprising that he should see it as his task to revolutionize all our habits, from where and when we drank, to how long we stayed married, who we went to bed with and what sort of punishments we faced if we broke the law. It was he, then plain Roy Jenkins, who devised a programme which had more effect on the way that life is lived in this country than the thoughts of any other post-war politician, including Margaret Thatcher. Much of his success has come from his ability to find and then exploit divisions and weaknesses in the Conservative Party, which for decades has been full of people who are not really Conservative at all. His 1959 triumph with the Obscene Publications Act took place, as he himself admits, because Tory MPs often could not be bothered to attend important committee meetings. On the crucial clause, allowing literary witnesses to testify to the artistic 'merit' of books, five Tory MPs defected to Roy's side. He had discovered something that would influence his whole career, that there was a cross-party consensus against the national status quo.

In 1965, as the dim and inept Sir Frank Soskice floundered at the Home Office, the youthful Jenkins (he was forty-five) actively wanted his job, because he knew it was central to what he hoped to do. He later wrote in his autobiography, 'The struggle for the Obscene Publications Bill in the late 1950s had led my mind on to Home Office questions beyond censorship, and in *The Labour Case*, my Penguin Special written for the 1959 general election, I had devoted one chapter, entitled "Is Britain Civilized?", to producing what was in effect an unauthorised programme for Home Office reform.'

The chapter in question is a revolutionary manifesto, opening with the grandiose claim that 'It is about the need to make this country a more civilized place in which to live. . . . It concerns many subjects which are normally regarded as outside the scope of party politics. But they are nevertheless at least as important as many of the matters which are regularly chewed over by party propagandists.'

Seeing how much Roy Jenkins would change Britain in the coming years, nobody could deny that he was right about this. Many of these issues are actually *more* important than normal party political issues—because they affect individuals more directly, and because there is far more scope for government to make a major difference by simply passing or repealing laws of this kind, than in tinkering with the economy. Jenkins's time at the Treasury, while significant, did not have anything like the lasting impact of his years as Home Secretary.

Lord Jenkins, who so often appears a relaxed and genial person, reveals himself here as a man of hot passions, much more his father's son than he appears to be.

'Hanging is a barbaric and useless penalty,' he impatiently maintains. 'The ghastly apparatus of the gallows continues to exist, and is used much more often than was thought likely. . . . Britain, despite our much-vaunted social and political maturity, still stands out as one of the few advanced countries which retains this presumptuously final penalty.'

As for the law on homosexuality, this is 'brutal and unfair', and he savages the then Tory government thus: 'What is particularly hypocritical about the Government's refusal to act on homosexual law reform is that none of its leading members (nor those of any other major institution in the national life) apply social disapproval to conduct which, for public consumption, they insist on keeping subject to the full rigours of the criminal law.'

Fulminating about the many other 'gross restrictions on individual liberty which are in urgent need of removal', Mr Jenkins listed 'the fantastic position by which the Lord Chamberlain, a Court official who may exceptionally have an intelligent playgoer's knowledge of the stage but never has anything more, possesses powers of absolute censorship over all the public theatres of London; and has frequently used it to force some of the most intelligent presentations into the semi-obscurity of private theatre clubs.'

Then 'there are the ridiculous and (fortunately) largely unenforceable Sunday observance laws. There are the betting laws, which make off-course betting perfectly all right for anyone who has a credit account with a bookmaker, but a criminal offence for someone who has not.'

And 'there are the licensing laws, which may have been necessary to cope with the mass drunkenness of the early part of this century, but which are today an unnecessary restriction and would not be tolerated by any other European country'.

The list of doomed legislation continues with 'the divorce laws, which involve both a great deal of unnecessary suffering and a great number of attempts (many of them successful) to deceive the courts. There are harsh and archaic abortion laws.'

Jenkins also attacked the statutes which in those days made attempted suicide a criminal offence (an interesting example of the pre-counselling culture at its flintiest) and 'the administration of the immigration laws (affecting foreigners, not Commonwealth citizens) which would often be more suitable to a police state, terrified of intellectual infection from the outside world, than to a Britain which is the traditional refuge of the oppressed'.

Jenkins said it was time for politics to be more concerned with such matters than before, though he did not explain why. Perhaps it was simply his instinct that the moment had arrived, and that the other side was not in the mood for a fight. He admitted that there was a 'radical wing' of the Tory Party which was sympathetic to his aims, but he insisted that the very nature of that Tory Party meant that only a Labour government could do these things.

He predicted that a Labour government could not necessarily achieve all these aims but added, so prophetically that it is hard not to think that he had hopes in this direction even in 1959, that 'A great deal would depend on the reforming zeal and liberal spirit of the man who became Home Secretary. And however well endowed he was with those qualities, he might still have difficulty on some points.'

There are many fascinating things in this short passage. The first and perhaps the most important is the sense that

Jenkins is shoving at a rotten, weakened gate which he knows will soon give way. Even its traditional defenders no longer believe in the things they are supposed to stand up for—a point Jenkins makes deftly in his reference to the laws on homosexuality. There is the feeling that *the time has come.* The old order is tottering, and new and determined men can demolish it and begin again.

It is also interesting that Jenkins has lumped together exactly the same set of measures that a reactionary would list today as the death blows to traditional British society. Few politicians, of either Left or Right, think in such a systematic way. Most are content to climb to office and become known for a well-conducted war or a neat piece of popular reform, or to sponsor a single bill. But even in 1959, Roy Jenkins was marshalling his tanks along a thousand-mile front, fully aware of the weight and size of the blow he meant to deal the enemy. A clever Tory opponent might, in 1959 or 1964, have dug out this chapter and portrayed Labour as the party that would abolish hanging, legalize homosexuality and weaken marriage. But most of the clever Tories tended to side with Mr Jenkins anyway, as we shall see. In fact it was only those widely condemned as stupid, outdated and prejudiced who would try to stand in his path, as he supervised the scheme he had so ably outlined.

Then there is the inescapable fact that Roy Jenkins was also the leader and linchpin of a foreign policy view which was and is equally hostile to traditional Britain. As the Europhile of Europhiles, his tactical cunning, influence and personal force were to do more to push Britain towards European integration than even Sir Edward Heath.

Meanwhile, what of the great Jenkins programme to transform Britain? The key to it was that it was a moral putsch by the liberal élite. Although Jenkins had the courage to set out his ideas in *The Labour Case,* few voters can have been aware of them, and they were not official government policy. As a result, no MP could ever be held to account for them at a general election, or ever has been. The fiction of a 'free vote' in which MPs' 'consciences' are respected is one of the most powerful propaganda weapons of the cultural revolution. All that the MPs are free of in these cases is any pressure whatever from their constituents, who have no way of punishing them individually or collectively for ignoring their wishes and opinions. Instead, they face the rival pressures of the liberal metropolitan élite, and of the BBC.

The tactics by which the Wilson government pushed through two of these measures (Abortion and Sexual Offences) are described by Jenkins himself with great candour in his autobiography:

> Neither was a Government bill, but they would not have got through had not I or someone of similar mind been Home Secretary. I could not have got the Cabinet to agree that they should bear the imprimatur of the Government. A substantial majority of ministers were in favour, but three or four were opposed, and another larger group wished the issues would go away....
>
> It was therefore necessary to proceed by stratagem, and the one which I adopted was that the Government, while nominally neutral, would free the back-bench sponsors of these measures of the normal bane of private members' bills, which is a shortage of parliamentary time. The Government would allow the House to sit for as long as was necessary to get the bills through. In addition, while members of the Cabinet would be free to vote against them, I would be free to speak (and vote, of course) in their favour from the despatch box and with all the briefing and with such authority as I could command as Home Secretary.

As Jenkins himself says, 'These arrangements ... gave the bills a virtual guarantee of passage', provided their supporters were willing to do the needful donkey-work. Which of course they were.

But these might not have been so easy if the hardest of all these issues had not already been cleared out of the way. The Wilson government's first Queen's Speech had surprised the nation with its pledge to allow time for 'a free decision by Parliament on the issue of Capital Punishment'. Only three months after Labour's narrow victory, on 21 December 1964, the decisive debate on hanging was opened by Sydney Silverman, who had been campaigning for this moment for more than a decade.

Describing the gallows as 'a grotesque barbarity', Silverman hinted broadly that this was really a government bill, just one that liberal Tories might feel free to vote for. 'I hope,' he said, 'we may count on the neutrality of the government being a benevolent neutrality.' Silverman gave a great hostage to fortune, declaring that there had never been a time in the history of this country when convictions for murder had reached hundreds a year—something which would take place less than twenty-five years after his bill was passed. But he had the best of the argument, tolerant, decent, cleverly and knowledgeably dismissive of the idea, then unprovable, that the rope was a unique deterrent. With few exceptions, his opponents were emotional, floundering and confused by the fact that they were forced into defending the messy and inconsistent law which then applied. This was the 1957 Homicide Act, a botched and unloved compromise which limited hanging to very few types of murder, mostly those involving police and prison officers. Few people realize that it was because of the 1957 Act that Myra Hindley and Ian Brady could not have been sentenced to death.* Pro-gallows MPs such as Brigadier Terence Clarke and Sir Richard Glyn were easily brushed aside by Mr Silverman, because *they* were arguing from instinct, prejudice and tradition, while he was arguing with moral force and intellect. Silverman could also tell them, quite accurately, that the death penalty no longer applied to many of the crimes they believed it should punish. The real battle had been lost seven years before.

Probably the most significant speech came from Sir Henry Brooke, the Tory Home Secretary who had become a hate-figure of the Left much as Michael Howard would be thirty years later. Brooke revealed that he had now become an abolitionist, partly because of his experience at the Home Office. It was as if Margaret Thatcher had come out in favour of unilateral disarmament, and symbolic of the crumbling of traditional beliefs at the very centre of the Tory Party. Mark Carlisle, another senior and respected Tory, also declared his support for abolition. It was left to Sir Peter Rawlinson to make the heavyweight case for keeping the noose.

It was and remains a good case, suggesting without alarmist words that abolition would change criminal behaviour, reminding MPs of the worries which had persuaded the Commons to retain the penalty for some crimes in 1957: 'Would there be an increase of violence or an increase in the use of firearms? We wondered whether in this country crime and criminal activities would develop as they have done overseas?' By this he meant 'gangs and gangsters, armed with guns'. 'And would there be an increased danger to the public, and would the police have to be armed?'

He claimed that the law had a great effect as it stood:

> Great care is and has been taken by professional criminals to avoid the risk of violence leading to death, because of the difference in the penalty which is paid.
>
> I believe we are witnessing an increase in professional crime, and that there is an extension of operations by organised gangs. I fear that the removal of capital punishment from this field of crime would introduce a risk of greater violence, the wider use of guns and greater danger to the public.

But what Sir Peter lacked was the passion and moral force of Sydney Silverman and his allies, a passion which had attracted many younger, brighter Tories into the abolitionist camp. Sir

Peter's arguments were purely utilitarian and practical. And, though he would be proved right by the passage of years, his approach had no power to influence the liberals. They were discussing the rules by which Britain was to be run from now on, rules which implicitly rejected the taking of life by the state, and which no longer really relied on the idea of punishment or even retribution.

The abolitionists' ideas were rooted in a post-Christian humanism which sought to perfect life on earth, rather than to govern a community of miserable sinners. The supporters of the Silverman bill were not really concerned about the possible bad consequences of getting rid of capital punishment. Though they would not admit it then or now, the truth was that they were prepared to accept the death of innocent people, the arming of the police and greater danger to policemen and prison officers. These were all sacrifices they were prepared to make, rather than allow something they believed to be a morally repulsive punishment to continue. Serious retentionists have the same problem, that they must accept the possibility of wrongful execution as the price of *their* principle. The 1957 Act had merely been a compromise along the way to the abolitionists' goal. Reformers were actually disappointed that executions continued after it was passed, having expected that they would quietly die out. Their disappointment would not last long.

Until 1964 the moral Left, though increasingly triumphant in the worlds of art, literature, religion and journalism, still had a weak grip upon parliament and the law. But the new House of Commons was the first in which modern liberal ideas could— just—summon a majority. From that point onwards, liberal post-Christian morality gradually increased its strength, with both Tory and Labour Parties quietly shedding their moral traditionalists—the old-fashioned, red-faced, incorruptible Cavaliers vanishing from the Tory benches, the temperance Methodists and working-class Catholics from Labour's side.

The abolition of the death penalty was the most significant

symbolic victory of the new order because it went to the heart of the difference between old and new. In a Christian society, execution merely refers the matter to a higher court, allowing the condemned man the chance of repentance in this life, and salvation in the world to come. But in a post-Christian society, the idea of a death penalty is quite abhorrent. A man's greatest possession is not his soul, which does not exist, but his life, which is all he has. In that case the very idea of execution is quite intolerable, even if the alternative is—as it turned out to be—a grave increase in armed crime and the gradual arming of the police force.

The argument between Christianity and liberalism had been quietly lost during the First World War, and particularly in the mud-pits of Passchendaele and the Somme, when men from the educated classes had seen so much death and so little mercy that they had come to hate killing of any sort, and had ceased for ever to believe in the certainties of the world before 1914. In the lingering afterglow of Christian belief, the old guard had been able to preserve some remnants of punishment and retribution. But in general the ruling élite could not justify such cruelties to themselves, and had come to despise the masses for clinging to their belief in the power of the noose. Until December 1964, they had never dared impose their own doubts and uncertainties upon the people who had elected them. The decision was a mighty victory of the élite over the people and of humanism over Christianity. With the shadow of the gallows removed, the new liberal cross-party majority had altered the whole purpose and nature of the penal system, and inaugurated a new era of loving the sinner while not caring all that much about the sin. Now the youthful Roy Jenkins, marching into the Home Office full of zeal, would lead them on to still greater triumphs, triumphs which have continued ever since under both parties, as the laws have grown more permissive and society more violent, selfish and chaotic.

SIXTEEN

Year Zero

BRITAIN IS THE ONLY VIRGIN in a continent of rape victims. Alone of all European countries, her recent past is unsullied by collaboration or even by dishonourable neutrality. She has paid an enormous price in blood and treasure for this privileged position, but her sacrifice in 1940 saved much of Europe from permanent tyranny of the worst kind, and altered the course of world history. Yet she acts as if she had something to be ashamed of. National pride is suspect, patriotism rarely expressed, the national flag can only be displayed ironically. A British citizen who behaved like an American, and hung the Union Flag over his porch, would be regarded as a more than slightly unbalanced eccentric, while the national anthem is widely despised and seldom sung. What remains of the national history on the school syllabus contains much heart-searching and regret, and very little pride.

We seem to be in the sort of demoralized period that often ends in revolution or collapse, but it is hard to see what has led to it. Before a nation suffers such a pre-revolutionary mood, it generally needs to pass through a disaster, some huge national reverse that leads to a loss of confidence among the rulers and a loss of deference among the ruled. Hitler exploited the resentment and suppressed rage which followed Germany's defeat in 1918. French institutions are damaged to this day by the experience of occupation and collaboration. The countries invaded and occupied in 1940 all have shameful memories, which explains why so many of them have enthusiastically buried their past beneath a layer of bland secular modernity. But why should Britain, undefeated, uninvaded, unbroken, have turned her back upon her history?

The uncomfortable truth is that Britain *was* defeated by her enemies, and then occupied by her friends, but managed to postpone the recognition of her reduced status for many decades. Britain lost the first part of the Second World War, which ended in the autumn of 1940. But, having been beaten back into her own territory, she was able to fight off the final humiliation of seeing a victorious foe parade through her cities, thanks to the lucky survival of her navy and the even luckier rebirth of her air force during a period when the rest of her national defence was scandalously neglected. She came frighteningly close to suing for peace in 1940, but avoided this mainly because she had a Prime Minister who was a living embodiment of the national history, and who refused to accept the 'inevitable' surrender pressed on him by 'moderate' and 'reasonable' politicians.

There then came a second half of the war, in which Britain fought as the involuntary ally of one former rival and one potential foe, the USA and the USSR, and in which she sustained terrible national defeats—in Hong Kong, Singapore and Tobruk. Those defeats would make it morally impossible for Britain to keep her Empire once the war was over, even if she had been rich enough to do so, and even if the USA had not actively sought to wind up the Empire as a political and trading association. They prepared the way for the humiliation at Suez fifteen years later, the last time a British government attempted to ignore the reality of this country's weakened position. The Japanese triumph in Singapore ended the British Indian and Far Eastern Empire, though there would be a half-hearted attempt to hold on to some of it once the war was over. It was also during this stage of the war that Britain fell under foreign occupation for the first time in her modern history, an occupation which was welcome and unavoidable, but which permanently affected the national state of mind.

The catastrophe of 1940 has until recently been concealed from the mass of the British public. Clive Ponting's merciless study of the dark days, *1940: Myth and Reality,* and Nicholas Harman's *Dunkirk: The Necessary Myth* have now lifted a corner of the dust-sheet which covers this complicated corner of the national lumber-room. But even half a century after these events, the disquieting truth is still quite understandably resisted by millions. In a world of broken faith, it is one thing that they can still believe in.

Winston Churchill's assertion that 1940 was 'our finest hour' and his understanding that 'never in the field of human conflict has so much been owed by so many to so few' during the Battle of Britain were *not* mere propaganda. Britain had been led into terrible danger by fools, and left herself virtually defenceless until the last minute, but she had a choice in 1940, and she chose the steep and rugged pathway rather than the easy exit. The Battle of Britain may have been won by luck as much as by judgement, but undoubtedly it was also won by courage and nerve. The British Expeditionary Force may have spent too much time retreating, and Dunkirk was certainly a miserable defeat and terrible loss, but the naval evacuation was a triumph of coolness under fire, and kept alive the hope that we might fight on. If Admiral Bertram Ramsay had failed in his task of evacuation, and the entire British Army had been held hostage by the Nazi authorities, surrender *would* have been inevitable. It was therefore right to bring British troops out of Dunkirk before evacuating the French, and right, if cynical, to refuse to plunge scarce RAF squadrons into the foredoomed Battle of France.

This is what is wrong with Clive Ponting's otherwise excellent piece of debunking. He guesses on the basis of strong circumstantial evidence that on 17 June 1940, Britain was fumbling towards peace negotiations with Germany. Certainly the Foreign Office minister Rab Butler seems to have tried to open communications with Berlin through Sweden, and there is strong circumstantial evidence that a message was sent via that route. But the records also suggest that Churchill *did* live up to his image as tenacious bulldog, and squashed the initiative with some force when he found out about it. The 'myths' of Dunkirk, the Battle of Britain and our 'Finest Hour' are therefore nothing less than the truth. Similarly, Ponting's account of national bankruptcy, which threatened on 22 August 1940, misses the point. He says: 'Britain would still face the ... dilemma of choosing between dependence on the United States or peace with Germany,' as if these were just equivalents with little difference between them. For any rational, democratic patriot, dependence on the USA would be a small price to pay for avoiding a peace with Germany that would only be the first stage in submitting to a German-ruled Europe. The USA's traditions, language and culture were fundamentally similar to our own, and had their roots in the same faith and the same experiences. It might have been better if we had been able to pursue an independent path, but by August 1940, that path had long been closed.

Most British people were unaware that their country was so close to national humiliation. However, our desperate military and financial plights *were* known to the governing class, who were profoundly affected by it for the rest of their lives. The later decision to build a British nuclear bomb—at all costs—was taken because politicians, scientists and civil servants alike recalled the terrifying summer and autumn of 1940, and wanted to ensure that Britain would always have an ultimate weapon in her hands if such danger threatened again. The realization that we were more or less defenceless and bankrupt ended the blithe Victorian self-confidence of our rulers, nurtured on fantasy and kept alive between the wars by complacency. Without Winston Churchill to rally national morale, the élite's near-panic would have infected the rest of the population, especially given the disloyalty and defeatism among the intelligentsia, many of them still refusing to support the war effort because of the Stalin-Hitler pact.

But this did not happen. Morale did not collapse, there was no serious movement for a negotiated peace, and the idea that Britain had saved herself by her exertions became such an important part of the national consciousness that it is, even now, difficult to believe that the truth was more complicated than that. For anyone from the wartime or post-war generation, it is almost physically distressing to read the evidence that respected British statesmen seriously contemplated a shameful peace with the Third Reich.

Because so few people knew the unpleasant facts, and because Churchill was such a superb propagandist, there were two completely different versions of 1940, one circulating among the rulers and one accepted by the ruled. Out of this was born a new division between the élite and the mass of the people—the élite knowing how close we had come to extinction, the people refusing to believe that such a thing could have happened.

But the masses were to have their own awakening not long afterwards. When American servicemen began arriving in Britain in 1942, much of the United Kingdom fell under a bizarre and unique form of military occupation. The occupiers were officially friends, often because they were ordered to be, and definitely allies. They spoke the same language but brought with them a completely different culture, different morals, different habits of courtship and even different tastes in food and drink, music and entertainment. Because many of them came from immigrant stock whose children had learned to be Americans more quickly than their parents, they showed less respect for old age and had a distinctive 'youth' culture quite unlike Britain's. They were richer, bigger, better fed, better dressed and better educated than their hosts, and they were subject to a different legal system; because their country was so rich and powerful Britain had no choice but to accept this rather colonial arrangement, which she had once imposed upon the Chinese in Shanghai. They even broke the iron monopoly of the BBC, insisting on their own separate network of radio stations. In all ways but one, they behaved liked a reasonably well-disciplined army of occupation, and many British people, including George Orwell, frankly viewed them as occupiers as well as saviours.

Too often this era is dismissed lightly with the old cliché that the American troops were 'overpaid, oversexed and over here'. Thanks to David Reynolds' book *Rich Relations: The American Occupation of Britain 1941–45*, we now have a serious account of this immensely influential period in the national life, one which changed the British people's view of themselves and turned the eyes of millions towards America as a place where life was more abundant and less bound in by history, tradition and class. More than fifty years after the American forces left, the radical journalist Jonathan Freedland urged in *Bring Home the Revolution* that this country should introduce American democratic methods and become a republic on the U.S. model. But what the British common people actually liked about America was its way of life, its food, its music, its language and its classlessness, not its way of choosing its town council, its judges or even its head of state.

They had already been exposed to a rather lurid idea of America through the cinema—even in the 1920s and 1930s it was noticeable that working-class audiences preferred American movies, while the middle class were happier with British-made films. Now real Americans, in huge numbers, arrived to live amidst the British. They came at a time when the differences between the two cultures were greater than ever. Rationed, blacked-out, bombed and shabby, urban Britain can seldom have looked so backward, dingy and forsaken as it did in the middle years of the war. Conscription of men and young women and the vast movement of female labour into munitions factories had led to great population shifts, as had evacuation. According to Reynolds, there were sixty million officially registered changes of address between 1939 and 1945 in a British population of thirty-eight million. Countless more must have happened without the authorities knowing anything about them. Husbands and fathers were absent from their homes, from the lives of their wives and their daughters. Peacetime rules of behaviour were relaxed, so that women went into pubs in large numbers for the first time since the nineteenth century. British army pay was pitifully low, leaving wives at home with only a few shillings a week to pay for food, clothes and heat. Almost everything worth having was rationed.

Into the midst of this came tens of thousands of boisterous, well-paid young men who were unimpressed by English landscape and heritage, whose manners and customs were entirely different, though their language was almost the same, and who seldom mingled with the British in their own homes. Unlike the Canadians, who had arrived earlier, Americans were seldom billeted with British families, and when they were, it was often in oppressive conditions which led to hostility. Their power to impress women and children, while infuriating younger men and the older generation, was huge. Reynolds shows that by the spring of 1944, there were several counties with an emergency population of at least sixty thousand Americans. London itself swarmed with U.S. troops on leave, looking for some escape from the bleak, dank dreariness of life in camps and raw new airbases. The total number of Americans in the UK at this time was more than 1.6 million, mostly active young men, at a time when Britain's active young men were mainly away from home.

Many of them were young men fated to be misunderstood. The anthropologist Margaret Mead made a serious study of the difference in British and American courtship patterns, pointing out that Britain's mainly single-sex schools produced a completely different relationship between young men and women. For Americans, 'dating' was a subtle game played by two people who knew the rules and were cynical. 'A really successful date is one in which the boy asks for everything and gets nothing except a lot of words.'

As Reynolds says: 'Mead's theory was an attempt to explain why GIs seemed oversexed to many English people and why local girls seemed cheap and forward to many GIs. It certainly *does* help to explain some of the misunderstandings. But many of the contacts between American servicemen and British women were perfectly straightforward, with both parties knowing exactly what they were doing.'

Reynolds also cites a British Home Office report from 1945, which concluded:

> To girls brought up on the cinema, who copied the dress, the hair styles and manners of Hollywood stars, the sudden influx of Americans, speaking like the films, who actually lived in the magic country and who had plenty of money, at once went to the girls' heads. The American attitude to women, their proneness to spoil a girl, to build up, exaggerate, talk big and act with generosity and flamboyance, helped to make them the most attractive boy friends.

And he records the enormous strain on many British couples caused by separations of as long as three years, softened only by brief and rare leave periods. In many cases, hurried marriages contracted early in the war simply could not stand up to this stress. There would be a terrible rise in the divorce rate immediately after the war. Many of those divorces—unusually—would be demanded by men who came home to find their wives had children by other men, often American servicemen.

Had these things happened at the hands of, say, German occupiers, it would have been easier for people to have seen the episode as a period of national humiliation and shame, but because the Americans were our closest allies, our 'cousins', and because they were our only hope of winning the war, such a revulsion never came, only awkwardness and occasional fights, combined with a rather touching and honourable refusal by Britons to countenance the U.S. Army's colour bar. Because the Americans came in peace and saved us from conquest, there could be no moment of release and regained national pride when they left. British mobs could hardly shave the heads of women who had slept with the Americans, or denounce them as collaborators.

Instead, millions of people learned from hard personal experience that Britain was very definitely no longer top nation, on the battlefield or in the competition for the fairer sex, as soldiers from another country swaggered and boozed and seduced their way through poverty-ravaged, bomb-damaged cities, buying up the few remaining consumer goods, bruising the pride of the men and awakening the fantasies of the women and children. There is a painful moment in John Schlesinger's film *Yanks,* when a middle-class English husband returns briefly from his naval duties for a staid and restrained weekend of tense reunion with his wife, who is betraying him with an American officer. The sound of Anglican hymns and the splendour of Royal Navy uniform serve as a reminder of the fast-disappearing Britain where such things would not have been possible.

The long-term effect of this era was partly a sort of class-based cargo cult, in which poorer Britons associated luxury, colour and affluence with America. Meanwhile, the middle classes and the intelligentsia tended to think of the U.S. influence as coarse and vulgar. While a few people formed close friendships with Americans, or even married them, most British people realized for the first time that America was wealthier, mightier, younger and more energetic than Britain. The display of American military power, as it rolled through the narrow roads of southern England in May 1944, must have been daunting as well as impressive. These were our allies and not our enemies, but such armed might was far beyond the capability of Britain, which must suddenly have looked small and weak to herself.

Such moments do not produce the same despair and self-loathing which follow actual defeat and real occupation by an enemy. It would be absurd to suggest that they do. However, they do have lasting effects on the view a people takes of itself, effects which slowly work their way through society.

By 1956 and the Suez episode, much of the governing élite had accepted that Britain could no longer act alone. Those, such as Anthony Eden, who did not accept this had personal, sentimental or other special reasons for deluding themselves that Britain was still a world power. Perhaps Eden believed that he could emulate Churchill and overcome unpleasant realities through sheer force of personality. If so, he ignored or forgot the half-American Churchill's great skills in influencing and cajoling the USA.

The mass of the public, however, had only just begun to understand the implications of American power. America's swift and ruthless (and, as it turned out, wrong) undermining of the British action must have helped to change that. But by then the Korean War and the Cold War had opened a new kind of relationship with America, in which we were the junior partner, but the most-valued junior partner, the only reliable friend in a Europe of unreliable and fractious allies.

Rivalries and resentments were largely forgotten as we settled into the cosy warmth and comfort of the long Cold War, where the other side were unmistakably wicked and our side just as unmistakably good. When Britain repeated the Suez operation in the Falkland Islands in 1982, it was with American help—including intelligence and emergency airlifts of munitions. The resentment had been buried, the panic of 1940 was recalled only by a few, and the British people saw the USA and its people as friends.

Only the Left, which had sympathized with the USSR during much of the Cold War, continued to resent Washington's power and the effects of American culture on the British way of life, claiming that our role as the USA's unsinkable aircraft carrier and as a base for spying on the Warsaw Pact was one-way exploitation, rather than a partnership which suited both sides well.

The first warning shiver was felt in the late 1960s, when the new generation had grown old enough to offer their first challenges to their parents—through fashion, popular music and, in the expanding universities, through a new independence of life. The 1967–73 explosion can now be seen as a warning of what would happen when the post-war generation eventually rose to power in Britain's institutions.

In his novel about the Sixties upheaval, *Places Where They Sing*, Simon Raven depicts a conversation between a left-wing Cambridge don, Tony Beck, and his brilliant revolutionary pupil, Hugh Balliston:

> Until just recently, whatever was the case with the world at large, there remained in privileged England enough national stability to make any kind of radical action unpopular and futile and therefore thoroughly impractical.... But ... the time for it is nearly over. The national, the purely local stability which made it possible for me to play [my game] in peace has been rotted right through to the piles and will soon collapse completely.... Even though I've been observing closely ... I'm not at all sure why or how this has happened. I suspect that British energies have been sapped by a mixture of guilt for an imperial past and resentment at imperial decline. But the important point is that it has happened and nothing can halt the process now, certainly not a flabby Labour government with half-baked right-wing policies and sentimental left-wing sympathies. From here on, the order of the day, in England as everywhere else, will

be crisis and flux: disobedience and mutiny on the part of
the so-called lower classes; despair and desertion on the part
of the upper. In short, Hugh, things are just going to fall
apart.

Raven, whose Alms for Oblivion series beautifully describes
the collapse and decline of the British upper class, in step with
the decline of the Empire, knew what he was talking about.
The national atmosphere in that period was a very strange one,
and continued to be until the Yom Kippur War of 1973, and
the 'oil shock' afterwards, calmed down the student generation
and perhaps persuaded them to forget immediate revolution
and move off into influential careers. Two great events of 1968
probably decided what their world-view would be. They were
finally divorced from any illusions about Soviet Communism
by the invasion of Czechoslovakia. And they were convinced
of their own glamour and brilliance by the Paris riots earlier in
the same year, riots which were really just a giant nose-thumb-
ing at the wartime generation. Shortly before this, the prosecution of Mick Jagger for drugs offences, followed by his release
after a *Times* leader attacked his conviction, convinced many
young people that the 'establishment', if it still existed, had lost
its nerve. Jagger was popular because he defied cultural conventions about clothes, hair, sex and manners, and appeared
dangerous. If authority shied away from punishing him when
it had the chance, then it was plainly because authority was
afraid of what he represented. So we reasoned, those of us who
were young and impressionable in the 1960s.

The period of conventional quiet among the young which
began in 1973 was misleading. The influences which were erod-
ing the older values were still at work, from the pill to rock
music, drugs and television. There was plenty of unsettling disruption elsewhere. The constant, and now largely forgotten,
strife in major industries gave an impression of national
instability. One week the postmen were on strike, next week

the dustmen. Almost all the major industries, plus hospitals and ambulance services—things we had always relied upon—became suspect. When the Thatcher government brought this to an end, it introduced a new type of destabilization, as its policies wiped out millions of traditional jobs. Mrs Thatcher's carelessness with traditions and institutions looked like necessary radicalism. But it helped to weaken the foundations of everything that had seemed permanent before.

The deep uncertainties about our national future did not surface again until the end of the Cold War abruptly awoke the ghosts of the 1940s. Suddenly without a common enemy, and under intense European pressure for integration with a new Continental superstate dominated by a hastily reunified Germany, Britain was brought back to the place she had escaped from fifty years before. We were alone in the world, unexpectedly insignificant, and lacking in confidence. Our armies in Germany were now useless and rather ludicrous. Our vast and expensive nuclear apparatus, designed to devastate a Soviet Union which no longer existed, was absurdly large for any imaginable use we might make of it. The supposed 'special relationship' with the USA was a delusion exposed by the lack of common interest once the Warsaw Pact was wound up. Later attempts to revive the link, in actions against the unconvincing bogy of Iraq, merely showed how puny and obsolete our military might was when set beside the colossal aircraft carriers and air fleets of the Americans.

And, while we were now a wealthy nation once again, we were not a confident one. Our national culture was far weaker in all classes than it had been during the war. The penetration of working-class culture by America, begun during the war, had continued through the cinema and television, and through the growing numbers of British people taking their holidays or working in the USA. Egalitarian governments had demolished many of the old landmarks of the class system, and segregation of the sexes, particularly at school age, was now quite unusual. The last generation which had been brought up in a specifically British way was growing old.

Among the middle class, the change was even more striking. Orwell's view that the intelligentsia were ashamed of Britain still held true. And it was more important because the intelligentsia had become far more influential. In the expanded education system, especially the universities, and in broadcasting, ideas which were once restricted to Bloomsbury were now the conventional wisdom of the day. Thanks to Continental holidays, the middle-class sort of holidays which involved renting houses in country villages and pretending to mingle with the natives, this generation was the first for centuries to feel at home on mainland Europe (working-class holidaymakers went to Spain, it is true, but took Britain with them and returned without any fellow-feeling for the Spaniards). They associated 'Europe' not—as their parents had done—with wobbly currencies, poverty, riots, dictators and wheezy plumbing, but rather with wine and pavement cafés and a spacious countryside. And they could see for themselves that many Continentals were richer than they were.

Old-fashioned British patriotism was driven back into besieged enclaves. English patriotism, which began a sort of rebirth, was still linked with football crowds and coarse hooliganism. As the idea of Britain weakened, older loyalties grew stronger again—especially in Scotland. Scotland's more idealist people had always been more sympathetic to socialist ideas than the English. Despite a brief period when Tory Unionism was popular among the Protestant working class, Scotland's establishment conservative party was, in truth, the Labour Party. A prolonged period of Tory rule from London, based on English votes, fed a desire for separatism, helped by the fact that the more Scotland voted against the Tories, the more subsidies Scotland received. Wales felt the same thing more mildly.

In Ireland, British governments were tiring of the cost, in lives and money, of keeping hold of the north-east corner of an island where they no longer had any 'selfish or strategic interest'. The USA, which had been highly sympathetic to Irish republicanism until Ireland chose neutrality in the Second World War, now felt free to follow its instincts again. Bill Clinton, it is true, was rapidly converted to the republican cause by his need to win back Catholic voters who had deserted his party over its abortion policy. But, judging by the behaviour of American conservative leaders such as Bob Dole, any U.S. administration in the post–Cold War period would have sympathized with the Teddy Kennedy point of view and urged Britain to deal with the IRA. Continental Europe's mainly Roman Catholic nations were also sympathetic to the republicans. And the EU itself, which for years lavishly subsidized the Irish Republic with British money, saw Ireland as an English-speaking ally in the battle to tame the UK and bring it closer to Brussels ways. The idea that Ireland could be reunited under *European* sovereignty has always been an unstated implication of calls for closer British integration in Europe.

The British governing classes could see that some sort of gradual handover of this troublesome territory to the Irish Republic would ease relations both with Washington and with the European Union, as well as saving billions of pounds in military and social spending. The British public, too, were weary of it. They had become a great deal less British in the period of cultural revolution, indeed far less British than the Ulster Protestants, a group of people who desperately wanted to be British, but who evoked no sense of fellow-feeling among their mainland cousins. On the contrary, most mainlanders found the Ulstermen tiresome, incomprehensible and old-fashioned, with their talk of Protestantism and the Battle of the Boyne and the Somme. Urged to abandon the Northern Irish in the name of 'peace', mainland voters barely blinked at the surrender, and mostly did not trouble to discover the details.

Meanwhile, a new ideology was growing among the Left, the idea that the United Kingdom was an artificial creation of the Hanoverian era, an invention whose time had gone. Linda Colley, in her influential book *Britons,* helped to make this idea highly fashionable. So, on a more populist level, did the film *Braveheart,* a misleading hymn to Scottish nationalism and a one-sided denunciation of English oppression and cruelty.

So Year Zero came at last, rather gently and gradually, after many of those who would have been most bitterly distressed by it were already dead. We were alone and faced with absorption into a European superstate, but millions did not care. We no longer spoke, dressed, ate or behaved as we used to, but the changes had worked their way through our society so quietly that we did not feel as if our way of life had been stolen. Our national constitution came under question, but few even thought that the 1688 settlement was important any more. Our monarchy, robbed of much of its role by the Tory decision to elect party leaders, went through an undignified frenzy of adultery, divorce and melodramatic death. And perhaps it was that death, with the grim reaper's dark ability to drag out our deepest feelings, which shocked millions into realizing that they now lived in a country that was not what it had once been, and would never be again.

CONCLUSION

Chainsaw Massacre

THE BRITISH CONSTITUTION grew like a forest, requiring long centuries and fertile earth to flourish and come to maturity. It was not built like a temple, deliberately designed and constructed in a short span of years, as its American equivalent was. It was not made up merely of written rules, but of habits of mind, of careful restraint, of ingenious balances which could be tipped by a single feather but were deliberately left undisturbed. It required a robust and independent press, and a critical opposition. Its much-mocked traditions and flummeries merely helped to explain to the people that its deepest principle was to honour the past, and to assume that the generation of the living neither knew everything, nor owned everything. Long before Isaiah Berlin told us, the people of Britain knew that there was no perfect solution to earthly problems, that different traditions and opinions must live side by side for civilized life to take place, that different parties or factions in the state might be better-fitted to solving different problems at different times—peace or war, health or prosperity, justice or liberty.

The British system did not only enshrine habeas corpus, trial by jury, common law and parliamentary democracy. It demanded freedom of speech and thought, protected inheritance and secured property. It gave every citizen a private life, every family its own small kingdom. It made each police officer the embodiment of the citizens' will, rather than a gendarme sent from above. It made liberty the property of the subject, to be lent to government between elections. It even made monarchy a subtle restraint on the power of the executive. It decreed that everything was permitted, unless specifically prohibited. It honoured dissent, loved eccentricity and despised conformity. It refused to make windows into men's souls, and punished them for what they did, not for what they were, let alone for what they thought or said. Above all, it relied upon its laws being written in the hearts of the British people, who both respected authority and guarded liberty, who alone of the peoples of Europe *volunteered* to fight for their King in 1914, and for that matter *volunteered* for their chosen side in that great convulsion of unselfishness, the General Strike of 1926.

Yet a forest that has taken centuries to grow can be cut down in weeks, or even hours, especially if the foresters have grown indolent and slack, and take their charge for granted. England, which has not seen a battle on its own soil since Sedgemoor in 1685, which had lived in peace and stability thanks to a settlement reached in 1688 which few had heard of or understood, had taken its peace, order and prosperity for granted. So had Wales, peaceful for even longer, and Scotland, which last heard the clash of steel at Culloden in 1746. When the British tradition was suddenly threatened by attractive-seeming ideas, innovations and philosophies, there was no one left to fight for the old order. When affluence encouraged individual independence and weakened the sense of mutual obligation, all classes began to forget the ties that had bound them together. Tory politicians might defend tradition's practical benefits, but they did not understand or cherish the beliefs in which they were rooted, or the complex compromises involved. Northern Ireland was the one place where British patriotism took the form of nervous and defensive nationalism.

Few on the mainland cared about that or tried to understand it, dismissing their Unionist cousins as concrete-headed fanatics who banged big drums and wore bowler hats.

The British Protestant settlement was so old and seemed so permanent that its supporters treated it as a fact of nature, a range of hills or a river, unchangeable, and safe to ignore. Influenced by a prosperity which was greater and longer than any known before, we became complacent about the underpinnings of civilized life. When the settlement began to be attacked, we thought the assaults were petty and doomed to failure.

So we allowed our patriotism to be turned into a joke, wise sexual restraint to be mocked as prudery, our families to be defamed as nests of violence, loathing and abuse, our literature to be tossed aside like so much garbage, and our church turned into a department of the Social Security system. We have responded to the challenge of Scottish and Welsh nationalism with subsidies rather than arguments. We let our schools become nurseries of resentment and ignorance, and humiliated our universities by forcing them to take unqualified students in large numbers. We compelled our armed services to become laboratories of sexual equality. We abandoned a coinage which, with its half-crowns, florins, latin inscriptions and complex arithmetic, both spoke of tradition and authority and required a serious education system to teach it. We did the same thing to weights and measures which stretched back into both the Middle Ages and the beloved countryside. Both were replaced by continental, republican measurements which require no knowledge or understanding, merely the normal complement of fingers.

We lost our nerve and our pride. We thought there was something wrong with our own country, and so we scanned the world for novelties to import and adopt. We tore up every familiar thing in our landscape, adopted a means of transport wholly unfitted to our small, crowded island, demolished the hearts of hundreds of handsome towns and cities, and in the meantime we castrated our criminal law, because we no longer knew what was right and what was wrong, and withdrew our police from the streets of the suburban wilderness we had made. The police themselves, increasingly bureaucratic and car-borne, no longer even tried to rely on the goodwill or consent of the public, and operated more and more as a militarized force, referring to the public as 'civilians', and festooned themselves with huge clubs, cans of CS gas, jangling handcuffs and semi-battledress uniforms. More and more of them carried firearms.

The most significant change for the great majority is that life is no longer so safe, so polite or so gentle as it once was. Especially on the edges of society, on the large housing estates, the breakdown of the family meant that tens of thousands of young people were being brought up by nobody, or by the television. Young males, especially, failed to grow up because they no longer needed to. The old disciplines of marriage, fatherhood and work had gone. The police, who had given up foot patrols in the optimistic days of the 1960s, responded to growing levels of petty crime by becoming a reactive service, rushing noisily to the scene after the deed was done, and then filling in forms. They now merely enforced the letter of a bureaucratic law rather than the spirit of an agreed and respected moral code. As a result, they often seemed frighteningly neutral between criminals and householders. There was an alarming growth in cases of law-abiding citizens, stretched to the limit, reacting with violence to vandalism or theft and finding themselves in the dock.

It is impossible to measure the connection between the collapse of the family, the growth of television, the decay of authority and the withering away of common citizenship. It is certain that crime is higher among the children of broken homes than among those from stable families, but so far the collapse of marriage has mostly affected the poor, who are of course least able to cope with it. They have also suffered most from the spread of illegal drugs, which are now on more-or-less open sale in most cities and outside many schools, and which certainly contribute to the explosion in petty theft that has affected the whole nation.

It seems plain that television has helped to make things worse in its role as third parent, amoral teacher and pornographer in both violence and sexual licence, gradually removing our natural disgust at these things. It has also done great damage by popularizing bad language—once a useful half-way mark between civility and violence because it was taboo, now just a coarse and depressing feature of life. It has helped to spread false ideas about society, through propagandist drama, and created a national conformism among the young, in taste, humour, morals and politics, that is quite unprecedented. The governing class brushed aside the wise caution of T. S. Eliot and others, and encouraged television without undertaking any study into its likely effects. They then made certain that it would pursue the lowest taste, by opening it to commercial competition and sacrificing the BBC monopoly.

One of the inspirations for this book was a research paper, 'Regulating for Changing Values', produced by the Broadcasting Standards Commission in May 1997. It concluded that 'People were confused about how they should live and that they were left adrift in an indeterminate sea of uncertainty, but all the time anchored by the pragmatic principle of protecting themselves and those close to them from harm.' In other words, every man for himself.

For those who fear a Hobbesian war of all against all, this finding is sinister and alarming. So is what followed:

This concentration on the self as at risk from harm is a mark of not trusting the world of others. Although respondents felt that they were decent and raised their children to behave in a decent manner towards others, their performance was not seen to receive support from the performance of the wider community.

There was a general feeling that the family was being forced back in on itself in terms of moral instruction. The existing culture outside the home, in the schools and in the everyday performances of others that they witnessed, such as the extension of courtesy and politeness, was antagonistic to the moral directives that they wished to give their children. Of particular importance in this direction was the cultural performance of television.

And all this was taking place in a landscape of change, change and more change. If you doubt that Britain has undergone a cultural revolution during this brief era, look and see how many things are no longer being used for their original purpose. Fertile fields are fallow, 'set aside' for subsidies. Hill farms are derelict, or converted into guesthouses. Seaside resorts have become colonies of dole-drawers and asylum-seekers. Old rectories and old village schools are rich businessmen's houses, old churches are 'arts centres', old markets are knick-knack-infested tourist traps. Then there are the 'old' police stations, fire stations, judges' lodgings, town halls and stations. And public houses which once bore royalist, patriotic or rustic names are now called such facetious, chaotic things as 'It's a Scream' or the 'Rat and Parrot' and celebrating nothing but trivial minds, puerile humour and booze. As if to prove that many people never wanted these changes, the few parts of the country which have been spared are filled with nostalgic summer visitors looking for a Britain which has ceased to exist. The village used to film a TV series set in the peaceful 1950s, *Heartbeat,* is now almost overwhelmed with people seeking in vain for a door into the lost past.

The old rewards of British life have also been taken away from one set of people and given to others. This is on sad display in the great Victorian suburbs of north Oxford, built for professional and academic families, and now beyond the means of all but the super-rich. The class system, which once rewarded education and diligence with status and wealth, now rewards only enterprise, a dangerous narrowness. Education alone will not get you a villa with two acres of garden, nor will it give you the wealth to buy your own children an education as good as the one you had. Knowledge, thought, understanding and wisdom are no longer valued. Comfortable, secure wealth comes only to those in what Stephen Pollard and Andrew Adonis describe as the Superclass—celebrity and political lawyers, television executives, senior broadcasters and show business successes—so well-paid that they actually have money to invest left over after tax and outgoings. This new and fashionable nobility is an aristocracy quite happy to join the radical movement, provided its own wealth is not threatened. Despite regular displays of tender conscience, many of its members have no true stake in society as a whole, being able to buy themselves out of the urban mess and the education disaster.

The reforms and the feverish, unsettling changes which have continued through the whole of the late twentieth century have so weakened the people's attachment to their traditions and institutions, their liberties and their independence, that it is now far easier than it would once have been for the Blair government to make a series of changes which amount to a slow-motion *coup d'état*. Its guiding spirits, whose ideas are those of Tom Paine even if they have never heard of him, have suddenly found themselves free to hack down all the institutions, habits and ideas which had withstood radical assault for two centuries and more. As the chainsaws whined and howled, and the great trees crashed down one by one, an indifferent public and a complaisant Fourth Estate looked on without lifting a finger to save the forest of law and custom which had protected them for so long from the cruelties and violence which other, less fortunate countries have undergone. Some even cheered as it fell, unaware of the cold harsh winds that would soon blow across the bare landscape.

The British cultural revolution has so far been free from direct violence. No elderly professors have been paraded through the streets in dunce's caps, nor have counter-revolutionary elements been thrown from the tops of high buildings or otherwise crippled and murdered. The violence has been done to *institutions* and to traditions and ways of doing things, to language, but not—yet—to people. I cannot guarantee that it will not lead to bloodshed in the end, as revolutionary ideas so often do, but it has been restrained up till now. For this has been a very *British* revolution, perhaps the last thing we shall do that *is* British.

We have abolished the very customs, manners, methods, standards and laws which have for centuries restrained us from the sort of barbaric behaviour that less happy lands suffer. We are about to break the ingenious and cunning constitutional bonds that have kept these islands at peace for centuries. We are entering what the Chinese call 'interesting times', and the future is worrying and uncertain. Pessimism is often decried as if it were a crime, but it has one great virtue, apart from the fact that it is seldom unjustified: it armours us against approaching danger, and sometimes allows us to anticipate peril before we have to meet it.

This was never meant to be a purely political book. It has concentrated on the upheavals in our society that have happened despite politics, under governments of both parties and often through 'private' bills and 'free' votes, or without votes at all, in TV executives' offices, in courtrooms, laboratories and boardrooms. It is intended to show that the cultural battle, ignored by most politicians, is often more decisive and important than the noisier clash of parties at Westminster. The changes it records and tries to explain, while not directly political themselves, have made it possible for a long-buried radical strain to climb out of its tomb and finish a revolution which first threatened this country during the Civil War, was defeated by the Restoration and headed off by the historic compromise of 1688. It rose again in the aftermath of the French and American revolutions, but was defeated by Church, King, Law, patriotism and tradition—which is why today's radicals loathe the United Kingdom so much. To them, it is the living disproof of all their theories: conservative and royalist but democratic, lawful but free, rooted in the past but capable of modernization. It ought not to exist, so they plan to make sure that it ceases to do so.

Society has been reconstructed so that the most abject conformism appears to be rebellious, casually clothed, loud-mouthed, safely undisciplined, speaking in the glottal accents of Estuary English. Real individualism, Tory individualism, on the other hand, is merely eccentric, barmy, bonkers, contemptible. The old Soviet Union had to pervert the whole science of psychiatry to classify its dissidents as mad. We, the soap-watching, admass conformist society,* happily join in to deride free thought and suppress heresy. And while we do it, we think we are being rebellious. What an achievement—the power of totalitarianism without the need to imprison, torture or exile.

The very geography in which tradition, custom, respect and experience were rooted has been ploughed up. The ancient landscape of the countryside, the almost as ancient pattern of our towns have been overlaid by a new pattern. And they have straightened out the rolling English road, of which Chesterton wrote: 'I knew no harm of Bonaparte, and plenty of the squire, and for to fight the Frenchies, I did not much desire, but I did bash their baggonets because they came arrayed, to straighten out the rolling road the English drunkard made.'

Our language, stripped of its literary references in a world where almost nobody has heard of Cranmer or Tyndale, and where Shakespeare is considered too rich a mixture for our young, has been rebuilt.

Our architecture, which once was full of messages of authority and faith, is now lumpish and unhistorical. If it embodies the worship of anything, it is the worship of money, power and technology, even of ugliness itself. Compare the Victorian Houses of Parliament to the curious birdcages, rhomboids and garages proposed for the new toy parliaments of Wales and Scotland.

Our British Protestant sexual morality, which once required marriage as the price of pleasure, now treats any sexual activity as a recreation. This allegedly liberates women from the slavery of the home, and men from the slavery of supporting a family. But in truth it imprisons children in a world where they always come second to adult pleasures, it imprisons women in endless competition with their sisters for fun—a competition in which the rich and beautiful are the only winners for as long as their wealth and beauty last and not a moment longer—and it imprisons men in an ultimately sterile quest for passing pleasure. But it is 'judgemental' to point any of this out.

In everything from children's magazines to advertisements, a message of hedonism and impatience is spread. The soap operas promote and bring into the mainstream such things as incest and transsexualism, and because so many of us no longer have real neighbours or neighbourhoods, we come to believe that the world around is full of such things, and to tell ourselves that we must accept a new morality because it is pointless to resist change.

Our religion, such as it is, has abandoned the only territory where it could not be challenged, the saving of souls, and has given up troubling our individual consciences. Instead, it has joined in the nationalization of the human conscience, so that a man's moral worth is now measured by the level of taxation he is willing to support, rather than by his faith or even his good works. Other tests—opposition to apartheid or General Pinochet—are valued more highly than personal adherance to the Ten Commandments or the Sermon on the Mount. An adulterer with the correct view on Nelson Mandela is preferable to a Mother Teresa who fails to criticize the currently unfashionable regimes of the world.

All these things in themselves are damaging to the stability of society. But taken together, as they have happened, they are devastating. This country *was* different from others. It was a multinational state, though not a multicultural one. It was a profoundly Christian society, in which religion was part of the language, of the state and of daily life in a way quite unique in Europe. It was a hierarchical country, in which people understood authority and respected it without grovelling to it, for it was also a society of individuals, nonconformists, dissenters, troublemakers, grumblers—self-reliant, given to banding together in unions, friendly societies and clubs, believing in law, but devoted to fairness. It was an educated, literate country with a strong musical tradition. Through its great literature, its verse and its hymns it had obtained an idea of itself that was comforting and powerful. It believed in the family and the home, that great zone of private life in which the state has no business.

Now, in a generation, all this has been demolished, concreted over, reformed out of existence. In some cases by accident, in some cases deliberately, in most cases irreversibly. The words which once bound us together are no longer understood when they are spoken, and the subtle invisible chains which bound us to the past, in Burke's compact of the dead, the living and the unborn, have been snapped.

Britain is, or soon will be, somewhere else: George Orwell's Airstrip One, or a series of regions in the European Federal State—Channelside, perhaps, as Kent and Sussex are merged with Pas-de-Calais, and a series of other unrecognizable and meaningless regions. For Britain, as she has been all these centuries, is far too big and powerful to be swallowed whole into the bland blend of the new multicultural Euroland.

But the puzzle is why this country of all countries, free, generous, just, democratic, cultured, honourable in its dealings, should have won the enmity of so many of its own citizens.

I believe that many people in the new and over-educated middle class resent the success, stability and prosperity of a nation state whose very existence denies their radical theories. We are a monarchy, yet not an autocracy. We were an empire, yet we have excellent relations with most of our former colonies. We are not modern politically, but we have successfully modernized our economy again and again. We have a class system and snobbery, yet there is no bar to talent. We are Christian, but we do not seek to make windows into men's souls. We are conservative, yet tolerant, capitalist, yet blessed with a social conscience. We have military skills, but do not use them to oppress our neighbours.

According to the radicalism born in Europe in the eighteenth century, none of this should be so. That radicalism, the secular religion of the power-hungry middle class, never quite succeeded here, and has never quite forgotten its defeat. Now it seeks to extinguish Britain, not by revolution, but by stealth.

The apparent rebirth of Conservatism in 1979 was a false dawn because the Thatcherite movement was not interested in morals or culture. It believed mainly in the cleansing power of the market, which has much to be said for it but which has no answers to many fundamental questions—and which cannot operate properly unless honesty and stability are enforced through both ethics and law. Worse, the Thatcher government unwittingly helped to destroy many of the things Conservatism once stood for. In eighteen years of power, an immense time, the Thatcher–Major government was unable to reverse a single part of the cultural revolution, not least because it barely tried, and did not understand it. It also unintentionally devastated many of the pillars of stability.

Selling council houses did sometimes break up communities. Breaking the power of the over-mighty manual unions did in the end destroy many of the last stockades of male employment, thus fatally weakening many working-class families.

Given the opportunity to return the BBC to impartiality and support for British culture, the Thatcher government chose instead to subject the corporation to accountants, while doing nothing to halt the long march of the cultural Left through its corridors. Abolishing the Greater London Council created the precedent for abolishing the House of Lords. In search of a guiding ideology, the Tories could come up with nothing better than the brute force of the market, whose inhuman logic of course ignores patriotism, morality, tradition and beauty, and elevates the businessman to the role of bishop, a role even he does not want. Some of its supporters could not see how baldly repulsive their pure doctrine was, even when it led them into 'libertarian' policies on the free sale of poisonous narcotics.

The furious socialist critics of Thatcherism were right to see something cruel and heedless in what was taking place. Sadly, they drew the wrong conclusions: that greater government intervention and higher taxes were the answer to a society drained of kindness and obligation. Because this decay in civilization became obvious during the Thatcher years, they blamed it exclusively on her policies, when it was also the fault of the permissive experiment of the 1960s, combined with the general collapse of self-confidence which followed the end of imperial glory. Nick Davies toured the crumbling edge of society for his book *Dark Heart,* and identified the growing barbarism of danger, crime and child prostitution in a superb piece of reporting. But he saw this as a result of government, when, in truth, government had merely made it worse. The real problem was that a free people needs to be a moral people, founded upon strong family and neighbourly ties, but these ties had been worn away by decades of cultural revolution.

In a curious and unintended way, Margaret Thatcher's years gave her opponents the chance to launch a *political* revolution to match the cultural one. It was she, by her attacks on institutions and customs she disliked, by her impatience with Parliament and Cabinet government, who alerted the Left to the great weapon they were neglecting. This point, that Lady Thatcher's government actually turned Britain into what Marxists had claimed it was, but which it had never actually been, is cleverly made in James Buchan's novel *Heart's Journey in Winter*. Labour's intellectuals, especially the Marxists and ex-Marxists among them, understood this paradox and acted upon it. Blair's government has wasted little time on the well-worn but inaccurate weapons of economic power, apart from quietly raising levels of taxation. Instead it has reached for the levers of *institutional* and *constitutional* change, tugging furiously at them from the moment of its election victory.

Many of these switches could be pulled without the need of Parliament, and the non-Parliamentary methods of the Blair regime were themselves an attack on the past.

1 May 1997 really *was* the start of a new era. The new Prime Minister's triumphal progress to Buckingham Palace and Downing Street was filmed from the air by sycophantic broadcasters as if a dull cortège of motor cars were a rebel army finally emerging from the sierras to occupy a conquered city. It would not have been surprising to see plumes of smoke from Whitehall courtyards, as the defeated regime burned its records. The broadcasters' instincts were, as it turned out, right. This was not merely a change of government, but something far more profound and disturbing.

Mr Blair's actual arrival at Number Ten, choreographed in every detail by Labour Party officials, was the first example in British history of a fake spontaneous demonstration. It consisted of Labour Party headquarters staff and their families, issued with special passes to the Downing Street high-security zone, marshalled by stage-managers wearing head microphones, and handed Union Flags to wave, as if they were patriots. Such people, in fact, generally despise the Union Flag, and it would be interesting to know what arguments were used to persuade them to wave an emblem they find embarrassing and kitsch. Those few observers who had visited dictatorships and people's democracies, and realized what was going on, were disturbed as they witnessed this sinister and fraudulent event. Many reporters did not appear to notice the fraud they were watching, and so became part of the deception.

Foreboding grew when the new Prime Minister addressed 'his' MPs and told them that they were, in effect, government employees, deputies whose job was to represent the state and party to the people rather than the other way round. This came soon after close aides of the Prime Minister had, through special Orders in Council, been appointed to high office in the civil service, ending in seconds a century of Whitehall neutrality. When the Prime Minister's close confidant and adviser, Peter Mandelson, mused that the era of representative democracy might be coming to an end, the pattern was clearer still. When Mr Blair and his wife walked out to meet the crowds during the State Opening of Parliament, deliberately stealing the occasion from the Queen, another side of the revolution— its assault on the monarchy—became suddenly obvious.

A nation whose sensibilities had been dulled by the affluence of the Thatcher years did not seem to mind about anything the government did unless it affected their pockets. So the new authorities took care to make no overt attack in that direction. The British had also been separated from their traditions, by the weakening of family ties, by the disruption of schools, by the virtual abolition of national history and literature, by the subsidization of teenage independence of parents through the universities, by the sexual revolution and all the other changes described above. So Mr Blair and his advisers felt free to take a bulldozer to the constitution.

In a few short months, they had held referendums in Scotland, Wales and London, establishing new tiers of government. These were portrayed as devolution, though their main effect was to take yet more power from Parliament and place it in the hands of the Labour Party, which believed it could control all the new bodies. What was far more important was that, because the changes were approved by referendum, Parliament could not repeal them. Another principle of the British constitution, that no one government could commit its successors, was destroyed. Worse still, these referendums were held without any of the rules of fairness long established in general elections. The government used taxpayers' money to urge people to vote in favour, and the broadcasting organizations were not obliged—as they are in the Irish Republic—to give equal time to both sides. The conduct of the Welsh referendum, in particular, would later be criticized by the Neil Committee on standards. Had it been conducted more fairly, it might well have gone the other way.

The government's attitude to the monarchy was more complicated. Some leading figures did not think it mattered at all, though there were many senior ministers who were privately republican and believed that the monarchy was an obstacle to executive power. The issue had not been debated in the Labour Party in public since the 1920s (when the debate lasted fifteen minutes), but the long years of opposition had allowed many 'think-tanks' to flourish, in which learned men sought to change the constitution to ensure that Labour was never out of office again. They also wanted to make sure that Continental ideas of liberty were built into the legal system, through the European Human Rights Convention. For the first time, the British people would have positive 'rights', which sounded attractive, but actually converted this country from one where all is permitted unless prohibited, to one where all is prohibited unless permitted. Incidentally, in a House of Commons ambush which the government did little to resist and nothing to reverse, anti-hanging MPs quietly used the Human Rights Bill to make it impossible for the House of Commons to reintroduce capital punishment, ever. This breach of a promise to review the issue in each Parliament passed almost unnoticed, but cemented the revolution in criminal law begun in 1957 with the Homicide Act.

The idea of achieving political ends through constitutional means gained strength in Labour circles partly because Mrs Thatcher had destroyed the nineteenth-century industrial and trade union base of the Labour Party. The unions and their block votes may have forced Labour to adopt dreary and impractical economic policies, but they had also given it a sort of working-class, monarchist patriotism. A man might be a militant shop steward, but that did not make him a social revolutionary. Ernest Bevin, a former leader of the Transport and General Workers' Union, had led the anti-pacifist forces in the 1930s Labour Party and was one of the keenest supporters of a British nuclear weapon in the post-war Labour government. In fact, Labour's need to appeal to trade unionists meant it had to forget the alleged 'Common Sense' of Tom Paine, and appeal instead to the British common sense of the working class. For the most part, they were even more mistrustful of foreign nations than the Tories. Accidentally, by breaking the connection between Labour and the workers, Margaret Thatcher had driven the Party back to its roots in eighteenth-century radicalism, roots almost completely forgotten in the long struggles over nationalization and industrial law.

The death of Princess Diana showed how far this rebirth of republican radicalism had already gone, though there were signs of what was to come from the very beginning of the Blair government. A strange mob convulsion among Diana's partisans, aided and abetted by the television coverage which suggested that the grief was more widespread than it was, gave the Prime Minister the chance to ride a wave of pro-Diana, anti-Charles and increasingly anti-Elizabeth sentiment. It is hard to tell how large this sentiment was, except that it was almost certainly not as great as it seemed at the time. It united, in an unlikely alliance, fanatical partisans of the Princess and the growing strand of republican thought in the Labour Party. Diana's supporters were themselves an odd collection of outcasts, who believed that she in some way spoke for them. She seemed popular among some racial minorities, perhaps those who felt excluded from the respectable mainstream, among the sexually unconventional because of her AIDS campaigning, and among single mothers and wronged women in general, of whom there were by this time an enormous number, thanks to the cultural revolution's creation of the single-parent state.

The Prime Minister himself was slow to see this, but his cleverer aides, who spotted it at once, equipped him with the phrase The People's Princess, found him a black tie, and sent him off to RAF Northolt to welcome Diana's broken body home, even though he had no constitutional role there at all and had barely known her. Mr Blair then made a 'Presidential' appearance at her funeral, not content to sit in his pew, but actually reading the main lesson. At the end of this episode, he had effectively established himself as a rival head of state, a role he underlined by his brusque visit to Balmoral during the mourning. It was during this period that the Royal Family seemed to accept the 'protection' of the government, in return for abandoning significant parts of its independence. The decision to fly the national flag over Buckingham Palace for the first time was a lasting symbol of the change. Other incidents in this strange unsettled period demonstrated the new relationship between monarchy and Downing Street. But in the post-Diana period, Downing Street sought, with growing confidence, to elbow the monarch aside.

During the Queen's golden wedding celebrations, Mr Blair acted as Her Majesty's unofficial escort as she moved among the crowds. He walked close behind her, sharing her day and shaking the hands of people who had come to see her. He later made a semi-literate speech at the celebration lunch, describing her patronizingly as 'the Best of British'. A few months afterwards, he created the post of First Lady of Britain for his wife, allowing her to act as hostess to other First Ladies aboard the Royal Train during the 'Group of Eight' economic summit.

Mrs Blair was technically a private citizen, since there had until then been no formal office of Prime Minister's consort. Other private citizens (including the author) who attempted to charter the train were rebuffed, presumably because they were a good deal more private than Mrs Blair. The Prime Minister also moved to share the aeroplanes used to fly the Queen and the Royal Family. However, he found they were not grand enough or fast enough for him, and took to flying abroad by Concorde whenever he could. He also took the first steps towards the creation of a British version of Air Force One, the U.S. Presidential plane. He asked for special beds to be installed, so that he could sleep in comfort on long flights. Meanwhile, the Royal Yacht *Britannia* was vindictively retired on the grounds of cost. If money was in such short supply, it was strange that enough could be found to put bronze cladding on a new office block for MPs at Westminster, at a cost of £34 million.

These actions marched in step with a Presidential method of government, gathering all power in the Premier's office. Partly because the government's main purpose was to win a second election, and partly because his Press Secretary Alastair Campbell was one of his most valued and influential advisers, it was the government press service which felt the change most acutely. In department after department, from the Treasury to the Northern Ireland office, established civil service press officers were pushed aside to make way for political appointees who were also political commissars. Requests for information were no longer treated with civil service impartiality, but subjected to political and propaganda considerations.

Cabinet meetings, already unwisely reduced in significance during the Thatcher years, became mere formalities sometimes lasting less than an hour. Mr Blair himself often did not bother to attend. Cabinet Ministers became, quite clearly, employees of the Prime Minister's office. When the Foreign Secretary, Robin Cook, was caught cheating on his wife many people were shocked that he was told to choose between divorcing her or abandoning his mistress, while he waited for a flight at Heathrow Airport. What was far more shocking was that the choice was forced on him by the Prime Minister's office, whose business it was not. One of the senior figures in the Cabinet was being treated like a wayward employee. Similarly, when the Welsh Secretary Ron Davies was robbed on Clapham Common in bizarre circumstances, he was, to all intents and purposes, dismissed by Downing Street.

The idea that the Prime Minister was Chief Executive spread into many other places. A senior civil servant, the Cabinet Secretary Sir Richard Wilson, allowed himself to be quoted praising Mr Blair's 'courage'. Other public officials lined up to applaud Mr Blair in the Downing Street garden, after the Premier had given a self-serving 'annual report' on his government. And Downing Street press officers, whose salaries are paid by the taxpayer, have told the author that 'I am paid by the Prime Minister', unaware that this is not merely untrue, but a breach of the constitution.

The point at which the new government cut most deeply into the forest of law and tradition was over Northern Ireland. Here was a clear conflict between law and crime, in which terrorist parties were seeking to gain concessions through murder and destruction. Within months of taking office, Mr Blair had invited the leaders of those terrorist parties to meet him personally in Downing Street, and agreed to release a large number of convicted criminals to secure an unreliable 'ceasefire' by the criminals. At the same time, he and his Northern Ireland Secretary, Marjorie Mowlam, had shown indifference and even hostility to the Unionist people of the province. It was made clear to the Orange Order that their freedom to march would be restricted from now on, and that the Royal Ulster Constabulary and the British Army would be used against them if they insisted on behaving as they had always done. At any time this would have been significant. At a time when mighty efforts were being made to bring the IRA's political tail, Sinn Fein, into talks, it was doubly so.

The former arrangement, under which the British government, the army and the police had been on the side of Union, or at least of law, was over. They were now on the side of a compromise which clearly spelt the end of the Union, and which over-rode the law. Mr Blair was careful to *appear* Unionist, in a way typical of his methods, and typical of the way in which the Labour movement has used his boyish, trustworthy public-school appearance and manners to reassure those who suspect that his party is a parcel of Levellers and Jacobins. The Prime Minister said that he believed that the Union would last at least for his lifetime. He did not say that he thought it *should* do so, or promise to ensure that it *would* do so, but was happy to let people infer this meaning from his neutral words. A few months later, the Irish Prime Minister, Bertie Ahern, predicted a United Ireland within fifteen years, and in this case there was no doubt that this was also his desire.

This collapse and surrender to lawlessness was possible mainly because the Conservative and Unionist Party had opened the door for it. Many years before, Tory Cabinet Ministers had held secret talks with people they believed to be delegates from the IRA. But this was nothing compared to the moves that were made under Mr John Major's government. Rapidly retreating from principle, Mr Major sought some form of words from Sinn Fein which would allow him to talk to them openly. This policy was rewarded with an IRA 'cease-fire', but no guarantee that it would be 'permanent'. When Mr Major did not run away fast enough, the 'cease-fire' ended with a bomb at Canary Wharf, in the City of London, which would have put an end to negotiations if they had been based on good faith or principle.

But as usual, they were not. The government was founding its policy on exhaustion, cost and fear. The IRA had proved, in earlier bombs in the City of London, that it could do enormous and expensive damage. Pressure from the United States to reach a settlement was great, because of the enormous debt which Bill Clinton owed to Irish-American voters and businessmen (they had won back Catholic working-class votes lost to the Democrats through their pro-abortion policy). Mr Major, who appeared to believe in nothing but good management, did not really know why Britain was in Northern Ireland or see that, by dealing with terrorists or granting local autonomy, he would unravel both the UK—which he claimed to love—and the rule of law. Sadly for him, his policy of retreat was not bold enough for the IRA, who failed to give him the 'peace' agreement he sought. They presumably suspected that they would get a better deal by waiting for a Labour government, which would not need the votes of the Ulster Unionist MPs at Westminster, or those of the dwindling number of serious Tory Unionist MPs on the mainland.

Northern Ireland was the harshest expression of the 1688 settlement that the Tories could no longer be bothered to support. As I have said, it was the only place on British territory where British patriotism took the form of nationalism, often clashing with a rival Irish nationalism. Mainly because of this, it was sometimes a good deal uglier and more violent than the settled islanders across the water would have liked. They did not want to see that they might have been more like the Orangemen if they had shared their territory with a rival culture. The Province was isolated from the British political mainstream and had—in an act of huge folly—been allowed its own local parliament and government when the Irish Free State was set up in 1921. When the London government imposed direct rule in 1972, it might have ended this anomaly for good, and brought Northern Ireland fully into Great Britain. However, neither Mrs Thatcher nor her Cabinet seem to have understood this as an issue of principle, and so wandered rather vaguely down the path of compromise with Dublin, through the Anglo-Irish agreement. It is doubtful if Margaret Thatcher knew what she was agreeing to, and in any case, with the Cold War still in progress and the USA staying out of the quarrel, it did not look likely that Northern Ireland would be presented to the Irish Republic in any future that it was then possible to foresee. Only lonely prophets, such as Ian Gow and Enoch Powell, and easily dismissed fanatics such as Ian Paisley, were aware of the danger. As for the British people, they mostly lacked the historical knowledge or concern, and—never having needed to consider the foundations of their own state— were bored and confused by Ulster fundamentalists of both sorts.

Those Ulster people who rejected violence, yet wished to remain British, were therefore well-prepared for what Mr Blair brought to them. They were willing to accept a suspect compromise if only because they could sense that rejection would result not in saving the status quo, but in more and fiercer pressure to give in. They must also have guessed that failure to give the expected 'Yes' answer to the referendum on the Belfast Agreement would mean that it was put to them again and again until they did so. The agreement itself, as few have noticed, contains provisions for referendums on the future of the Province *every seven years* if necessary. It is not stated, but clearly implied, that these referendums will go on until they come up with the 'right' answer, i.e. incorporation in the Republic. And after that there will be no more. As no British constitutional experts have noted, but some Irish ones have, this means that Northern Ireland is no longer under the sovereignty of the UK Parliament. That Parliament is now obliged by treaty to cede the territory, as soon as the 'Yes' faction wins a referendum.

This process was in many ways a dress rehearsal for the coming referendum on entry to the European Economic and Monetary Union. The Protestants of Ulster are the first group of people to learn that they are no longer allowed to be British, but the rest of the people of the United Kingdom are fated to undergo the same shock in the next decade or so. Several weapons were used and will be used again: the full force of government moral and financial support on the side of a 'Yes' vote, aided by media which do not even attempt balance. The monarchy may also be brought into the campaign if the Northern Ireland precedent is followed. Just after the Ulster agreement was reached, the Queen issued a statement welcoming the agreement—*not*, significantly, the fact that an agreement had been reached, but the agreement itself. Since the document involved the release of hundreds of convicted criminals and was opposed by several parties, including the entirely constitutional UK Unionist Party, in Ulster, and by many citizens in all parts of the UK, this was a shocking departure from Royal impartiality. It was the worst such breach of the constitution since King George VI foolishly endorsed the Munich agreement in 1938—though in that case there was no vote taking place, so there was no suspicion of the throne seeking to influence the democratic process.

As preparations go ahead for the next phase of the political revolution—the creation of English regions under closed-list party rule, the abolition of the unpredictable first-past-the-post system of electing the Commons, the attempt to present European economic and monetary union as a *fait accompli*—the government is also tidying up other awkward areas. The hereditary peers were stripped of their powers not because they were undemocratic, but because they are the last people sitting and voting at Westminster who cannot be brought under party control. A life peer is no more democratic than a hereditary one. But he is more likely to be obliged to the Party which gave him his title.

In two years or less, this government will face a general election which will decide the future of Britain. If it wins, Party rule will swiftly replace Parliamentary rule, through proportional representation and the centralized control of MP candidate selection, and Britain will take her place as a full member

of the European Superstate, yielding one of the great pillars of
sovereignty to a foreign power for the first time since King
Charles II signed the secret Treaty of Dover and became a
salaried employee of Louis XIV of France. This will be done
by the Blair government's favourite method: the plebiscite in
which the voters are required to approve a decision already
taken by the executive. Unfair referendums, in which the BBC
are not required to show balance and the government is allowed
to spend taxpayers' money on endorsing its own case, will be
held to rush the country into the Euro and into proportional
representation, and to ratify the new government-controlled
House of Lords.

These changes, once made, will be irreversible by any democratic process now in existence. They will mark the end of a
period of national history stretching back at least to the time
of Henry VIII and the Reformation, and much longer by some
calculations. Britain, or its component parts, will rejoin the
continental mainstream as a client of continental powers. In
an age when sea power has been superseded, there is no possibility that, should she wish to regain her independence, she
will be able to do so.

The riddle now before us is whether the British people any
longer possess the will or the identity to resist this project, or
whether they will sink, exhausted and grateful, into the mushy
embrace of the new Europe.

The issue of European integration unites all the threads of
the cultural revolution into one. The things which made Britain
different were the things which made it different *from the Continent*. An old and respectable tradition believes that England's
Tudor breach with the Continent was a mistake, that the Anglican rupture with Rome was an error, that Europe would have
been better off with England as an integrated part of the continental system, rather than an outsider stirring up trouble in
Europe to protect its own independence. From its attitudes to
sex and marriage to its literature and its coinage, its food and

the shape of its cities, Britain had chosen different solutions from those favoured across the Channel and beyond the Rhine, ones which were more individual and self-reliant, which depended more upon individual conscience and liberty, and less upon imposed authority. This tradition views Britain's alliance with the USA—with some justice—as a one-sided friendship, far more 'special' on our side of the Atlantic than on theirs. It takes little account of the cultural ties which make the USA such an attractive ally and trading partner.

Until the cultural revolution, this opinion was a minority view even in the governing élite. However, the overthrow of traditional belief has made it far more acceptable to younger people of all classes, unschooled in tradition as they are. The end of the Cold War, and the apparent success of the European Union in the short term, has also made a European connection more attractive and the U.S. relationship less urgent. At the same time, the sense of national decline, the growth in foolish and bad behaviour by prominent figures, especially in the Royal Family, have persuaded many that—since this country is so poorly run—it would be no bad thing if we gave more authority to the wise, cool heads of Europe. After all, nobody can claim that, for example, Germany is badly governed, crime-infested or poor by comparison with Britain.

In its convulsions over the gun massacre of schoolchildren by a perverted maniac at Dunblane, and the knife murder of the London headmaster Philip Lawrence, British society showed that it had changed in two important ways. It was far more easily manipulated by emotion, and had forgotten its instinctive self-reliance and suspicion of authority. The idea that the right response to these tragedies was a ban on the holding of guns or knives by law-abiding citizens was, on the face of it, demented. Such measures would simply reserve such weapons for law-breakers. Yet these bans were passed into law with almost no opposition. As in the post-Diana period, a sort of dictatorship of grief frightened many people into silence. A similar illogical panic authorized the slaughter of thousands of perfectly healthy cattle, because the British people preferred to hand over their right to decide what they ate to the state, rather than take an infinitesimal risk of contracting a disease which may or may not be passed through infected beef. And after the Omagh bomb in Northern Ireland, which took place despite enormous concessions to terror factions, the revulsion of public opinion was used to pass laws allowing courts to convict suspects on little more than the say-so of a police officer. The British people seemed to have forgotten their attachment to liberty, at the same time as they forgot their history and their geography and their literature.

And yet it is not certain that the struggle is finished or that the modernizers have already won. The radicals have completed their long march through the institutions so that the education industry, much of the media and especially the broadcasting networks are largely in the hands of liberal conformism. 'Political correctness', a very unfunny project to make it impossible to express certain ideas, has been alarmingly successful.

Even so, when the issue of the national future is presented in plain view, as the irreversible abolition of independence through the scrapping of the national currency, a majority recoil in mistrust and suspicion. No serious independent nation manages without a currency—because it is not a symbol of nationhood, like a flag or an anthem, but a fact of nationhood, like a legal system, a frontier or an army. After years when the opponents of the cultural revolution have fought their little isolated skirmishes and lost them, here at last is a full-scale battle against a recognizable threat to our entire way of life. It is as if the conservative elements in society have been hacking at a fogbank with blunt cutlasses, to all appearances attacking an imagined foe. Suddenly, the fog lifts, and the great scaly monster of national abolition is revealed in all its ugly menace.

In the tremendous debate which must now begin on this, the most important decision the British people will take in this generation and many others, all the other reforms and upheavals in our daily life are involved. If we are what we used to be, then this is a last unrepeatable moment at which we can halt our extinction as a culture and a nation. We have been so safe from such threats for so long that most of us have never felt the insecure, passionate form of nationalism which is all too familiar to Poles, Frenchmen and other less fortunate peoples. If we do not wish to experience it, if we believe that our society has already abandoned too many of its restraints and good manners, this is the opportunity to halt the process, re-examine what we have been and might be again, and to reassert a culture which has done the world a great deal more good than harm.

This appeal is not just directed to those many millions who feel that they have become foreigners in their own land and wish with each succeeding day that they could turn the clock back, though they have for far too long been deprived of a voice by the political party which should have defended them and has ignored them instead. I believe that many who think of themselves as socialists and radicals must now also suspect that they have pushed the clock too far forwards, and that the very people they hoped to help have been plunged into a new darkness of insecurity, ignorance, crime and despair. I do not see why, because I may disagree with them profoundly about some of the great issues before us, we should be divided in the face of a common enemy. We can and should combine to express our joint concern for our fellow-creatures and fellow-citizens.

It is dangerous for the country that the citizens who care most about it are still divided by sterile name-calling which dates from the Thatcher period. Both Left and Right were wrong about the Thatcher government, which turns out to have been a much more complicated thing than it seemed at the time. I have quite deliberately aired some serious conservative criticisms of Mrs Thatcher, because her moral and cultural failures had serious consequences for her own cause as well as for the whole country. In return, I ask the Left to begin to reconsider its own record, especially in damaging the family, ruining the schools and making Britain a land fit for pornographers. If the decay of obligation, duty and morality continues, danger and misery will soon be hammering at the front doors of all of us, Left and Right alike. The longer we leave it, the more illiberal, costly and nasty the ultimate solution will have to be. We have a common interest in climbing out of our trenches and honestly re-examining our opinions. This, by the way, is not to suggest some mindless big tent or grand coalition in which there is no more argument. It is to suggest that we need to protect and rebuild the unseen web of goodness which is essential for a free and democratic nation to continue to exist.

The history of the world so far suggests that the nation-state is the largest unit in which it is possible to be unselfish to any effect. Within that state, of course, family disagreements can freely continue. But if we give up our nationhood, as the government now wants us to do, we will all of us, socialist or conservative, lose the right to influence the fate of our country. It will not matter if we want lower taxes or higher ones, more hospitals or more warships, smaller school classes or a new selective state education system. Under the plans for Economic and Monetary Union, we will pass these decisions to a supranational power where we will always be a minority voice, and where our specific British traditions are despised or unknown.

This enormous decision provides us with an opportunity to reconsider many things, not least the foundations which lie beneath our ancient and honourable country. In the brief space left before the next general election, I urge all responsible citizens to consider whether they wish to endorse the burial of a great and civilized nation, or whether they wish to halt a process which they never asked for or voted for, or were even asked if they wanted, which has brought about misery, decadence and ignorance, and which threatens to abolish one of the happiest, fairest and kindest societies which has ever existed in this imperfect world.

Notes

23: *Belisha beacons,* named after the 1930s Transport Minister Leslie Hore-Belisha, were (and in a few places still are) yellow flashing globes mounted on tall striped poles at either side of a crosswalk. Drivers are supposed to stop at these crossings if they see a pedestrian waiting to cross, and until quite recently all drivers voluntarily did so. However, as courtesy and good manners declined and traffic grew heavier, most of these crossings have now been replaced by mandatory traffic signals.

33: *Mary Whitehouse,* a schoolteacher, began a national protest in the early 1960s against what she viewed as the growing amount of swearing, sexual innuendo, and portrayal of sexual material on British mainstream TV. Her campaign attracted widespread public support, and the Post Office at one time had to make special deliveries of letters to her house. But her campaign completely failed to alter the direction of British TV.

38 and 66: *Comprehensive schools, grammar schools, eleven-plus examination.* Grammar schools in Britain were selective secondary schools taking children from the age of eleven to eighteen. Entry was gained by passing an examination known as the 'eleven-plus'. These schools provided a high level of education at no charge, and by the 1960s were beginning to supplant most of the so-called 'public' (i.e. private, fee-paying)

schools, especially in gaining college places. 'Secondary moderns' provided a more basic secondary education for those who failed the 'eleven-plus'. Most of their pupils left at fifteen, but some did go on to university.

The comprehensive project was launched in 1968 by the Labour government, supposedly as an anti-elitist policy. The then Education Secretary, Anthony Crosland, vowed to 'close down every ****ing grammar school in England'. In the next twenty years he very nearly succeeded. Of the thousands of grammar schools at the time, only 164 are now left. The all-ability 'comprehensives' which replaced them are vastly variable in quality, and the best are open only to those living in the wealthy districts from which they take their pupils.

There is now no way in which most poor British families can get a first-class education for their children. Many quite affluent districts have very poor state education, and as a result many people of fairly modest incomes spend heavily on sending their children to independent fee-paying schools. Few of these are now of the Eton type (i.e. boarding, highly traditional and aristocratic). Most are fairly similar to the old grammar schools, the only difference being that they cost around $12,000 a year per child, and often more.

42: The *Jarrow March* was a famous protest against unemployment in the 1930s, processing from Jarrow, a small shipbuilding town in north-east England, to London. It is still widely remembered. The marchers were welcomed everywhere they went, and aroused the pity and sympathy of people in the south of England, which at the time was far more prosperous than the north. Jarrow had been wholly dependent upon shipbuilding, and the closure of the Palmers yard threw the entire male population out of work. It was known as 'the town that was murdered'.

What is surprising is that at the same time, new light industries were springing up in the south, and for a large part of the country the 1930s were a period of unheard-of prosperity, accompanied by a huge boom in house-building. People in different parts of the country had very different experiences of the 1930s. Rearmament, postwar prosperity and the welfare state have blunted those differences, and though Jarrow is still far from prosperous, almost every house is newly built and survivors of the march would not recognise it as the same place.

51: *Tom Brown and his employees. Tom Brown's Schooldays* was the classic novel of English boarding school life by Thomas Hughes. Its most famous character, apart from the admirably Christian young gentleman Brown, is the atrocious bully Harry Flashman, whose equally fictional later life has been cleverly chronicled in the novels of George MacDonald Fraser. Brown is referred to here as the typical English gentleman.

54, 55, 57: *O levels, GCE, GCSE, A levels.* The General Certificate of Education (GCE), introduced in the 1950s, examined children at two levels: 'O' (ordinary) and 'A' (advanced). A child was considered to have had a rounded education if he achieved five or six 'O' levels at high or medium grades by the age of sixteen. Subject categories included English literature, English language, elementary mathematics, physics, chemistry, biology, French, German, history and geography. Many secondary moderns (while they still existed) and comprehensives offered a lower-grade examination, the Certificate of Secondary Education (CSE). A top-grade CSE was equivalent to a basic pass at 'O' level. If a child planned to go on to university, he would be expected to take three 'A' levels, often in the same or similar subject fields, and usually specialising in either sciences or arts. These examinations usually consisted of three-hour unprepared papers which tested memory, depth of learning, writing skills and the ability to work under pressure.

In the 1980s egalitarians, distressed by the fact that millions of pupils were leaving school with no 'O' levels at all, introduced a different kind of examination, known as the General Certificate of Secondary Education (GCSE). This merged the GCE and CSE. It also introduced a great deal more continuous assessment of coursework, and required much less rigorous forms of knowledge. For instance, foreign language papers, which had once required students to know detailed grammar and vocabulary, now concentrated on practical tests of spoken language. Books could be taken into some exams, as could pocket calculators. There was substantial 'grade inflation' with vastly increased numbers of pupils scoring high grades. This was actually cited by the education establishment as proof that education was improving. As GCSE students were being less rigorously tested in their middle years at school, there was a consequent effect on 'A' levels, which became easier and are about to be replaced with new, weaker examinations. However, they will still be called 'A' levels.

89: *Papa and Nicole* are characters in a series of TV advertisements for French cars. The *Eurostar* is the super-fast train which runs between London and Paris beneath the channel. At present, due to the backward state of British railways, it can run at full speed only on the French side, and is an embarrassing symbol of French engineering prowess and British backwardness.

91: *Last Night of the Proms* is a rowdy and good-humoured event which takes place each September in London's Royal Albert Hall, with much waving of Union Jacks and singing of patriotic songs. It is the traditional end of a season of classical music concerts broadcast on the BBC and originally founded by the conductor Sir Henry Wood to offer classical music to a mass audience.

   The song 'Land of Hope and Glory', set to one of Edward Elgar's Pomp and Circumstance marches, became a sort of alternative national anthem after it was sung at Edward VII's coronation in 1902. Its words—'Land of Hope and Glory, mother of the free, how shall we extol thee, who are born of thee. Wider still and wider may thy bounds be set. God, who made thee mighty, make thee mightier yet'—are now seen as outdated and absurd by many (including me), especially given the disappearance of the British Empire in the ensuing fifty years.

97: *semis and detached houses.* Equivalent to duplexes and single-family dwellings.

105: *an old Hansard.* Equivalent to the Congressional Record.

105: *a beaming Roy Jenkins.* Home Secretary; see chapter 15.

135: *licence fee.* A tax on TV owners collected by the government and handed to the British Broadcasting Corporation.

138: *Chris Evans,* a talented TV and radio presenter of programmes for teenagers, is famous for his coarse behaviour in and out of the studio.

138: *'Disgusted, Tunbridge Wells'* is a British national cliché, the mythical signature of an angry elderly person who has written to the newspapers to protest against some outrage of the modern world. Tunbridge Wells is a spa town in Kent, once famous for its large population of militantly conservative retired military men and their fearsome lady wives.

138: *Mr William Hague in a baseball cap.* Mr William Hague is the leader of the Conservative Party, leader of the official Opposition and the principal challenger to Mr Tony Blair at the next British general election. Though young, Mr Hague is bald and studious, and in an attempt to seem cool and funky he appeared in a baseball cap at a photo op, which backfired on him as badly as Michael Dukakis's ride in a tank.

149: *Lord Home,* also known as Sir Alec Douglas-Home, was Conservative Prime Minister of the UK, 1963–64, after which he narrowly lost the election to Labour, then led by Harold Wilson. A Scottish aristocrat, Lord Home had renounced his peerage to become Prime Minister (by 1963 it was not acceptable for a British Prime Minister to be a member of the House of Lords; he had to be in the by then far more powerful House of Commons). Home, who spent his summer holidays shooting grouse on the Scottish moors, had the ill-luck to resemble a skull, and his old-fashioned gentlemanly qualities seemed out of place in 1960s Britain. He was mercilessly mocked as a braying, brainless buffoon, who tried to manage the economy by making calculations with matchsticks. He later became Foreign Secretary and was acknowledged by his former critics to have been unfairly maligned.

154: *Reithian idea.* Sir John Reith, later Lord Reith, was a stern Scottish Presbyterian who was the first Director General of the BBC, and who believed that it should use its immense monopoly power to foster high culture, morality and Christian values.

160: *W. H. Smith* is Britain's national chain of newspaper and magazine shops, with outlets in almost every high street and at railroad stations. Most British magazine sales are through shops rather than subscriptions, and a W. H. Smith ban was a major impediment to mass sales.

208 and 269: *Myra Hindley and Ian Brady* are Britain's two most famous murderers, and are both still in prison thirty-six years after their crimes. They kidnapped children, subjected them to sexual and sadistic torture, and tape-recorded their cries for mercy. Some of their victims, buried on a remote piece of moorland, have never been found. Many people were horrified that they could not be sentenced to death. Brady has gone mad during his imprisonment and is now confined in a

special hospital for the criminally insane. Hindley has become, or claims to have become, a devout Roman Catholic and still seeks to be released. One of the reasons for the authorities' refusal to consider this is that they fear she would not be safe if she were free. The case led to a complete change in British parents' willingness to allow their children to roam streets and countryside unsupervised, effectively ending childhood freedom.

215: *New Lad's monthly.* In the early 1990s a series of magazines with titles such as *Loaded* were launched, aimed at men in their late teens or early twenties, aggressively 'laddish', i.e. coarse about sex and drinking, and full of provocative pictures of women which would have been considered outrageous by both puritans and feminists, but because they were 'ironic' were now acceptable. These successful publications were known as 'New Lads' magazines.

227: *Neighbours* takes place in an Australian suburb and deals with the lives and tribulations of mainly young, lower middle or working class Australians. Sexual and similar matters are openly and frankly discussed, and though the programme is not pornographic or offensive by modern standards, it is certainly not designed for young children.

297: *admass* is a term used by 1960s British sociologists to describe the mass audience aimed at (and captured) by early TV advertising.

Acknowledgements

This book has its roots in more than twenty privileged years spent on the staff of the *Daily Express,* with my nose pressed eagerly against the window-pane of history. The ideas behind it were formed in many places: hanging around the dingy meeting halls of the Labour movement or the lobby of the House of Commons, lying in the mud to avoid Soviet bullets in Vilnius, experiencing total lawlessness in Mogadishu, running away from the People's Police in East Berlin, sneaking into the occupied shipyards of Gdansk, rubbing Gerry Adams up the wrong way in Kansas, seeing a man executed in the Death House in Jackson, Georgia, watching Margaret Thatcher firing live ammunition on the north German plain, searching for the Tsar's bones in a snowy forest outside Sverdlovsk, being told to sit down and stop being bad by Tony Blair.

During that time many people, editors, colleagues, rivals and others have aided, encouraged, advised and rescued me, argued with me, sent me into trouble (usually at my own request) or got me out of it. Some of them urged me to write a book, and some of them helped me to do it. Many of them may not have realised that they had a part in shaping what follows, and I only hope they will have some pleasure in discovering that they did. I am sorry that these acknowledgements come too late for Arthur Firth and George Gale. My thanks to: Richard Addis, Tim Garton Ash, Piers Blofeld, Tom Bowring, Rosie Boycott, John Campion, Barrie Devney, John

Downing, Douglas Dupree, Alan Frame, Jonathan Freedland, David Goodhart, Derek Jameson, Bruce Kemble, Mary Kenny, Geoffrey Levy, Nicholas Lloyd, Chris McGovern, Robbie Millen, David Miller, Igor Monichev, Conor O'Clery, Valerie Riches, David and Tamara Ross, Antonia Salt, Nick Seaton, Dennis Sewell, Bob Tyrrell, Justin Walford and Jack Warden. If there is any credit for what follows, then they should share it. If there is any blame, it is all mine. But my greatest thanks must go to my wife, Eve, for her companionship, support and comfort and her unfailing readiness to advance towards the sound of gunfire.

Works Cited

Alice in Genderland. National Association for the Teaching of English, 1985.

Ambler, Eric. *Uncommon Danger.* First published 1937; Penguin edn, 1960.

Amis, Kingsley. *Russian Hide and Seek.* Hutchinson, 1980.

——*Take a Girl Like You.* Victor Gollancz, 1960.

Atkin, Paul. Chapter in *Sex Education and Schools: Tried but Untested.* Family Education Trust, 1995.

Bennett, Alan. *Forty Years On.* Faber and Faber, 1968.

Betjeman, John. 'The Planster's Vision.' In *New Bats in Old Belfries.* John Murray, 1945.

Beyond the Fringe. New York: Samuel French Inc, 1964. Reprinted by permission of the Peter Fraser and Dunlop Group Limited.

The Blue Guide to England. John Murray, 1920.

The Blue Guide to England. A&C Black, 1995.

Booth and Brown, eds. *Teaching GCSE History.* History Association, 1986.

Briggs, Asa. *History of Broadcasting,* Vol. 5. Oxford University Press, 1995.

Buchan, James. *Heart's Journey in Winter.* Harvill Press, 1995.

Carstairs, Morris. *This Island Now.* Penguin, 1962.

Carter, C. C. and H. C. Brentnall. *Man the World Over.* Basil Blackwell, 1952.

The Church and Marriage. Church of England, 1956.

Cole, Margaret. *What Is a Comprehensive School?* London Labour Party, 1953.

Colley, Linda. *Britons*. Vintage, 1996.

Cox, Brian. *Cox on the Battle for the English Curriculum*. Hodder and Stoughton, 1995.

—— *An English Curriculum for the 1990s*. Hodder and Stoughton, 1991.

Dance, E. H. *History for a United World*. Harrap, 1971.

—— *History the Betrayer*. Hutchinson, 1960.

Davies, Nick. *Dark Heart: The Shocking Truth about Hidden Britain*. Chatto and Windus, 1997.

DeMarco, Neil and Richard Radway. *The Twentieth Century World*. Cheltenham: Stanley Thorne, 1995.

Dickinson, A. K., ed. *Empathy and History in the Classroom*. Heinemann, 1984.

Dickinson, A. K. and P. J. Lee. *History Teaching and Historical Understanding*. Heinemann, 1978.

Drabble, Margaret. *The Millstone*. Penguin, 1965.

Eagleton, Terry. *William Shakespeare*. Basil Blackwell, 1986.

Ellis, Robert. *Was There a Mid-17th-century English Revolution?* Cheltenham: Stanley Thorne, 1995.

Fienburgh, Wilfred. *No Love for Johnnie*. Hutchinson, 1959.

Freedland, Jonathan. *Bring Home the Revolution*. Fourth Estate, 1998.

From the Workhouse to the Workplace. National Council for One-Parent Families, 1993.

Halberstam, David. *The Fifties*. Villard Books, 1993.

Harman, Nicholas. *Dunkirk: The Necessary Myth*. Hodder and Stroughton, 1980.

Hoggett, Brenda. 'Ends and Means: The Utility of Marriage as a Legal Institution'. In *Marriage and Cohabitation in Contemporary Society*, ed. J. M. Ekalaar and S. N. Katz. Butterworth, 1980.

Howard, Roland. *The Rise and Fall of the Nine o'Clock Service*. Mowbray, 1996.

James, P. D. *Cover Her Face*. Faber and Faber, 1989.

Jasper, Ronald. *The Development of the Anglican Liturgy 1662–1980*. SPCK, 1986.

Jenkins, Roy. *The Labour Case*. Penguin Special, 1959.

———— *A Life at the Centre*. Macmillan, 1991.

Kress, Gunther. *Writing the Future: English and the Production of a Culture of Innovation*. Sheffield: NATE, 1995.

Lawrence, D. H. *Apropos Lady Chatterley's Lover*. Mandrake Press, 1930.

Leach, Edmund. *A Runaway World?* BBC, 1967.

Macdonald, Hamish. *From Workshop to Empire*. Cheltenham: Stanley Thorne, 1995.

Marenbon, John. *English, Our English: The New Orthodoxy Examined*. CPS, 1987.

Marshall, H. E. *Our Island Story*. Thomas Nelson, n.d.

Mead, Margaret. Articles in *Current Affairs*, 11 March 1944, and in *New York Times Magazine*, 19 March 1944.

Orwell, George. *The Collected Essays, Journalism and Letters of George Orwell*, Vol. 2, *My Country Right or Left*. Penguin, 1970.

———— *The Road to Wigan Pier*. Victor Gollancz, 1937.

Pickles, Thomas. *Europe*. J. M. Dent, 1932.

———— *North America*. J. M. Dent, 1963

The Plowden Report. Report of the Central Advisory Council on Education. HMSO, 1967.

Ponting, Clive. *1940: Myth and Reality*. Hamish Hamilton, 1990.

Postman, Neil. *Amusing Ourselves to Death*. Heinemann, 1986.

———— *The Disappearance of Childhood*. W. H. Allen, 1983.

Putting Asunder: A Divorce Law for Contemporary Society. SPCK, 1966.

Raven, Simon. *Places Where They Sing*. London: Anthony Blond, 1970.

'Regulating for Changing Values'. Report for the BSC by Matthew Kieran and others. Institute of Communication Studies, University of Leeds, 1997.

Reynolds, David. *Rich Relations: The American Occupation of Britain 1941–1945*. Harper Collins, 1996.

Richards and Hunt. *An Illustrated History of Modern Britain*. Longman, 1983.

Riches, Valerie. *Sex and Social Engineering*. Family Education Trust, 1994.

Santayana, George. 'The Weather in his Soul'. In *Soliloquies in England*. Constable and Co., 1922.

Tenen, Isidore. *This England*. Macmillan, 1944.

Wilson, H. H. *Pressure Group: The Campaign for Commercial TV*. Secker and Warburg, 1961.

Woolf, Virginia. *Letters of Virginia Woolf 1923–29*. Vol. 3, *A Change in Perspective*. Edited by Nigel Nicolson. Hogarth Press, 1977.